Experience and Being

Northwestern University
STUDIES IN *Phenomenology &*
Existential Philosophy

Calvin O. Schrag

Experience and Being

Prolegomena to a
Future Ontology

NORTHWESTERN UNIVERSITY PRESS

1 9 6 9   EVANSTON

Calvin O. Schrag is Professor of Philosophy
at Purdue University and author of
Existence and Freedom:
Towards an Ontology of Human Finitude

IN MEMORY
OF MY FATHER:
A NONPROFESSIONAL PHILOSOPHER

Contents

Preface

THERE ARE ALWAYS many motives and reasons which induce one to undertake a particular study. Some of these may escape one's own reflective awareness, and in any case it would be extraordinarily difficult, to say nothing of the dubious desirability, to enumerate and catalogue the manifold influences and expectations which lie behind any given project. Yet there are certain formative influences and projected expectations which stand out, and assuredly the reader has the right to require that I give some account of my general plan. The principal design which underlies this work is twofold. In the course of my previous investigations and studies of phenomenology and existentialism, I have been impressed with the seminal insights that these movements offer and at the same time dismayed with the obscurities that often accompany these insights. Convinced that many of these obscurities are accidental accompaniments and not essential ingredients of the attitude, methodology, and program of phenomenology and existentialism, I have projected in this present study a revision of the phenomenological and existential approaches through the elaboration of a new philosophy of experience. This program of revisionism, it is hoped, will both provide a systematic clarification of some of the more durable insights of recent phenomenology and existentialism and move in the direction of critical independence. Coupled with this design is an effort to reformulate the question of being in experiential terms and to sketch prolegomena for a future ontology of experience. I have come to the conclusion that such a future ontology, if it is to retain its liaison with experience, can no longer take as normative the inquiry-standpoint and categorial schemes of traditional metaphysics. Hence the movement toward a new ontology of experience must, in the first instance, be understood as a movement beyond metaphysics. This movement is discussed in Part III and the distinguishing features of a possible ontology of experience are suggested.

It would not be far amiss to say that the general thesis of the book is that one of the main tasks of philosophy is the elucidation of experience. Philosophical reflection, in one of its more dominant expressions, is reflection in and about experience. But general theses have a way of being very general, and to inform the reader that one's book is about experience is to do little more than initiate a barrage of questions as to the meaning and use of experience. It is precisely here that the problem lies. The book begins and ends with an interrogation of the meaning of experience. As every schoolboy knows, many views of experience have been proposed in the exciting, if at times tortuous, history of philosophical thought. Admittedly the most prominent of these views is the use and delimitation of experience by the three great British empiricists, Locke, Berkeley, and Hume. But we have become heir to another species of empiricism, more *radical* in intention and result than that espoused by the British empiricists. This is the empiricism of William James's philosophy of experience. There is also the much discussed existential posturing of experience by such seminal thinkers as Kierkegaard and Nietzsche. Heidegger, although his central philosophical project remains of a somewhat different sort, has offered numerous suggestions for both a critique of traditional empiricism and a formulation of a new approach to the structure of experience. Not to be neglected are certain writings of Husserl and, in particular, the works of Merleau-Ponty, in which the notion of *lived experience* is explored and developed. It is also my contention that insufficient attention has been given to the role of experience in the thought of the Anglo-American philosopher, Alfred North Whitehead. It is unfortunate (and for this misfortune Whitehead is himself partly responsible) that the metaphysical scaffolding of his speculative cosmology has virtually eclipsed his seminal insights into the dynamics and texture of experience. What is sorely needed in Whitehead scholarship today is a reexamination of his philosophy in light of his theory of experience.

These are only some of the philosophers who have been

attentive to the role of experience in philosophical reflection. There are many others. Although the "philosophy of experience" is, strictly speaking, an emergent within modern and contemporary philosophy, the ancients and the medievals were not oblivious to the contributions of experience. They too need to be critically consulted in our effort to clarify the dynamics and structure of experience. On the one hand our project consists of an attempt to establish a critical dialogue with those philosophers, mostly contemporary, who propose a return to experience. On the other hand we intend to carry through a systematic approach to the question about the structure experience in the hope of doing justice to its breadth and depth, safeguarding its richly variegated character, and clarifying its ontological features.

There are many individuals to whom I am indebted for various kinds of help in the writing of this book. No doubt many of my colleagues and former students at Purdue University, Northwestern University, and Indiana University will find in some of the following pages insights and ideas which came to fruition through critical discussions with them. To these colleagues and students especially I express my sincere thanks. In particular I owe debts of gratitude to my Purdue colleagues, Professors Richard F. Grabau, Francis H. Parker, and William L. Rowe, for their helpful suggestions in the discussion of various parts of the manuscript. I am most grateful to Purdue University for granting me a sabbatical leave and to the Guggenheim Foundation for a generous stipend which made possible the launching of this project. I am also heavily indebted to the National Foundation on the Arts and Humanities for an additional grant which enabled me to complete the book. *The Philosophy Forum* has kindly given me permission to use parts of my article, "The Phenomenon of Embodied Speech," published in 1969 (vol. VII, no. 4). Some ideas which I discuss in Chapter 8 were developed in my essay "Re-thinking Metaphysics," in *Heidegger and the Quest for Truth*, ed. M. S. Frings (Chicago: Quadrangle, 1968). Finally, it is fitting that two other individuals be acknowledged in an expression of thanks: Mrs. Helen Allison for her technical help with the preparation of the manuscript, and Mr. Samuel Barnett for his careful and competent reading and correction of the proofs.

C. O. S.

Experience and Being

Introduction

THE WORDS "EXPERIENCE" AND "BEING" have been in the philosophical vocabulary for some time. On certain occasions one or the other has provided the terminological pivot for philosophical investigation and construction. At other times their use has been avoided in philosophical discourse because of their alleged generality and apparent ambiguity which make it difficult to know clearly what is at stake in their employment. The word "experience" is used in many different contexts, and the word "being" appears so fluid and open-ended that it stands in danger of becoming a vacuous concept. There is indeed evidence that the multifaceted and ambiguous character of language about experience and being has often gone unrecognized in traditional philosophy. This unfortunate fact should be acknowledged, and an effort should be made to strive for clarity and lucidity to the extent that they can be achieved. Yet it needs to be recognized that clarity is itself an open-ended concept whose applicability varies from context to context, depending upon the phenomena under investigation. These phenomena seem to exhibit a certain resiliency which not only sets limits on the degree of clarity but may require a specification of types of clarity and types of meaning.

The recognition of the initial generality, ambiguity, and vagueness of the term "experience" would not in itself provide sufficient grounds for its deletion from philosophical discourse. There is indeed a singular advantage in the use of the language of experience as a philosophical point of departure. The term itself conveys the unity of insight and action, perception and conception, knowledge and valuation, theory and practice. Expe-

[3]

rience has to do both with seeing into a situation and acting within it. It includes in its range perceptual acts and the anticipation of concepts. It involves both the knowledge and evaluation of objects, events, and situations. Thus experience in its primitive presence lies beyond any conflict between theory and practice, subject and object, intellect and will. It is with this notion of experience in its primitive presence that philosophical reflection begins, projecting as its peculiar task the penetration of experience with lucidity. Philosophy, in one of its central functions, thus becomes the elucidation of experience. This experience, as we have indicated, is presented in a strikingly ambiguous manner, as a multifaceted complex of living relationships and intentionalities of thought. Thus the word "experience" may well be ambiguous, because what it intends and expresses is ambiguous. Any pejorative assessment of this ambiguity, however, would be premature. There are different types of ambiguity. Some are rich and revealing, expressing the multidimensionality of a state of affairs; others are impoverished and obscuring, concealing rather than revealing. Philosophical reflection thus needs to assume the task of elucidating this ambiguity as it shows itself in the concreteness of lived experience. Ambiguity which is rendered lucid is no longer simple ambiguity. It is ambiguity transfigured and, in some sense, understood.

The process of elucidation which we are here proposing is one of clarification by means of distinctions. Many nonphilosophers are troubled, and at times offended, by the welter of distinctions, both fine and coarse, that abound in the writings of professional philosophers. But the hard fact remains that what is needed, particularly for elucidating primordial experience, is not fewer but more distinctions. The plethora of configurations, developments, and textures within experience require for their understanding a careful placing of distinctions whereby that which is presented in its variety and intermingling can be grasped with respect to both its conjunctions and disjunctions. The use of distinctions is the very stuff of philosophy. Distinctions have their origin in reflection, and reflection is a process which goes on and on. Distinctions thus provide philosophy with its creative impetus, but also, paradoxically, they constitute its chief peril. Distinctions can go wrong and solidify into bogus dichotomies. It is one of my contentions that precisely this misuse of distinctions accounts for many mistakes in the traditional views of experience. Perception and conception, knowledge and valuation, subject and object may be illuminating distinctions; when they are transformed into bogus dichotomies, however, the interlacing and connectedness of that which is distinguished within experience is concealed, and the stage is set for half-truths and reductivisms. The task is to elucidate experience in such a manner that distinctions within experience become visible in their interplay and interpenetration. Each distinction should be traced back to its source in the primitive presentment of experience and its validity should be determined by the extent to which it illuminates correlative and implicatory distinctions.

A deeply ingrained tendency to move in the direction either of absolute objectivity or of absolute subjectivity has characterized much of the development of modern and contemporary philosophy. This tendency has been present both in those philosophers who are ready to engage in bold metaphysical speculation and in those who are much more cautious with respect to metaphysical matters and remain content to tidy up their epistemological criteria and concepts. The dilemma of being impaled either on the horn of absolute objectivity or on that of absolute subjectivity is well illustrated in the metaphysical debate between deductive idealism and reductive naturalism. In both of these the subject-object distinction is reified into a dichotomy and legislated as normative, setting the stage for giving precedence either to the subject or to the object. Deductive idealism follows the path of absolutizing the subject; reductive naturalism takes the other road and grants priority to the object. The problem which this dilemma creates for these diverse metaphysical programs is that of establishing some commerce and connection between that which they have transformed into insular entities. Deductive idealism seeks to do this by taking a stand on subjectivity and then deriving the object from the subject. But the sad history of idealism is that it has been unable to burst the cocoon of its subjectivity, and has come to rest in a hermetically sealed, interiorized experience. In this process of interiorization, the object as presented in its objectivity is lost. The object in idealism achieves only the status of an object-for-a-subject. Reductive naturalism, impaled on the other horn of the dilemma, moves in the direction of absolute objectivity. Using the objectivity of the given as its philosophical springboard, it leaps to objective qualities and relations and searches for the subject within the maze of interrelated objective qualities. But the irony of this search is that it never discovers the subject as subject. What it finds, not surprisingly, is a subject reduced to an object. Reductive naturalism requires that the subject justify his existence through objective determinations, and what is left after the justification is completed is an entity constituted by objective qualities and relations. Deductive idealism is destined to conceal the object; reductive naturalism is destined to conceal the subject. Neither subject nor object is permitted to show itself as it emerges from a more primordial level of experience. The conditions which give rise to objectification and subjectification remain unexplicated. The basic error of both idealism and naturalism is that their peculiar inquiry-standpoint is defined through the use of a bogus dichotomy. What is required is the elucidation of a commerce with the experienced world which is older than subjectivistic and objectivistic categories, which precedes the thematic constitution of both, and which undercuts the dilemma as it is traditionally formulated.

The acceptance of the subject-object dichotomy as normative by idealists and naturalists leads to other difficulties within their respective programs. The naturalist is unable to conceal his metaphysical prejudice that being is all of one piece, reducible to objectifiable entities and events. Being and nature, in the last analysis, become convertible. The central, and insufficiently examined, presupposition in the program of viewing all being as an expression of nature is that there is an unbroken solidarity of man and nature. It is no accident that John Dewey chose the title *Experience and Nature* for his most metaphysical book. Admittedly Dewey uses the concept of nature in its broadest range of meaning, thus obviating the faults of materialistic naturalism. Yet Dewey, and many of his pragmatist successors, never fully succeeded in doing justice to the historical deployment of experience. The meaning of being is not exhausted by its expression in nature. Indeed the primordial sense of being may need to be sought elsewhere, in ruminations which lead us to the hither side of the metaphysical dichotomy of nature and history. It is this and related issues which will become our primary topic in Part III of this study.

It should be clear from what has been said above why it was necessary to title this book *Experience and Being* rather than

Experience and Nature. Significant also is the fact that I have avoided the title *Experience and History*. Since the time of Hegel there has been an active interest in the foundations of historical knowledge and the mode of historical being. The development of this interest led to the inauguration of historicism as a kind of counterplay against naturalism. Thinkers of the historicist tradition focused their attention on the historical subject, who emerged in the designs of historicism as an abstracted and disembodied generator of meanings liberated from his confinement in nature. But historicism, in developing out of idealism, inherited its peculiar problems. An overt activism, either intellectual or voluntaristic; the interiorization of experience; and a neglect of the facticity of nature—all underlie the program of historicism as they did that of idealism. The experienced phenomenal world becomes an "inner world." The world has an interior but no exterior, and the only access to it is that of radical introspection or inward intellectual intuition. The facticity of man's natural environment is dissolved by an absolute freedom, and the finitude of the concrete experiencer goes unacknowledged, for the most part. Idealism, after having absolutized interiority and activity, is unable to account for exteriority and passivity. Naturalism, after having absolutized exteriority and passivity, is unable to account for interiority and activity. Thus the two forms of metaphysics find themselves pierced with the respective horns of the traditional dilemma of subjectivity vs. objectivity, and experience and being suffer the consequences. At this juncture we must pose a number of questions. Is this dilemma fact or fiction? Is the dichotomy of subject and object genuine or bogus? Is it possible to elucidate the concrete movement of experience and the sense of being from an inquiry-standpoint other than that of traditional idealism and naturalism? In the discussion that follows these and related questions become themes for inquiry.

The fate of the more epistemologically oriented philosophies in their use of the subject-object dichotomy is in many respects similar to that of deductive idealism and reductive naturalism. In this tradition the dichotomy is put into play in the very formulation of the so-called "problem of knowledge." The tendency to view experience as contributory to epistemological designs has been widespread and remarkably influential since the emergence and development of British empiricism. The epistemological inquiry-standpoint of the three great British empiricists is already made explicit in the titles of their more important works—Locke's *Essay Concerning Human Understanding*, Berkeley's *Treatise Concerning the Principles of Human Knowledge*, and Hume's *An Enquiry Concerning the Human Understanding*. In this tradition experience is tailored to fit an epistemological theory and construed as an act of knowledge, defined as some species of connection between a knowing subject and a knowable object. The model on which the classical empiricist's theory is constructed is one in which the subject passively receives impressions and sensations which impinge upon him. Perceptual experience *happens to us*. Like sleep, it overcomes us. It is not at all difficult to see how, with the use of this model, the more skeptical exponents of empiricism were led to question the status of the objects of knowledge themselves and recommend a substitution of sense-data language for object language. But the problem which the sense-data theory is invoked to resolve is itself created by a prior sedimentation of the subject-object distinction.

Kant, in spite of his "Copernican revolution" which provided modern philosophy with its "transcendental turn" and allegedly definitive answer to Hume, remained notably in debt to the British empiricists. Not only did he inherit their preoccupation with the problem of knowledge, but he also appropriated virtually wholesale their atomistic view of perceptual experience. The peculiar task which he set for himself in his first *Critique* was to show how the manifold of atomized sensory experience, itself chaotic and disarrayed, required the conceptualization of an active transcendental ego to set it in order and thus determine it with respect to its proper objects of knowledge. Granting that knowledge *begins* with perceptual experience, Kant was concerned to show that properly speaking it cannot be said to *arise* from perceptual experience. Perception, understood as the reception of sensory data, is dumb. It may indeed be the first step toward knowledge but it displays no intrinsic power of sense giving. Percepts without concepts are empty or devoid of meaning. Perceptual experience must wait upon the constituting activity of a transcendental ego, which has at its command ready-made categories with which to organize the fragments received from the sensory manifold. Although Kant, more incisively than any previous philosopher, explored the conditions which first make objectivity and subjectivity possible, his atomistic and nonintentional view of perceptual experience kept him from successfully surmounting the bogus dichotomies of perception and conception, passivity and activity. Perception, he agreed with the British empiricists, is that which happens to us; conception is that which we do, as active and constituting transcendental ego. There is a sense in which, in the philosophy of Kant, these dichotomies become internalized, creating a tension which carries through the interplay of empirical and idealistic elements within Kant's philosophy itself. But the dichotomies remain in force and the question remains as to whether and how they can be surmounted.

We position ourselves in the discussion that follows against the traditional metaphysical and epistemological uses of experience and undertake a recovery of experience in its lived concreteness. Our primary interest lies with the vitalistic and vibrant resonance of experience, with experience as that which man *lives through*. This experience must be allowed to speak for itself and show itself in its various aspects within the actual context of human life. An elucidation of experience that retains its hold on the phenomena as presented cannot legislate methodological formulae and metaphysical schemes in advance. Such formulae and schemes would only prescribe beforehand what one is to find when one looks. Our interrogation of the dynamics and structure of experience will be guided by the phenomena, by "that which shows itself," in its variegated intensities and intentionalities. It is a *phenomenology of experience* that is attempted in the following pages. The reader will discern a rather far-reaching indebtedness of the author to contemporary German and French phenomenology. But he will also discern, if he is attentive, a process of critical revision at work. The transcendental phenomenology of the early Husserl, the hermeneutical phenomenology of Heidegger's *Being and Time*, and the existential phenomenology of Merleau-Ponty need to be acknowledged as notable advances in the program of getting to the "data themselves." But philosophical insight and understanding is never simply the sum of sedimented results that occur at the end of a movement or period. They are the peculiar fruits of the exercise of creative imagination and discovery. The primary task of philosophy is to achieve insight rather than to provide information. At the moment that philosophy becomes a technique of information retrieval which devotes itself to the collection of historically transmitted bits of knowledge, it barters its birthright. Admittedly it is our destiny to begin our philosophizing through a communication with the tradition, and as Karl Jaspers has pointed out, our questions are already shaped by the interplay of historical traditions. This, however, is only to say—and assuredly this needs to be said—that we never stand at the beginning. We always begin *in medias res*. And it is precisely through the exercise of philosophical imagination that our historical destiny is reopened and transfigured, making possible the disclosure of new insights and perspectives.

We appeal to this power of philosophical imagination and freedom in our project of revisionism. In the process we will seek to prune phenomenology of its idealistic vocabulary as it was formulated in the early writings of Husserl. We will critically investigate the meaning and use of the transcendental ego and dissociate ourselves from an egological point of departure. We will raise questions about Merleau-Ponty's "primacy of perception" and suggest reasons for putting in its stead the "primacy of experience." We will think through some of the questions that Heidegger has asked but emerge with different recommendations for their productive pursuit. Our effort to formulate a phenomenology of experience and sketch its ontological features will thus proceed in dialogue with the rich variety of phenomenologies which have emerged on the contemporary scene, but in this dialogue we will retain a critical distance.

A final introductory point would appear to be in order. Our elucidation of experience will proceed under the directive of the systematic principle, by which we mean, basically, the effort to describe and analyze how one portion of experience connects with another and to discern the concrete conditions which underlie our predicative judgments about any given segment of experience. We propose this use of the systematic principle, however, in full awareness of, and at least partial sympathy with, Nietzsche's warning that the "will to system" is a philosophical disease. Yet we maintain that there is an unmistakable distinction between the procedure of systematic reflection and elucidation and the boldly speculative construction of an architectonic system. Kierkegaard, for example, rejects rather spiritedly Hegel's alleged accomplishments in his *Science of Logic,* but his attack on "the System" proceeds in a quite systematic and internally consistent manner. Reflection within and about experience can proceed systematically without having the results of reflection taken up into a final and completed categorial scheme. It is the latter which occasions the claim of absolute knowledge, and this, although it may well remain a possibility for God, does not appear to be a possibility for finite man. As philosophers of experience we stand squarely positioned in that experience which we seek to elucidate. A standpoint outside of experience, however desirable, appears not to be readily available. We are thus constrained to abandon what Merleau-Ponty has appropriately labeled the philosophy of the "God-like survey," and concern ourselves with the perspectives of finite man. The reflections of the philosopher are themselves determined by his situational finitude. Even when he reflects about the infinite, or goes one better and encounters the infinite in a mystical union, he does his reflecting and encountering as a finite being under the conditions of a variant existence. It is this awareness of finitude, of which one decisive index is the experience of anxiety, that keeps our systematic elucidations from congealing into a completed and closed system of truths. As we shall see in the discussion which ensues, this fact of finitude becomes a key organizing notion for our phenomenology of experience and hence needs be given thematic consideration. Abhorring systems while striving for the clarity of systematic presentation, our elucidation offers no *philosophia perennis* and no *summa philosophica*. It offers an invitation to the reader, in the spirit of Kierkegaard, to examine and judge for himself.

PART I

The Dynamics and Structure of Experience

1 / Experience
as a Dynamic Field

Experience as a whole is a process in time,
whereby innumerable particular terms lapse
and are superseded by others that follow
upon them by transitions which, whether
disjunctive or conjunctive in context, are
themselves experiences, and must in general
be accounted at least as real as the terms
which they relate.
    —William James, *Essays in Radical Empiricism*

[1] THE CONFIGURATIVE CHARACTER OF EXPERIENCE

PHILOSOPHERS OF VARIOUS SORTS, throughout the
vast history of their discipline, have had much to say about
the nature and role of experience. Even the most ardent of the
rationalists, the Hegels and the Spinozas, have been forced to
recognize the contributions of experience. Before Hegel systema-
tizes the rationalists' dream in his *Science of Logic* he writes a
Phenomenology of Spirit, in which the resonance of experience,
in its presentational concreteness and existential pathos, still
plays a dominant role. One could argue, and it would seem to us
convincingly, that this dominant role of experience was too
hastily forgotten by Hegel. The fact remains, however, that his
early writings elucidate with a dialectical profundity the wander-
ings of the concretely embodied unhappy consciousness. It is the
tragic resonance of experience that is of particular interest to the
early Hegel, and it may well be that existentialist critics have too

readily dismissed the youthful Hegel's explorations of the concrete life of consciousness. Spinoza fashions a magnificent metaphysics of substance, *ad geometrico,* but at the existential source
of this metaphysical flight is the pathos of an *amor fati* pulsating
in the finite veins of the metaphysical architect. The phenomena
of experience may be taken up into a rational or speculative
system. In the process of their rationalization they may become
disfigured, banished, or buried; but like specters in the night
they return to haunt the speculative mansions from which they
have been extruded.

William James, in his struggle to retain a hold on the "world
of pure experience," [1] and Merleau-Ponty, in his proposal that
"experience anticipates a philosophy and philosophy is merely an
elucidated experience," [2] seem to us to focus most clearly the
theme of inquiry that is at issue. There is also the claim by
Whitehead, which is usually overlooked by his interpreters, that
"the elucidation of immediate experience is the sole justification
for any thought." [3] As we have already suggested, there is an
aspect of Whitehead's philosophy which has received all too little
attention by his interpreters. This has to do with his acknowledgment and discussion of the need to render an account of the
infinitely varied components of experience. In an illuminating
and generally neglected passage, Whitehead states one of his
main philosophical requirements:

> Nothing can be omitted, experience drunk and experience sober,
> experience sleeping and experience waking, experience drowsy and
> experience wide-awake, experience self-conscious and experience
> self-forgetful, experience intellectual and experience physical, ex-
> perience religious and experience sceptical, experience anxious
> and experience care-free, experience anticipatory and experience
> retrospective, experience happy and experience grieving, experi-
> ence dominated by emotion and experience under self-restraint,
> experience in the light and experience in the dark, experience
> normal and experience abnormal.[4]

1. *Essays in Radical Empiricism* (New York: Longmans, Green,
1942), pp. 39–91.
2. *Phenomenology of Perception,* trans. Colin Smith (New York:
Humanities Press, 1962), p. 63.
3. *Process and Reality* (New York: Humanities Press, 1929), p.
6.
4. *Adventures of Ideas* (New York: Macmillan, 1933), pp.
290–91.

James, Merleau-Ponty, and Whitehead are philosophical mid-
wives who have aided us in giving birth to the formulation of our
central thesis. It is from experience that philosophical reflection
arises, and it is to experience that reflection must return for its
justification. Experience is the soil in which philosophical insights and truths germinate and grow. As a plant plucked from
the soil in which its roots are nourished wilts and eventually
dies, so philosophical reflection cut off from the vibrant source
of experience succumbs in a shroud of anemic and lifeless cata-
gories.

The first suggestion that we wish to develop in our exploration and elucidation of experience is that fewer distortions are
likely if experience is understood as a dynamic field. The articulation of experience as a field constitutes, as it were, our point of
departure. In this point of departure certain ontological features
are already implicitly present. Hence, the third part of our study
in which the outlines of a possible ontology of world experience
are sketched is already present in the first part. And it can be no
other way; for if reflection on the problem of being is to avoid its
traditional fate of evaporating into empty concepts it must redis-
cover its genealogy in primordial experience. We speak of experience as a dynamic field. Why this particular formulation rather
than another? What advantage is achieved in speaking of experience in this manner? Are not the uses of the term "field," both in
its everyday expression and in its more technical usages, so
varied that no single meaning can be attached to them? What,
after all, does a baseball field have in common with a magnetic
field, or a field of corn with a sociometric field of correlations? It
is hence of singular importance that the use of a field vocabulary
in connection with the elucidation of experience be clarified with
respect to its context and range of meaning. Our first elucidatory
remark might best be stated negatively. To speak of an experiential field or a field of experience is to suggest an alternative to
speaking of experience as a juxtaposition of discrete elements.
Experience in its primordial presentment, we suggest, is not a
granular arrangement of psychic data or an atomistic accumulation of sensations and images. There has been a widespread
tendency in traditional theories of experience to view experience
as broken up into discrete units, like grains of sand. These
granular units are assumed to be scrambled or wholly disconnected, passively presented to an experiencer who then has the

burden of arranging them into some kind of conceptual unity. The field theory of experience, generally stated, is proposed as an alternative to the granular theory.

In the way of a more positive and specific explication of what is at stake in the field notion of experience, it needs to be said that experience is *configurative* and *multidimensional*. In speaking of experience as a configuration we mean that it is an interlacing of the constituents of experience. These constituents we understand to include experiencer, act of experiencing, figure, and background. The presentational complex of the experiential field is that of *experiencer-experiencing-figure-with-background*. The insertion of hyphens between the words is neither arbitrary nor accidental. They are grammatical indices of the bonds or connective tissues within experience and are essential for grasping the field notion itself. Experience, in its lived concreteness, is the act of experiencing figures (objects, events, situations, persons, moods, chimeras, hallucinations) not in isolation but contextualized within both determinate and indeterminate backgrounds. Every experience has its figure and background. The configurative character of experience constitutes the *primary* topic of attention in a phenomenology of experience. Herein resides the originary character of experience as an organic unity of experiencer and perceived objects, encountered persons, attendant values, manipulated tools, and situations of involvement. From this organic unity, through the exercise of reflection, *secondary* topics can be selected for the focus of attention. Particular figures can be analyzed and distinguished in terms of their peculiar modes of presentment. The determinants and texture of the particular background can be explicated. The act of experiencing and the experiencer himself can be rendered thematic as specific topics of attention, examined, described, analyzed, and interpreted. Philosophical elucidation moves back and forth between its primary and secondary topics of attention.

In speaking of experience as multidimensional we are referring to the plurality of postures that it can assume. Indeed there seems not to be any one all-encompassing and clearly demarcated field of experience but rather fields in the plural, and fields within fields. There is the perceptual field, and within the perceptual field there are visual, auditory, tactile, and olfactory fields, and what might be called a field of taste. Each of these fields displays peculiar figures and distinctive backgrounds, and in each the perceiver is already situated in a particular manner. Merleau-Ponty in his discussion of the "phenomenal field" has provided an exceptionally illuminating treatment of the deployment and structure of perception. The phenomenal field, according to Merleau-Ponty, is neither an "outer world" of objectively reconstituted properties and relations nor is it an abstracted "inner world" accessible only by introspection. He provides a description of the perceived world as present in lived-through experience. Perceptual consciousness, it is maintained, is never enclosed within itself, exiled from the world. It is from the beginning lodged in the world as an intentional bond with figures positioned against a background.[5] However, Merleau-Ponty is led, for reasons never fully justified or even made clear, to the conclusion that the visual field has a privileged status in comparison with its kindred configurations. This elevation of sight to a position of privilege is made explicit in the following passage:

> It is true that the senses should not be put on the same basis, as if they were all equally capable of objectivity and accessible to intentionality. Experience does not present them to us as equivalent: I think that visual experience is truer than tactile experience, that it garners within itself its own truth and adds to it, because its richer structure offers me modalities of being unsuspected by touch.[6]

It is not readily evident why visual experience should be "truer" or display a "richer structure" than do the other forms of perception. Admittedly sight has the advantage of more directly providing conditions for objectification than do the other senses, but it is also, by virtue of this, the most distant and disembodied of the senses and hence the more prone to become separated from the concrete experiencer and his dynamic life-world. What is required is a reinsertion of sight into the full-bodied *aisthesis* which mediates all of the senses. This full-bodied *aisthesis,* so overtly manifest particularly in tactile sensation, continues to be operative in the visual field, and by virtue of it sight retains its liaison with the other senses. From this, however, we are not permitted to conclude that Merleau-Ponty's position must be inverted and priority given to the nonvisual fields. Touch and

5. *Phenomenology of Perception,* pp. 52–63.
6. *Ibid.,* p. 234 n.

hearing, for example, are neither "truer" nor "richer" in structure than sight. We are contesting the elevation of any one of the senses above the other. We find no meaning in the claim that one might be truer or richer in structure than the others. The tyranny of sight over the other senses must be combated. Sight without the full-bodied *aisthesis* of the other senses divests experience of its vibrancy, as the other senses without the distance of sight tend to enslave experience in an unredeemed immediacy.

The multidimensional texture of experience is displayed not only in its plurality of perceptual fields but also in the variegated deployment of conceptual and valuational fields. Conceiving and valuing, as assuredly as perceiving, occur within a figure-ground context. Experience is always broader in its range than the reach of perceptual fields, and there may be some problems in a doctrine of the "primacy of perception" as set forth by Merleau-Ponty. It is important, however, that Merleau-Ponty's doctrine not be misunderstood. He never claimed for perception a primacy in the sense of an exclusive source of knowledge and truth. By the "primacy of perception" he meant rather that perception displays a figure-ground relation and an intentional structure revealing its intended figures, rediscovered at every level of experience.[7] Yet the fact remains that Merleau-Ponty is committed to a view in which perception assumes a status of privilege in disclosing the figure-ground structure. But the figure-ground structure is as readily discernible in conception and valuation as in perception. More precisely, the figure-ground structure is manifest in the configurative development of experience as a reciprocating movement of perception, conception, and valuation. The connections between perception, conception, and valuation are more intimately reciprocal than Merleau-Ponty seems ready to acknowledge. Anticipatory concepts and attendant values play a role in perception, and, reciprocally, perception nourishes concept and value formation. Man's total behavior infects the phenomenal fields of experience, accounts for their interplay, and contributes to their sense. Distortion and misunderstanding could thus best be avoided by speaking of the "primacy of experience" rather than the "primacy of perception." Each of the emergent fields of experience can be thematized and ren-

7. *The Primacy of Perception*, ed. James M. Edie (Evanston: Northwestern University Press, 1964), p. 34.

dered explicit through an elucidation of their peculiar figures and backgrounds and their intentional structure, and this explication and elucidation is able to proceed without reductivism only if the primordial reciprocity of perception, conception, and valuation is held in attention and acknowledged.

William James, in developing his notions of the "field of consciousness" and the "fringes of consciousness," had already suggested a path of inquiry that moved in the direction of what we have called the field theory of experience. James too was dissatisfied with the granular theory. He spoke of the "pulverization" of experience by the British empiricists, and argued for a more radical empiricism which at the same time would do justice to the depth and varieties of experience, cognizant of its conjunctions and colorful configurations.[8] In many ways James anticipated the phenomenology of Merleau-Ponty, in which the figure-ground correlation assumes a role of crucial importance. According to James, every undivided portion of experience has its peculiar phenomena surrounded by fringes which reach into vague horizons and indeterminate backgrounds and make possible the expansion of meaning or sense. At the same time, however, James seems to retain a firmer grasp of the originative fecundity and breadth of lived experience than does Merleau-Ponty, for he is not as intent on finding a paradigm structure within the varieties of experience. With his healthy pluralism he is more cognizant of the wide range of solicitations, he abandons the search for transcendental unities (from which Merleau-Ponty is not yet sufficiently liberated), and he is able to grant to each dimension of experience a more explicit freedom to thrive. Although he says less about the visual field than does Merleau-Ponty, James is more aware of the breadth and richness of experience relative to its value-bearing intentionalities.

The point of central importance in regard to the contributions of James and Merleau-Ponty is that they have both grasped and given expression to the configurative and multidimensional character of experience, and have brought to the light of day some of the bogus dichotomies that have arrested many traditional views of experience. There is no warrant for any *solidified* distinction between interiority and exteriority, activity and receptivity, subjectivity and objectivity. Admittedly the distinc-

8. *Essays in Radical Empiricism*, p. 43.

tions are already present, if only in a latent way, but they are present only as tendencies and polarities within any given configuration of experience. They do not show themselves as insulated facts walled off from one another. It is not as though the figures of experience were passively received by a receptor, posited as things exterior to a given mental interior. Behavioral know-how, anticipations, and valuations already infect the figures and contribute conditions for meaning. Nor is it as though the figures were constituted by an insulated affector, implying an interiorization of that which is exterior. The figures of experience offer a certain resistance and their sense cannot be exhausted by any particular perceptual, conceptual, or valuational perspective. The sedimentation and consequent dichotomization of the distinctions of receptor and affector, passivity and activity, interiority and exteriority, fixes the destinies of both objective empiricism and subjective idealism. Traditional empiricism objectifies experience and makes it a matter of passively receiving exterior figures, construed principally as atomistic impressions or dead sensory qualities. It thus fails to acknowledge the configurative character of experience, and ironically loses the experiencer, for the experiencer is relegated to an interior region which itself cannot be accounted for by an inspection of passively received external facts. Subjective idealism follows the other path. It subjectivizes experience, interiorizes the phenomenal field, and confers upon the lonely epistemological subject the task of creating the forms of experience. But this epistemological subject is itself without life and body, functioning as an alleged universal condition for knowledge. The end result of traditional idealism is thus not substantially different from that of traditional empiricism. Both sacrifice the living, embodied, world-attached experiencer. In seeking to uncover the phenomenal-complex of experience as a field—as a configuration of full-bodied *aisthesis*, conceptual anticipation, and value-bearing behavior—we are staging a return to the source that precedes the objectivizing of traditional empiricism and the subjectivizing of traditional idealism.

[2] EXPERIENCE AS PROCESS

WE HAVE DISCUSSED what we consider to be at issue in speaking of experience as a field, distinguishing our approach to experience as a configuration of experiencing-figure-with-background from those approaches in which experience is viewed as a juxtaposition of discrete and granular elements. In this section our task is to elucidate, in a preliminary way, the dynamic feature of experience. Experience is a *dynamic* field. What does the adjective add to the meaning of the noun? In what way can its meaning be expanded through further elucidation? What new features are brought to light in the use of the term "dynamic" as a characteristic of experience?

The expansion of meaning in the expression "dynamic field" has basically to do with the introduction of the determinant of process so as to secure our view of experience from the threat of substantialization. Experience is an ongoing process rather than a static arrangement of parts. The phenomenal field never comes to rest as a concluded and finished state of affairs. It is given over to passage, development, movement, evolution, and the emergence of the new. Experience is a *streaming* presence as well as a configurative presence. The mixing of metaphors whereby experience is depicted at once as a field and as a stream is required by the phenomena themselves. The phenomenal field is at the same time a phenomenal stream. The configurations of experience are always on the way, accumulating new and at times unexpected textures of meaning. We are thus required to speak of a double perspective, by virtue of which experience is viewed both as a configuration and as a process. In speaking of the configurative character of experience we are presupposing something about the deployment of experienced space; in speaking of experience as a process or a streaming presence we are presupposing something about the role and character of experienced time. Hence, our elucidation of experience as a dynamic field opens our project of inquiry in such a manner that the explication of time and space as the fundamental horizon-forms of experience is anticipated. This will become our theme of inquiry in the succeeding chapter.

The phenomenal field of experiencing-figure-with-background is presented not as a substantive entity, defined by fixed and invariant qualities, but rather as a process of becoming in which variable figures appear against indeterminate and changing backgrounds. Experience is infected with process. James had already made this insight central to his philosophy of radical empiricism when he wrote:

According to my view experience as a whole is a process in time, whereby innumerable particular terms lapse and are superseded by others that follow upon them by transitions which, whether disjunctive or conjunctive in content, are themselves experiences.[9]

Whitehead's approach to experience, which at crucial points exhibits remarkable similarities to that of James, also finds in the designation of process a central distinguishing feature of experience. "Process is the becoming of experience," he says.[10] According to Whitehead experience is an occasioning of events which partakes of novelty and creativity borne by a temporal becoming. Whitehead speaks of "occasions of experience" as the primary figures, as it were, of his creative universe, and with this new vocabulary he attempts to uproot the notion that experience is a collocation of fixed and permanent particles. All of this is part of Whitehead's herculean project of replacing the traditional philosophy of substance with a philosophy of process. Philosophical reflection, through which experience achieves its elucidation, is no longer bound to substance-attribute modes of thought. It moves in the milieu of a new inquiry-standpoint and new categorial formulations. A similar concern to render explicit the process character of experience is evident in some of the later writings of Edmund Husserl. In his *Krisis* he articulates experience as a "streaming life of consciousness" (*strömendes Bewusstseinsleben*).[11] This articulation precedes, says Husserl, any talk about psychic dispositions and personality properties. The language of dispositions and properties presupposes the phenomenon of a streaming and vital consciousness. Recurring characterizations of experience as a process of "streaming-in" (*Einströmen*) and a "streaming presence" (*strömende Gegenwart*) are found in his unpublished manuscripts.[12] Husserl, like

9. *Ibid.*, p. 62.

10. *Process and Reality*, p. 252. Cf. p. 207: "These aspects can be summed up in the statement that experience involves a becoming, that becoming means that something becomes, and that what becomes involves repetition transformed into novel immediacy."

11. *Die Krisis der europäischen Wissenschaften und die tranzendentale Phänomenologie* (The Hague: Martinus Nijhoff, 1954), p. 233; English translation, *The Crisis of European Sciences and Transcendental Phenomenology*, by David Carr (Evanston: Northwestern University Press, 1969).

12. This is particularly the case in the collected manuscripts entitled "*Zeitkonstitution als formale Konstitution*," designated as

James and Whitehead, thus points our attention to the pervasive fact of process and clears the path for a new approach to experience in which the intrinsic dynamism of the phenomenal field is acknowledged and given a decisive role to play.

As philosophers of experience it is now our task to explore the clearing opened up by some of our predecessors and see where our explorations lead. What precisely is meant by the declaration that experience is a process or that the configurative structure of experience is imbued with dynamism? What is maintained by such a thesis and what historical distortions are combated in its claims? We suggest that three interrelated features, in particular, constitute the meaning of process or dynamism as applied to experience. These three features have to do with the fluidity, temporality, and historicality of experience.

The phenomenal field is fluid. It has no fixed or stable coordinates. It is precisely the dissolution of that which is fixed and stable that is at issue in talking about the fluidity of experience. This fluidity, and herein resides its decisiveness, extends to all of the constituents of the configurative complex of experience. More is involved than a simple acknowledgment of a change in the figures of experience and the modification of their sense. The experiencer, the background, and the modes of conjunction and disjunction are subject to fluidity as well. The determinations of the background vary in accordance with the particular perceptual, conceptual, and valuational perspectives that are assumed. The experiencer, inserted in the world as a project always on the way, comports his body and uses his utensils and funded experience to relate himself to his natural and social world in varied modalities. Fluidity permeates all of the constituents of experience. This permeating fluidity, however, is not to be confused with an abstractable quality residing in a particular. Fluidity is not localized within particular objects and events as an isolable quality. Hence we err if we look for fluidity in a quality attached to the abstracted constituents of the field of experience. Fluidity is a characteristic of the field itself, determining the multiple variations that occur within it.

The desubstantializing of experience through the elucidation and description of its fluidity should not be confused with the

---

"*Manuskripten C,*" currently housed at the Husserl-Archives at the University of Louvain, Belgium.

recognition of change in its classical formulation, or with the Bergsonian notion of the flux of consciousness. The classical doctrine of change is said to have its founder in Heraclitus and his well-known maxims "All things flow" and "You cannot step into the same river twice." Thus, Heraclitus allegedly discovered —or rediscovered, as may have well been the case—the reality of change. But the change which Heraclitus brought to our attention was that of a peculiarly limited genre. It was change in the form of cosmic succession, change abstracted from objects and things observed in their various species of alteration and displacement. Change came into its own, but it did so as a cosmological principle of explanation, applicable chiefly to the region of objects and things rather than the region of persons and actions. This approach to change—as a problem for cosmology—became normative in the classical period of Greek philosophy and received its sharpest articulation in the philosophy of Aristotle. Plato had maintained that although change needs to be acknowledged it must be acknowledged as unreal and hence unintelligible. Only that which is permanent and abides is privy to the penetrating light of the intellect. Aristotle, the student, inverted the doctrine of his teacher. Change is real, and the task of the philosopher is to render it intelligible. Aristotle performs this task by setting forth a classification of the different types of change (substantive, quantitative, qualitative, and locomotive) and delineating the peculiar structure of change (a supposite and two opposites) in whose terms change can be rendered intelligible as the displacement of forms. Yet for all of Aristotle's incisiveness in rendering change intelligible, his approach remained limited to considerations arising from cosmological interests. In the development of these interests a particular inquiry-standpoint is assumed. Attention is focused on that which is exterior. At issue is the understanding of change in entities that populate the "outer world." The dichotomies of exterior and interior, outer and inner, objective and subjective are thus already structured in Aristotle's doctrine of change, and he opts for the exterior and the objective. His doctrine of change thus offers an explanation of cosmic succession by virtue of which the alteration and displacement of entities in an external world can be understood. Aristotle's change remains the abstract movement of entities in objectified space. The concrete movement which characterizes perceptual experience, embodied existence, and the intentional vectors of the phenomenal field either remains hidden in the classical doctrine of change, or is indeed excluded. What needs to be articulated, according to our view, is the concrete movement of bodily engagement with its variant figures, which is operative in the constitution and emergence of objects and provides the conditions for objectification itself. This articulation antedates the familiar dichotomies of subject and object, interior and exterior. The fluidity of experience as process is not the change of objective, exterior cosmic succession.[13]

Bergson, in his exploration of the immediate data of consciousness, marks out another path of inquiry. Although in a very general and minutely informative way he agrees with Plato that change is unintelligible while accepting Aristotle's claim that it is real, nonetheless, the inquiry-standpoint that Bergson assumes is somewhat removed from that of the Greeks. He looks for the supreme instance and standard of process in the interior of consciousness, accessible only through an act of introspective intuition. In the interior of consciousness he finds only a flux of becoming, an uninterrupted flow devoid of distinctions. Change becomes interiorized and subjectivized in a rather decisive manner. Change as external and cosmic succession is redefined and becomes the *duré* of internal consciousness. The result of this is that change and movement are indeed desubstantialized and experience is rendered fluid in a radical way. But this rendering fluid proceeds by doing violence to the primitive presentment of experience as a field in which the subjective and objective are bonded by an operating intentionality, and in which the interior and exterior appear as late emergents, always requiring the field notion in order to be specified. Process as a feature of experience no more originates from the "inside" than from the "outside." It permeates the figure-ground structure of experience at a level on

13. A critical analysis and assessment of Aristotle's doctrine of change would carry us quite beyond the limits of our project. It needs to be pointed out, however, that not only is Aristotle's doctrine cosmological, it is bound up with a *particular* cosmology—one buttressed by the metaphysical category of substance. A possible alternative to the substance-oriented cosmology of Aristotle would be Whitehead's cosmology of "creative advance." A thorough examination and critical assessment of Aristotle's doctrine would thus need to proceed in awareness of other possible methodologies and perspectives for handling the cosmological problem; but this, as we have indicated, is not within the focus of interest in the present study.

which distinctions have not yet solidified into dichotomies. The fluidity of the phenomenal field shows itself only after the conflict of cosmological and psychological prejudices is suspended.

The second and related aspect of our effort to become clear as to the description of experience as a process has to do with the role of time. Time infects every act of perception and underlies every value-laden project. Experience would seem to be time-bound from start to finish, making it necessary to speak of the phenomenal field as a *temporalized field.* Indeed in speaking of the *presence* of an experienced figure, be it an object, event, or situation, we already find ourselves, upon reflection, involved in discourse about time. There is a twofold meaning in the use of "presence" when one speaks of the primitive presence of the experiential field. There is first the sense of presence as *appearance.* Something present is something that appears, becomes open to sight and inspection, and is placed within the focus of attention. Presence is that which is *presented.* But there is also the explicit temporal reference in the meaning of presence, indicating the "now" of experience, the moment of disclosure in which that which is presented comes to view. At every point of arbitrary division of our conscious life one can become aware of living in a temporal presence, in a "now" which pervades one's thought and action. The peculiar status of this "now," its connection with past and future and the various layers of meaning which attach to it, constitutes one of the more intriguing issues in any philosophy of experience and will require patient and careful scrutiny in the following chapter. At this juncture we are only concerned to locate the source of the issues in a more general characterization of experience. The two senses of presence which we have indicated are interrelated. That which is rendered present announces its appearance within a temporal horizon which encompasses experiencer, figure, and background. It is vitally important, however, that this temporal presence not be too quickly construed as an isolated and atomistic instant, as an abstracted space-time point. In the presentational immediacy of lived experience the "now" does not seem to appear this way at all. It remains part of a past which keeps arriving and part of a future which keeps advancing. The presence of the "nows" of experience thus exhibits an existential breadth which expands both into the past and into the future. Past and future enter into the constitution of the lived present.

Experience is a process of arriving from a past and moving into a future. The experiential field has the character of being imbued with a past—a living past which continues to impregnate the present and contribute to its significance. The present, as it were, retains the past. Correspondingly, it anticipates the future. This anticipation marks out possible configurations of perception, thought, and action yet to be realized and thus also contributes to the structure of meaning which surrounds the present. The pushes and pulls of the past and future as they interpenetrate in the present engender within the fabric of experience a vibrant and dynamic movement. To speak of experience as process is to recognize this temporal resonance.

The third aspect of the meaning of process has to do with the historical feature of lived-through experience. The elucidation of the historical texture contributes a perspective of meaning which is not as such entailed from a recognition of the fluidity and temporality of experience. James and Whitehead are quite cognizant of the fluid and temporal character of experience, but they have given precious little attention to the historical deployment of the experiential field. For suggestions along this line we need to consult different thinkers and different traditions—thinkers and traditions given considerably less attention in Anglo-American philosophical circles. Marx, Dilthey, and Heidegger, from quite different points of view, have seriously addressed themselves to the historical texture of lived experience. Marx projected a return to the historical experience of man's socioeconomic development. Dilthey, one of the founding fathers of hermeneutics as a philosophical problem, laid the foundations for a "critique of historical reason" which was to provide the interpretive concepts for an imaginative understanding (*Verstehen*) of the lived experiences which inform the aesthetic and religious world views of man. Heidegger, in *Being and Time*, sought to provide a fresh approach to the questions of existence, being, and time by taking as his point of departure a hermeneutical analysis of *Dasein*. Marx, Dilthey, and Heidegger have, each in his own way, grasped the significance of the historical expression of experience and discerned its relevance for philosophical method.

The historicality of experience, like its fluidity and temporality, is a contextual feature which extends to all of the constituents and connections within the phenomenal field. It bears upon the experiencer, the figures of experience, and the background. It provides the perspective for viewing the experiencer as both a product of his heritage and a bearer of historical decisions. Man is at the same time a creature and a creator of history. The profusion of historical meaning is not the result of the activity and decision-making power of man alone. Historical meaning also rests on a figure-ground structure. The figures of historical experience, the events in the life of a person and a community, are always positioned against a background of remembered happenings and anticipated purposes. Historical meaning emerges from the configurative unity of the constituents of the phenomenal field. It is the result neither of the constituting activity of an abstracted "historical subject" nor of the passive reception of abstracted objective facts. Experience as historical process displays intentionalities which precede any sorting out of subjective and objective elements. Historicality spreads its mantle over the interlacing constituents and manifold postures of the phenomenal field.

There is very little in our experience, if there is anything at all, that escapes the clutch of history. The very language that we use in the speech which articulates our experience carries with it a horizon of historical meanings. Our perceiving, thinking, and valuing proceed within historical contexts, not simply in the sense that the thoughts and values of our predecessors continue to figure as formative influences but in the more fundamental sense that perception, thought, and valuation are at once recollective and projective in character. Admittedly, the truth criteria of certain abstractive and objectifying modes of thought, as is notably the case in mathematics, are not subject to the variance of history. But even in the projects of objectifying modes of thought, certain layers of historical meaning remain in the background. This is discernible not only when one undertakes an objective-historical inquiry into the origins and developments of mathematics and science but, more fundamentally, when one addresses himself to issues having to do with the *value* of mathematics and science within the wider context of the cultural life of man.

In our preliminary elucidations of the historical feature of experience we can do little more than suggest certain themes for further inquiry—historical time and space, hermeneutical thinking, the historical character of the experiencer, and the connection between nature and history—to be pursued in the course of subsequent exploration and explication. But already in these preliminary elucidations it should be evident that the acknowledgment of historicality as a feature of lived experience provides our phenomenology of experience with a broader methodological foundation. Phenomenology, if it is to do justice to the manner of appearance of that which shows itself, cannot remain a project of pure description nor content itself with revising the inquiry-standpoint and concepts of transcendental philosophy. Descriptive and transcendental phenomenology must make way for hermeneutical phenomenology. There is no description without interpretation, and every interpretation occurs within a context in which some sense of the historical is already in force.

[3] THE RESILIENCY OF THE CONCRETE

IT COULD WELL BE SAID that the early Hegel discovered the concrete. *The Phenomenology of Spirit* is the story of the concrete, historical becoming of consciousness. But it also needs to be said that Hegel later moved from the terrain that he had discovered and explored to regions of more lofty abstraction. The homeland of *The Phenomenology of Spirit* is forsaken for the ethereal region of pure thought mapped out in the *Science of Logic*. Hegel, by now, has been sufficiently chided for submerging the concrete in his awesome feats of speculative construction, and it would be tedious to rehearse the accumulated attacks upon his system. What is of interest, however, is that subsequent philosophers, interested in remaining in touch with experience, have taken over the search for the concrete and have made this search the point of departure for their philosophical reflection. Husserl, in one of his later writings, speaks of the paramount role of the concrete in philosophical investigation. "Actual discovery," he says, "is a matter of concrete, extremely subtle and differentiated work." [14] This demand is reminiscent of Whitehead's insistence that the success of philosophical reflection is to be measured by the degree that it is able to avoid the "fallacy of misplaced concreteness." Abstractions have their place, and philosophy could hardly function without the use of abstractions,

14. "Die wirkliche Entdeckung ist Sache den konkreten, höchst diffizilen und differenzierten Arbeit" (*Krisis*, p. 260).

but Whitehead's caution with respect to the unwitting substitution of the abstract for the concrete and the possible failure to recognize the degrees of abstraction in speaking of matters of fact is well to be heeded. Heidegger's effort to explicate the existentialist (*existenzial*) structures of *Dasein* as they show themselves in the existential (*existenziell*) concreteness of human choice affords another illustration of a preoccupation with the search for the concrete. Heidegger, like Hegel, may not always remain true to his original insight, but the drive to discover the concrete is there. James, Jaspers, Merleau-Ponty, and Ricoeur are some other contemporary philosophers who have given sustained attention to the solicitation of the concrete within experience. It could indeed be said that the distinctive viewpoint of contemporary existentialism and phenomenology revolves around the search for the concrete.[15] In the background of the repeated appeals and demands voiced by these thinkers we discern a hard fact of experience itself—a fact which we shall name the *resiliency of the concrete*. The concreteness of lived experience can be philosophically forgotten. There is ample evidence that this may happen. But it does not permit itself to be submerged for long, and in the end resists removal by dubiously auspicious abstractions. It is thus required of a philosophy of experience that some account and some clarification of the status of the concrete and its bearing on philosophical reflection be given.

But is not the task which we have set ourselves an impossible one? Is not every elucidation of the concrete a speaking *about* it, and does this not already place us at a distance from the concrete, be it a concrete perceptual experience or a concrete bodily movement, and inevitably introduce some level of abstraction? Elucidating an experienced event or situation is not simply reenacting it. It involves an attentive focus upon it and a speaking about it in the hope of discovering its peculiar texture or character. Admittedly there is some play between our thinking and speaking on the one hand and that which is the topic of thought and speech on the other. We will account for this through the movement of transcendence which impregnates thinking and speaking. But there seem to be no good reasons for legislating a

15. William Barrett has developed this viewpoint as it relates to existentialism in *What Is Existentialism?* (New York: Grove Press, 1964).

diremption of thought and topic of thought, speech and that about which one speaks. Such a diremption would violate what we will later establish as the intentional character of thinking and speaking. In reflecting on the concrete and speaking about it we do not therefore necessarily conceal it. On the contrary, by virtue of the intentionality of thought and speech the concrete is first brought to light and explicated.

We direct our attention to the presence of the concrete. In what does this presence consist? How can it be circumscribed? What does the word itself mean and what is the sense of its use? To speak of that which is present as the concrete is in the first instance to speak of that which is in the act or process of "growing together." The word itself is of Latin origin, derived from the infinitive *concrescere,* meaning simply "to grow together." Although etymology never answers any philosophical problems, it may be a helpful guide in placing us on the proper path. Speaking of *the concrete* is already a grammatical abstraction. What is at issue is the *event of concretion,* the process in which the constituents of experience in some sense mix and mingle and conspire as an appearance or a phenomenon. We are thus able to see how the configurative and process character of experience, which we have discussed in the preceding sections, can properly be understood as the presentation of events of concretion. To speak of the concrete is to articulate the presence of the experiential field as a process in which experiencer, figure, and background conspire or grow together. The dynamic phenomenal field is determined by concreteness.

Concreteness, in its fundamental sense, is thus the presence of that which grows together. Proceeding with our elucidation we are now able to relate the meaning of concreteness to an old and familiar notion in philosophy, *the given,* and, hopefully, we can clarify its use and function. Philosophers have been prone to speak of the *given* within experience, if for no other reason than the recognition that philosophical reflection proceeds not within a vacuum but in response to solicitations of some kind or other. But to speak of a given for philosophical reflection is only to begin the inquiry. What promising candidates qualify as the given? What precisely is it that is given? The tendency, particularly in empirically oriented philosophies, has been to specify as the given certain elemental units—either material particles, facts of physiology, or atomistic sense-data—all of which display a rather high degree of abstraction. These elemental units, somehow serialized in time and juxtaposed in space, are then made to function as building blocks for theories of perception, knowledge, and the nature of man. But it is precisely this notion of an elemental givenness that is rendered problematic in our new approach to experience. Experience viewed as a dynamic field determined by concreteness allows no such elemental givenness on the primordial level. The concrete is the given of experience, but the concrete is never primordially given as an isolated granule or an atomistic unit of experience. Elemental givenness needs to be replaced by *global* givenness. That which is given within primordial experience is always a concrete global configuration.

The concretely given global configuration, with its interwoven constituents and vital conjunctions, is given as an implicit structure of meaning. The point which needs to be underscored at this juncture is that meaning is not found in passively received figures of experience whose meaning then is simply read off by an observer; nor is it the result of the constituting activity of an epistemological subject. Meaning is spread out over the global configuration of experience, and is the result of its configurative development rather than of any particular constituents of the field. The proponents of idealism saw clearly enough the problems with respect to the use of the given in traditional empiricism, but in forging their own answer they tended to construe meaning as an achievement of transcendental consciousness. For idealism the given is the qualification of experience with respect to its passivity, but no meaning is invested in the given. Meaning is the achievement of transcendental consciousness as it apprehends the given as given-for-it. According to Kant the structure of meaning resides *a priori* in the mind and is supplied through the activity of pure understanding. On this point the line of demarcation between Kant and Husserl, at least in the earlier works, is precariously thin. Admittedly, Husserl never conceived of meaning and order as given beforehand by a disengaged mind that manufactures its categories, but he did retain the doctrine of the transcendental ego and ascribed to it a resident power of constituting meaning out of disordered raw material. The whole tradition of idealism (to which Husserl is only partly an heir) has invested all too much power in the constitutive activity of a universal consciousness, which then becomes the absolute source of order and meaning. What is overlooked in this tradition is the possibility of dealing with the inherent problems of traditional empiricism in another manner—not by an appeal to a transcendental source of meaning but through a re-examination of the given. Such a re-examination, as we have seen, will yield a global configuration with implicit meanings rather than a juxtaposition of scrambled sense-impressions without connective tissues. The given already secretes meaning. It has, as James pointed out, its conjunctive relations which are every bit as real as the terms that they relate. Yet, it must be remembered that the structure of meaning in the globally given is only implicit, thus defining the task of philosophical reflection as that of a continuing explication of the implicit. A more thorough investigation of this structure of meaning, which it is the task of philosophy to explicate, will have to wait until our discussion of the intentional structure of experience in Chapter 3.

Our discussion of the concrete as a configurative event, presented as a global given, leads quite naturally to the questions "How is this concreteness delivered?" or "In what manner is it rendered present to the experiencer?" In addressing ourselves to these questions we will again make use of a traditional notion, one with an erratic and none-too-well-defined history, in the hope of salvaging it and revaluing it as stable philosophical currency. This is the notion of immediacy. The notion of immediacy has often been used in close conjunction with the notion of givenness, producing such locutions as "immediately given," "the given of immediacy," "given in immediate perception," and the like. The varied and often tortuous uses of immediacy have resulted in a kind of crisis in our concepts and our language and demand an effort to rescue them from their obscurities and distortions.

The distinction between the immediate and the mediated has been in philosophy for some time now, particularly since the advent of modern philosophy. Philosophers of various persuasions have either made explicit use of the language of immediacy and mediation or have betrayed in their formulations that the distinction remains in force. Philosophers as diverse in their outlooks as Hegel and Hume have spoken of that which is immediate, although the immediacy in Hegel's philosophy is hardly that in Hume's. Hegel makes use of immediacy principally in the interests of a metaphysical theory. This metaphysical theory, as is well known, provides a picture of reality coming to fulfillment in a system of concepts by virtue of which the merely existent is "taken up" into the system and comprehended. The history of this process of conceptualization is basically that of universalizing through dialectical mediation the immediacy of the merely existent so as to achieve the fulfilled immediacy of comprehensive concepts (*Begriffe*). Hume places immediacy not in the service of a metaphysical project but rather in the service of an epistemological inquiry which investigates the origin of simple and complex ideas. Hegel ends up with the fulfilled immediacy of the universal concept, generated by a universal consciousness that has the power to discern the universal in the particularity of bare immediacy. Hume remains cautious about the language of fulfilled immediacy and universal concepts, and settles for the immediacy of particulars—atomistic sense-impressions.

To clearly understand the propriety of the use of the vocabulary of immediacy, it is first mandatory that one suspend the metaphysical and epistemological inquiry-standpoints assumed by Hegel and Hume. The elucidation of experience in its initial stages must free itself from the designs of traditional metaphysics and epistemology and wait patiently for suggestions as to how the problems of being and knowledge can be most productively pursued. Because of the accumulated varieties and confusions in the use of the language of immediacy, there might be some merit in circumventing its use entirely. There are, however, certain aspects of experience that can be elucidated if its meaning is carefully delineated.

The immediate, as applied to experience, has to do with that which is *directly* presented, without the intervention of a "go-between" or a "by virtue of which . . . ." The deliverance of the concrete is direct rather than circuitous, following neither the lure of abstracted sense-data nor the vapor of mediating concepts. Concreteness is delivered in its immediacy through a response to the invitation, "Look and see." This should not, however, be construed as an invitation to look for passively given qualities or static states of mind. Because of the historicality of the concrete there can be no simple reception of figures of experience. In seeing one is already interpreting. Every description is mixed with interpretation and projective understanding. The main issue thus has to do with what happens in our looking and seeing. In what manner does the seeing of phenomena develop? How is the concrete directly delivered and disclosed?

The crucial aspect of this deliverance and disclosure has to do with the factor of time. To speak of the immediate is already to speak of time. The immediate is confronted in a *moment* of time. But this moment of time is not an abstracted instant of serial succession. It is a moment with fringes and a temporal background of past and future. The immediacy of the concrete is thus already a temporalized immediacy, a presence surrounded with retentions and protentions. There is no perception of the immediate in an instant, abstracted and cut off from the flow of the past through the present into the future. What is required for the elucidation of the immediacy of the given is a view of time other than that of mere serial succession in which past, present, and future are pulverized into discrete and granular units which succeed each other in an endless coming to be and passing away. The presence of immediacy is an *ecstatic* presence—a presence which stands out into a future and stretches back into a past. Immediacy, in the tradition, is for the most part determined by the concept of time as simple serial succession and becomes in the end a mere residue and fixed result of a temporal passage. The degree to which immediacy can be salvaged as a descriptive notion for the presence of the concrete must be measured by its success in avoiding the serial notion of time whereby the immediate becomes an instantaneous present devoid of duration. The immediate as an event of a configurative process of experience has a different temporal texture, ecstatic or existential in character. Thus confusion might be avoided in speaking of *existential* immediacy so as to distinguish our usage from the traditional usage borne by an abstract view of perception and an abstract view of time.

In the preceding paragraphs we have sought to elucidate the interrelated notions of concreteness, givenness, and immediacy in light of our earlier discussion of the configurative and process character of experience. We will now endeavor to illustrate some of the above elucidations through an analysis and description of the not uncommon experience of perceiving a lamp on a table. In selecting this particular example we have already set certain limits on the range of attention, focusing our attention on a specific configuration of experience, the perceptual field, as distinct from let us say the field of practical activity (building a book shelf), or the valuational field (judging an act of murder), or the field of personal, situational involvement (being in a state of anxiety), or some other field. Realizing that a certain arbitrariness in selection of illustrations is unavoidable, we will nonetheless attempt to show that there is a kind of compenetration of all fields of experience in the deployment of any particular one. The perceptual field is already layered, so to speak, with determinations of the other fields. There is first to be noted the figure-ground relation which obtains in our perception of a lamp on a table. The lamp is seen as a figure-with-a-background. The lamp is on a table, the table is in a room, the room is in a house, the house is on a lot, the lot is in a city, and the city is in a country. The background, or more precisely backgrounds, have an indeterminate and receding character, each copresent in the perception of the lamp and at the same time pointing beyond themselves, implicating other figures along the way. Let us say that we are so positioned that we see the lamp from the front. As seen from the front, a copresence of profiles surrounding the figure, as well as a copresence of backgrounds, have already made their appearance. The lamp shows itself from the front as a figure with a back, top and bottom, left and right sides. It is already an artificial construction to speak of seeing the front as a cluster of isolated sense-data which then mysteriously point to possible perceptions of other sense data which would, if made actual, constitute the perception of back, side, or top. Strictly speaking one does not perceive the front of the lamp; one perceives the lamp against its background from the front. The perception of the lamp from the front is part of an intentional structure of perception which already links the front to other visual profiles. It is not as though the front of the lamp were a juxtaposition of mute sense-data waiting to be connected with other sense-data so as to achieve significance. Perception in its initial upsurge is already bathed with significance, infected with meaning as a result of the intentional vectors that reveal the copresent profiles.

In all this the configurative character of experience is discernible. The givenness of the lamp is a *global* givenness, and the growing together of the profiles of the figure and the surrounding background in the *act-of-perception* defines the concreteness of the experience. This givenness and concreteness, however, is not delivered in an instantaneous present. Its immediacy is that of an existential immediacy wherein anticipations and recollections are already at work. The perception of the lamp in its configurative presentment is at once anticipatory and recollective. The lateral and rear sides are present as anticipations in the perception of the lamp from the front, and in the duration of perception the past continues to structure the texture of the present. Perceptual configurations are thus also perceptual processes displaying a peculiar synthesis of time.

But have we not erred in illustrating our elucidation of experience with an example from perceptual experience in which the primary focus falls on the visual field? Is not sight the most distant of the senses, the most susceptible to abstraction and objectification? Ought we not heed the urging of Heidegger and look for the deliverance of the concrete in the immediacy of man's practical projects, deployed within a field of tools and utensils? In the act of hammering, says Heidegger, there is a kind of uninterrupted attunement of man with the world as a field or configuration of instruments. The hammer is "at hand" (*zuhanden*), unmolested by theoretical reflection, at every stage of the process indissolubly linked with the preoccupations of the user and his projected purposes. In the act of hammering there is no explicit theoretical awareness of the hammer, no distance between the hammer and its user has yet developed. A *concrescence* of preoccupations, utensil, implicated materials, anticipations, and purposes, in which distinctions have not yet come to settle, takes place. But suddenly the hammer breaks, no longer performs its function, and obtrudes on the user and his well-ordered project. With this obtrusion a new mode of world-relatedness emerges. The hammer emerges as a thing, an entity positioned over against the user as an impediment or an *ob-ject,* a brute something which is merely "on hand" (*vorhanden*). Now for the first time the figure of experience makes its appearance as an object, something "on hand" to be reckoned with.

Admittedly, Heidegger has sketched in an illuminating manner the genealogy of objectivity as it takes its rise from the intrusion of discontinuities in our practical, everyday, workaday world. Whether this is the only path of genetic development that objectivity follows is, of course, quite another matter, and there are times when Heidegger himself suggests that it is not. Assuredly, if we never experienced reversals and frustrations in our practical life and never experienced a crisis in our concepts, we would have little occasion to reflect upon our predicament and put our conceptual schemes in order. The objectification occasioned by critical reflection would thus seem to be imbedded in a more primordial, prereflective comportment. Yet one needs to proceed with caution in setting one configurative complex or field of experience over against another as somehow more basic or primary. There is neither a "primacy of perception" nor a primacy of utensil-oriented praxis. The task is not to set one over the other but to discern their compenetration in lived experience, allowing only the primacy of experience.

A patient analysis of our example would illustrate this compenetration. The perception of the lamp is inseparable from project-oriented behavior. The lamp presented in the existential immediacy of lived concreteness is never simply an object to be gazed at. Such a mode of awareness may indeed be instated, but it is a derivation from a more primordial experiencing of the lamp. In the perception of the lamp, practical and aesthetic factors are already in play. The lamp as seen is also an electrical appliance which illuminates the room. It provides decor for the table and contributes to the aesthetic balance of the room. It is a treasure to be cared for, kept out of the reach of destructive children. Historical meanings surround it; its design reveals the period of its construction. The perceived lamp is never simply the sum of its abstracted material properties. It is part of an interpenetrating figure-ground complex which not only opens itself to a variety of visual profiles but to a rich abundance of praxis-oriented, aesthetic, and historical perspectives of meaning as well.

The concrete experiencer is always already inserted in one or a number of these varied and changing perspectives. The interests and concerns of the perceiver are already at work in the emergence of meaning which infects the perceptual event. This is not to say that the perceiver is in some way the single author of the emergent meaning (as idealism would maintain). It is rather that the involvement of the perceiver marks out certain possible meanings and excludes others in his reading of the solicitations from the immediate presentment of figure against background. The connoisseur of art finds in the perception of the lamp a different sector of meaning than does the electrician. The tired husband for whom the lamp is present as a means of providing the proper light for the reading of the evening newspaper expresses an attunement with the lamp significantly different from that established by his three-year-old child, for whom it is the threat of being burned. The housewife, as she arranges the furniture, experiences another perspective of the lamp; the carpet cleaner, for whom the lamp and the table are pieces to be moved to facilitate the execution of his task, illustrates yet another perspective. For all of these the lamp is already charged with meaning, global in structure and variant in character. It is at this point that the vocabulary of essentialism seems to break down. There appears to be no one stable *essence* (structure of meaning) of the lamp. It is a figure with a plurality of profiles and perspectives, each of them indissolubly linked with a contextualized background and with the behavior of the experiencer.

[4] THE EXPERIENCED WORLD

IN THE PRECEDING SECTIONS we have marked out certain paths of inquiry which point in the direction of a revisionary philosophy of experience. This revised empiricism replaces the granular model with a field notion; static qualities make way for events in dynamic process; experienced time takes the place of the abstracted time of serial succession; the concrete is explicated as a global rather than an elemental given; and immediacy is located in the existential presence of the experiencer's attunement with the contents of experience. In this section we will attempt to knit together some of the threads of inquiry that we have unraveled. Here we introduce the locution "the experienced world," and by it we indicate the totality or encompassing of the varied contents, constituents, and structures of experience. In speaking of the experienced world we are not speaking of the world as an object of reference. It is neither a particular entity, which would indeed be of a rather odd sort, nor is it a class of particular entities. It is an encompassing notion which includes within it the distinctions of individual and class, particular and universal, specific and generic. Admittedly, the world can be sliced in such a manner that it becomes intelligible to speak of it as a region of objects, a region of events, a region of situations, and the like. There are, if you will, numerous versions of the world, but the meaning of world as experienced is never exhausted or conclusively defined by any of its versions. In particular, our usage of the expression "world" indicates the interplay of the configurative with the process character of experience; it designates the interconnection of the deployment of experience as a field with the fact of dynamic process, and at the same time signifies the concrete deliverance of this interplay and interconnection to an engaged experiencer.

The usage which we are suggesting is not, it would seem, entirely novel. William James, to whom all philosophers of experience continue to stand in debt, had already cleared a place for the "experienced world" in his radical empiricism. Speaking to the point at issue he writes as follows:

> The individualized self, which I believe to be the only thing properly called self, is a part of the content of the world experienced. The world experienced (otherwise called the 'field of consciousness') comes at all times with our body as its centre, centre of vision, centre of action, centre of interest.[16]

In this passage and in others similar to it, James suggests a relatively untried notion of the world. He portrays the world as a totality of concentric fields—fields of vision, action, and interest —each of which is anchored in an embodied experiencer. James is here at the same time opening new paths for reflection on experience and anticipating explorations carried through by contemporary phenomenology and existentialism. We of course know that Husserl read James and admired his genius. However, to speak of historical influence and appropriation is quite another matter. In any case, the issue at stake is not one to be resolved through the delineation of lines of historical influence, interesting and valuable though such a project might be. The requirement is that of engaging in a dialogue with one's philosophical predecessors so as to follow experience back to its source, elucidate its texture and movement, and suggest new formulations and insights in a continuing quest for meaning.

The distinctive and richest contributions of James, Husserl, Heidegger, and Merleau-Ponty may well reside in their pioneering explorations of the experienced world. Husserl, particularly

16. *Essays in Radical Empiricism*, p. 170 n.

in his later writings, placed the notion of the *Lebenswelt* solidly in the center of his phenomenological investigations. Even the writings of his early and middle period, although allegedly dominated by the guiding motif of a *strenge Wissenschaft,* contain intermittent suggestions that the exploration of the concrete life-world provides the unifying theme of his philosophy. The life-world, in the phenomenology of Husserl, is the world prepredicatively manifest in the perceptions, decisions, and valuations of an intentional consciousness. This is the world present to consciousness as a field of human affairs in which various tasks and activities are already under way. This is the world of pretheoretical involvement, preceding not only the abstracted world-region of science but also the eidetically reduced world of the predicative judgment.[17] Heidegger, who in the period of his *Being and Time* was able to acknowledge an inestimable debt to his former teacher, proceeds from Husserl's foundational explorations and provides a more specifically existentialist reading of the life-world. The world as described by Heidegger is in its initial presentation the world of concerned *Dasein,* in which the moods of anxiety and guilt find a natural habitat and in which an irremovable being-unto-death leaves its telltale mark on all life and existence. Heidegger at the same time intensifies the dimension of finitude as a determining feature of man's being-in-the-world and widens the gap between the world as existentially apprehended and the world as objectively known. The break with Descartes' fateful interpretation of the world as a totality of extended substances is more sharply drawn by Heidegger than by Husserl, leading Heidegger perilously close to a disastrous diremption of *Dasein* and objective nature. Merleau-Ponty, philosophizing in the spirit of both Husserl and Heidegger, sets forth an existential phenomenology in which Husserl's *Lebenswelt* and Heidegger's *in-der Welt-sein* are repostured as *le monde perçu.* This perceived world is structured by a lived time and a lived space centered in a lived body. The world as perceived by an embodied experiencer remains, according to Merleau-Ponty, an unfinished business and an existential task, a plethora of projects to be assumed time and again rather than an accomplished state of affairs, a horizon of comportment in

17. See esp. *Erfahrung und Urteil: Untersuchungen zur Genealogie der Logik,* ed. and comp. Ludwig Landgrebe (Hamburg: Claassen, 1964), pt. I: "Die Vorprädikative [Receptive] Erfahrung."

which the liaison between experiencer and contents precedes the objectification of categorial thought. The suggestions and insights of James, Husserl, Heidegger, and Merleau-Ponty that emerge in their explorations of the experienced world need to be developed and critically assessed. Their challenge to find sense in the world of immediate experience is avoided only at peril to philosophy itself. But their challenge can be accepted without becoming enslaved to the analytical schema and doctrinal details of their respective programs.

There has been a pronounced tendency in the history of philosophy to approach the world as a cosmological issue. In such an approach the world as "cosmos" is pictured as an external totality of entities within an objective extensive continuum of time and space. The peculiar and ironic destiny of such a world-picture is that it has no place for the experiencer. The experiencer is exiled from the world, banished to some inaccessible region of nonextended, incorporeal substantive mind or to a transcendental island. The world is viewed as an external totality of entities somehow presented to an internal mind, self, or consciousness. Self and world are split and separated in accordance with the dichotomies of internal and external, subject and object. The experienced world is older than this split and precedes these dichotomies. The experiencer is a participant within the world rather than an entity set over against it. He is already lodged in a world of proximate concerns when he begins to inquire about it. Our use of the locution "the experienced world," in one of its meanings, is intended to clear the path for the return of the exiled experiencer to the world. The experiencer is always inserted in one or a number of fields of vision, action, and valuation, and this totality of the experiencer and his fields of concern and involvement is what we understand by the experienced world.

This experienced world with the experiencer at its center is never presented as a block universe with clearly definable contours. It is a world in process, displaying in its unfolding a plurality of versions. Indeed the world is experienced only as it displays itself in one or a combination of versions. This experience is expressed in such everyday locutions as "He is in the world of sports," "He has become a member of the academic world," "Decisions become increasingly complex in the world of finance," "Life is a struggle in the world of politics," and the like.

In each of these expressions a portion of experience is already rendered intelligible, and a version of the world comes to the fore. We can also proceed to talk of the "world of the child," "the world of the hermit," "the world of the psychotic," and with these expressions communicate contents and textures of experience that are readily understood. Our analysis and elucidation can proceed further through a specification of configurations of objects, events, and situations encompassed by these various versions of world. It must be remembered, however, that our use of the vocabulary of objects, events, and situations is accompanied by shifts in focus of attention; and if these shifts are not recognized and their attendant contexts not acknowledged, then the way is paved for various species of reductivisms and their unwarranted restrictions of the breadth of experience, to say nothing of the crisis of concepts that almost inevitably ensues. Through a strict adherence to the primacy of experience that flows through the various versions of the world, the tendency to reduce the meaning of world to any one set of determinations is avoided.

A further exploration of the configurative and dynamic experience that appears in each of the world versions as revealed in ordinary and everyday speech brings to light a dual character and movement. World experience is seen to include both prereflective and reflective experiencing and nonthematic and thematic significance. World experience has both a *prereflective-nonthematic* side and a *reflective-thematic* side. What needs to be underscored at the outset is that the reflective-thematic is still part of the cloth of experience. Reflection about or on experience is a movement which proceeds within experience. The essential connection between reflection and experience must be maintained. Kierkegaard launched his bold attack against Hegel's doctrine of "pure thought" because it severed this connection. The life and experience of the concrete thinker becomes a matter of indifference for the designs of pure thought. Kierkegaard sought to restore the intimate connection of reflection and experience in his return to the "subjective thinker." The subjective thinker reflects on experience within experience. He penetrates and elucidates the existential crannies of experience with thought. This defines the movement of Socratic and Kierkegaardian reflection as contrasted with the Hegelian reflection of pure thought.

A further exploration of this reflection, which remains anchored in experience, is required. Every stream of reflective awareness is awareness of or about a reflected content or figure, which constitutes its thematic focus. Reflective consciousness is intentional in character, and, as we will see in Chapter 3, there are various types of intentionality. The intentional character of reflection gives birth to the distinction between the *act of reflection* and the *reflected on*. Reflection is not a movement within interiorized thought which somehow turns back upon itself so as to reproduce its original operation. It is already directed toward the various figures of experience, to the *reflected on*. Reflection is already projected into the world. Husserl is correct when he describes reflection as a consideration and explication of what is to be found in experience rather than a repetition of the experiential process.[18] The process of experience is distinct from the act of reflection on the process. Yet this is a distinction without separation, and Husserl all too hurriedly positions the act of reflection at a distance from the process reflected on and too quickly retreats to a transcendental standpoint. The task, which is not an easy one, is to remain with the phenomena while reflecting upon them, recognizing that both the reflective act by an engaged experiencer and the reflected phenomena occur as events within the stream of experience. Merleau-Ponty, in my estimation, comes closer to achieving this than does Husserl. For Merleau-Ponty, reflection "grasps its object as it comes into being and as it appears to the person experiencing it, with the atmosphere of meaning then surrounding it, and which tries to infiltrate into that atmosphere." [19] Reflection occurs within a field in which both the act of reflecting and the reflected on are constitutive moments.

The reflective-thematic, however, is not the only possible structuring of world experience. There is also what we have called the prereflective-nonthematic. These two structural features are interwoven. They constitute, as it were, an existential cross section of the experienced world, interpenetrating in such a manner that it needs to be said that man lives both structures in every occasion of experience. The peculiar relation between these two structures as being one of distinctness without separa-

18. *Cartesian Meditations: An Introduction to Phenomenology*, trans. Dorion Cairns (The Hague: Martinus Nijhoff, 1960), p. 34.
19. *Phenomenology of Perception*, p. 120.

bility requires further elucidation. The use of the prefix "pre-" in the grammatical construction "prereflective" should not be construed to mean that the prereflective and the reflective are successive levels of experience within a serial time sequence. The prereflective-nonthematic is not serially prior to the reflective-thematic; neither is it genetically earlier or historically more primitive. Admittedly anthropologists find that the consciousness of primitive peoples is geared more to legend and myth than to scientific explanation, and psychologists speak of the emergence and the development of abstraction in the maturation of the child. But these interpretations are the result of a derivative application of the distinction at issue. It is likely that even in the originary experience of primitive man and the child the prereflective and the reflective interplay as they do in civilized man and the adult, the difference residing in the configurative forms of experience that emerge as a result of this interplay.

The original distinction has to do with a distinction of direction and deployment of two structural moments within world experience. As structural moments one is not serially prior to the other, although both are temporalized within their structures. It is not as though prereflective experience provided the nonthematic raw material of sense-data, emotive qualities, and inclinations which are then organized by a reflective ego. To express the distinction in such a manner would be to commit the fallacy of idealism. They both display organizational syntheses of their own, they both share in the configurative and process character of experience, and they both emerge within the complex of "experiencing-figure-with-background." In prereflective experience, the organizational synthesis is such that the configurative complex is undisturbed by explicit reflective discrimination of textures of figures and types of backgrounds. Admittedly, reflection is already implicitly at work even in prereflective experience, for prereflective experience can never be severed from the continuing contribution of past reflected experience. But the prereflective moment of experience does not congeal as an explicating and discriminating focus of attention. In prereflective experience, discriminating determinations are latent; in reflective experience they move about freely and occasion the attentive focusing of experiencer, figure, and background as explicit themes.

We are now in position to gather up some of our foregoing

elucidations and suggestions and propose a more general circumscription of the thrust of meaning involved in our use of the Jamesian phrase, "the experienced world." *The experienced world is a concretely delivered configurative field and dynamic process of prereflective and reflective experiencing, intentionally directed to figures and backgrounds, affording both nonthematic and thematic significance, with an engaged and embodied experiencer at its center.* With this multidimensional meaning of the experienced world we are able to safeguard the unity of action and insight, perception and conception, valuation and knowledge, which is implied in the word "experience" itself. An inquiry-standpoint is thus proposed from which the well-worn and, for the most part, unfruitful dichotomies of theory and practice, fact and value, exterior and interior, object and subject are suspended, making possible an inquiry as to their source and genealogy in a more primordial deployment of experience.

The peculiar posturing of the intentionalities of prereflective and reflective experience in the manifestation of felt, willed, and noetic meanings will need to be described and explicated in detail. This will constitute the topic of attention in our discussion of the intentional structure of experience in Chapter 3. However, before proceeding to an investigation of the intentional structure of experience, a preliminary task awaits our attention—the elucidation of time and space as the horizon-forms of experience. There have been recurring allusions to the temporal and spatial character of experience in the present chapter. We must now examine in some respectable detail the textures of time and space and elucidate their status and roles in the dynamics and structure of world experience.

2 / The Temporality and Spatiality of Experience

The space and time which I inhabit are in their different ways indeterminate horizons which contain various points of view. The synthesis of time like that of space is a task that always needs to be performed afresh.
—M. Merleau-Ponty, *Phénoménologie de la perception*

[1] TIME AND SPACE AS HORIZON-FORMS

THE EXPERIENCED WORLD is a configurative field and dynamic process at once temporalized and spatialized. World experience moves within temporal and spatial horizons. We speak of time and space as *horizon-forms,* and with this formulation we intend to suggest both the lived character and holistic structure of time and space. As horizons, time and space are dwellings or abodes, inhabited by a world-experiencer, which exhibit peculiar markings, signs, and intentionalities. As forms, they are structural wholes which display a forming and unifying function, synthesizing places and directions, interweaving past, present, and future. The characterization of time and space as forms should not be construed as a designation of logical conditions or dead frames for conceptualization. One might avoid this misunderstanding by speaking of them as *forming* rather than as *formal* in character. It is by virtue of this character that the unifying, synthesizing, and organizing of meanings in world experience are able to proceed. Horizon and form, in our understanding and use of these terms, are correlative notions, interdependently characterizing time and space as living realities within the phenomenal field, vitalizing and structuring world experience.

We agree with Kant that time and space are in some way at the basis of experience, but we find his analysis of them too restrictive and abstract. Kant never succeeds in making explicit the role of time and space in the concrete development of lived-through experience. He is interested in these forms primarily so as to account for a stage in the achievement of transcendental knowledge. Their significance resides in providing *a priori* forms for sensibility upon which the categorial operation of the mind works. In our phenomenology of experience, time and space carry a more specifically existential and ontological significance. They are ingredients within the dynamic structure of experience itself, rather than transcendental and *a priori* conditions for the possibility of experience. They pervade the configurative complex of "experiencing-figure-with-background" and provide the contexts for its deployment. Yet it was the genius of Kant to perceive that any elucidation of experience which is interested in the genealogy of its organization must begin with an examination of the forms of time and space. We thus remain true to Kant's original insight, but we substitute a configurative and intentional view of world experience for his more granular and non-intentional view (particularly as concerns his approach to perceptual experience), and we seek to liberate his forms of time and space from their epistemological servitude. It may well be that what is required is a "rewriting" of Kant's "Transcendental Aesthetic," as well as the whole *Critique,* from a more specifically phenomenological perspective. Through such a project the foundations and primal structures of world experience could be elucidated and clarified.

Our present task is to work out a descriptive and interpretive account of time and space as horizon-forms of world experience. We will proceed with our task with Whitehead's caution concerning the fallacy of misplaced concreteness clearly in mind. Geared toward an ontology of the concrete, our philosophical project requires that we disclose the temporality and spatiality of experience in their primordial concreteness. This demands the avoidance of some common and well-established approaches to the issue, not because these approaches are unjustified in themselves, but because a more fundamental understanding of time and space within the context of lived experience is sought. Our discussion properly begins with a delimitation of the scope of our inquiry, distinguishing our approach rather sharply from the traditional representational views of time and space. Before time and space can be *re*-presented through scientific, logical, and metaphysical categorial determinations they are *presented* in the dynamic development of world experience and need to be disclosed in their presentational immediacy.

In the representational view, time is conceptualized as a serial order and represented as a succession of *nows* measuring the movement of objects across space. Time is objectified and abstractly pictured as a flow of postulated entities which succeed each other in a determined order of coming to be and passing away. Time is segmented into units to which are assigned the values of past, present, and future, and the passage of time is represented by a numerical sequence. Although suitable for scientific calculation, such a view of time does not approximate the concrete temporal movements of the embodied experiencer in his contextual alliance with the life-world. The advantage of the representational view of time, with its expressed objectivity, resides in its utility for measurement. Representational time can be applied in the interests of measurement and practical manipulation. Thus one comes to speak of calendrical and clock time, the time of hourglasses, stopwatches, and timetables. The practical advantage of this applied and mechanical time is self-evident. However, this practical advantage carries with it a disadvantage. Mechanical time is measured backwards, while concretely lived time moves forward. Thus, the measuring of time reverses and transforms the original experience of time.[1]

1. Erwin W. Straus in his essay titled "Chronognosy and Chronopathy" has given some attention to the "inversion" which results from the measurement of time. "Statements about measured times are made in the past tense; we say the 100-yard race *was* run in 10 seconds, or the time of the Kentucky Derby was 2:01:4/5. Whenever a numerical value for the variable 't' (time) has been determined, such factum has been established in hindsight. This does not mean that at the finish the timekeeper remembers the start; rather both end and beginning are visualized in retrospection. Measurement of

Herein resides the main limitation in the application of representational time. Although providing chronometrical instruments of extraordinary value, it conceals time as a horizon-form of world experience if it is proffered as the sole and absolute perspective on time. There are various perspectives on time, various levels of abstraction, and various types of temporalization. Even standardized clock time is subject to variance in its practical applicability, when for example a segment of society switches from standard to daylight saving time in order to make objective time more in accord with the projects of existential time. It would thus seem that existential time, or the time in which man dwells and carries through his varied projects, enjoys a priority—although not a privilege of absoluteness—over the ticking-off of seconds and the numerical march of the calendar. All artifacts of instrumental and mechanical time are by-products of a process of dissection in which the time of immediate experience is rendered into granular units through an abstraction from its holistic structure. It may be too bold in this instance to say that "to dissect is to kill," but it must be said that the dissection of existential time transforms it in such a way that a second reflection is required to apprehend it in its primordial holism and directionality.

It is common knowledge that one of the more fateful consequences of the representational view of time, particularly as it received expression in traditional empiricism, is the atomization of time, following from a more general atomization of experience. Experience, as viewed in traditional empiricism, becomes riveted in a space-time point, in a here-now which has neither spatial nor temporal fringes. It was thus that traditional empiricism was forced to find its final criterion for experience in the serial succession of encapsulated sense-data. Time, in such a scheme of things, becomes a succession of instantaneous nows which provide the loci for the isolated sense data. The *lived passage* of time is substituted for the mere subjective determination to pass from one isolated sense-datum to another. From

time requires an *inversion* whereby the initial sequence ABCD is virtually turned in the opposite direction DCBA. In such a retrospective view the original experience is transformed and com-prehended" (*Phenomenology, Pure and Applied: The First Lexington Conference,* ed. Erwin W. Straus [Pittsburgh: Duquesne University Press, 1964], p. 154).

Hume to logical positivism, this view of experience, with its implicatory serial and subjectivistic view of time, remains normative. Whitehead's characterization of Hume's view of experience would thus seem to be fully justified: "Hume's impressions are self-contained, and he can find no temporal relationship other than mere serial order." [2] Given the atomistic view of experience in traditional empiricism, the pulverization of time into a series of discrete instants was unavoidable. It was thus that James's new approach to time came as a breath of philosophically fresh air. James could not locate the instantaneous present in the process of world experience, so he suggested the notion of the "specious present." The specious present is not a "knife-edge" somehow situated between an instantaneous now that has just gone by and one which is about to come. The specious present has an existential breadth or thickness by virtue of which it reaches backward and forward. It partakes of the immediate past and spills over into the immediate future. It unites experience already lived with experience yet to be lived. The specious present is situated along a horizon that marks out a living past and a living future. [3]

2. Alfred North Whitehead, *Process and Reality* (New York: Humanities Press, 1929), p. 208.
3. The nature of the specious present is given particular attention in James's *Principles of Psychology* (New York: Henry Holt, 1929), vol. I, chap. 15, "The Perception of Time." Here he discusses the specious present as the "practically cognized present" which is "no knife-edge, but a saddle-back, with a certain breadth of its own on which we sit perched, and from which we look in two directions into time" (p. 608). Again, he speaks of the specious present as having "a vaguely vanishing backward and forward fringe" (p. 613). A comparison of James's approach with Husserl's phenomenological approach to time would become relevant at this point. It is, of course, well known that Husserl quite openly acknowledged his debt to James. In his *Logische Untersuchungen* (2d ed., 3 vols., [Halle: Max Niemeyer, 1913]) he refers to "James' geniale Beobachtungen auf dem Gebiet der deskriptiven Psychologie der Vorstellungs-erlebnisse" (II, 208). In his "Persönliche Aufzeichungen," *Philosophy and Phenomenological Research*, XVI (1956), 295, he has this to say about James: "James' Psychologie, von der ich nur einiges und ganz weniges lesen konnte, gab einige Blitze. Ich sah, wie ein kuhner und origineller Mann sich durch keine Tradition binden liess und, was er schaute, wirklich festzuhalten und zu beschreiben suchte." Then there is the evidence from Husserl's intensive markings in his copy of James's *Principles of Psychology*. What precisely were the lines of

We have indicated above the path of our analysis and elucidation of time as a horizon-form by distinguishing it from the representational view of time. The initial elucidation of space as a horizon-form must proceed in a similar way. Space as a dwelling which vitalizes and structures world experience, which assigns values to concrete bodily movements and historical anticipations, is not encompassed within the determinations of representational space. Experienced space is not an extensive continuum, represented as a container in which physical objects and events are assigned a place. Such a representation occurs only on the level of cosmological abstraction, where the figures of world experience are converted into objects and conceptualized in their objectivity. We also need to differentiate the phenomenological view from the logical representation of space (through the use of the categories of traditional logic) as an inclusive genus under which segmented particulars are collected or subsumed. This is but another expression of the representational view. Even the advance of transcendental logic, in which space is understood as a necessary *condition* for experience, although approximating more closely the spatiality of world experience, does not penetrate to the meaning which is at stake in our analysis. Admittedly, space can be legitimately approached in the above senses, but preceding all of these senses there is a primordial sense of space, indicating a texture and manner of world experience itself. As Merleau-Ponty expressed it: "Space is not the setting (real or logical) in which things are arranged, but the means whereby the positing of things becomes possible." [4] The representational view construes space as a "set-

influence and parallelism in the thought of these two philosophers? The full discussion of this question is, of course, outside the scope of this book, but of particular interest would be comparisons of James's "specious present" with Husserl's *"strömende Gegenwart"* and of James's "backward and forward fringe" with Husserl's "retention" and "protention." Herbert Spiegelberg carries through a brief but illuminating discussion of the influence of James on Husserl's phenomenology in his book, *The Phenomenological Movement* (The Hague: Martinus Nijhoff, 1960), I, 111–17. For a more detailed discussion of the striking similarities between James and Husserl, see Alfred Schütz, "William James's Conception of the Stream of Thought Phenomenologically Interpreted," *Philosophy and Phenomenological Research*, I (1941), pp. 442–52.

4. *Phenomenology of Perception*, trans. Colin Smith (New York: Humanities Press, 1962), p. 243.

ting"—a matrix or a continuum—which provides loci for the identification of objects. In the phenomenological view, space is a lived horizon along which things and persons are perceived and valued. Phenomenological space is the forerunner of representational space.

We have seen that representational time provides the theoretical basis for clock and calendrical time. A similar function is performed by representational space. Representational space finds its practical applicability in the construction and use of maps and charts. It thus yields "mapped space" as representational time yields "clock time." But mapped space, like clock time, is removed from the original presentation of the phenomenon. One does not reside between the markings on maps and one does not journey across a summation of metrical points. Markings on maps and metrical points are lifeless abstractions and arbitrary constructions for the convenience of measurement. Space as a horizon-form of world experience is presupposed by them, and first provides the living context out of which they are abstracted.

In the above explorations we have performed our first task in the elucidation of time and space as horizon-forms—that of distinguishing our experiential view of time and space from the representational view. Representational time and space are *derived* rather than *presented;* they are derived through the employment of scientific, logical, or metaphysical categories. This is not to say that the validity of the procedures for deriving representational time and space is contested as such.[5] What is at stake is the question of the existential genealogy of time and space as represented objects, real or logical. Their genealogy cannot be discovered in the representations themselves. Before scientific and logical *judgments about* time and space can be fully comprehended as to their source, the immediate *experience of* time and space in the concrete movements of world orienta-

5. This is a point which remains problematic in Heidegger's philosophy of time. He seems to waver between the view that representational time is, by its very nature, condemned to unauthenticity and the view that within its restricted limits it possesses a "natural justification" ("Die vulgäre Zeitvorstellung hat ihr natürliches Recht," *Sein und Zeit*, 7th ed. [Tübingen: Max Niemeyer, 1953], p. 426). For a discussion of Heidegger's philosophy of time, see Calvin O. Schrag, *Existence and Freedom* (Evanston: Northwestern University Press, 1961), chap. 5.

tion must be explicated. If properly conducted, such an elucidation will lead us to the existential origin and foundation of any representational view. Presentation is phenomenologically prior to representation.

Our further elucidation and explication of the temporality and spatiality of world experience will proceed with attention to the following issues: a comprehension of the gestaltist structure of time and space as horizon-forms, an understanding of the lived coordinates which obtain in the presentational immediacy of time and space, and an acknowledgment of the ineradicable finitude of time and space. It is to a discussion of the first of these issues that we now turn.

[2] THE GESTALTISM OF TIME AND SPACE

TIME AND SPACE provide experience with its qualifications of now and here. Every undivided portion of world experience is occasioned within the horizon-form of time, which enables the experience to be presented as a "now experience." Correspondingly, it is occasioned within the horizon-form of space by virtue of which experience unfolds as a "here experience." World experience finds its existential anchorage in the "now" and "here."

"Now" and "here," as phenomenological data, are vectorially expansive. They are characterized by existential breadth and thickness. The now is experienced as a living present which reaches back to the past and expands into the future. It has fringes which interlace with the already experienced and the yet-to-be-experienced. The now as living present never appears as an isolated and atomistic instant. Likewise, the here in which all experience is rooted partakes of breadth and thickness, vectorially connected with variant "theres" that surround it and define it as a here-with-an-environment. As the now of experience is never phenomenologically present as an atomistic instant, so the here of experience is never phenomenologically present as an atomistic point.

Any elucidation of the now experience, which lies at the basis of the temporality of world experience, needs to proceed with the initial characterization of its vectorial expansiveness in mind. Only then can one penetrate to the phenomenon of time as a living reality, a phenomenon manifest as a structural inter-dependence of cross-referential values. Heidegger speaks of the "ecstasies" of temporality, indicating by this somewhat unfamiliar terminology that the three values of time coexist and inter-penetrate. This coexistence of the temporal ecstasies determines world experience as an interpenetrating complex of memories and anticipations invading the present. The now of experience suffers the pressure of the past and the beckoning of the future. Present sensations, feelings, volitions, and conceptions carry with them recollections of the already experienced and anticipations of the yet-to-be-experienced. World experience, presented in the living present, is ever in process of arriving from a past and moving into a future. Thus we come upon the retentional-presentational-protentional structure as the basic structure of temporalized world experience. This constitutes the gestaltism of time as a horizon-form.

The interdependence and coexistence of the values of time (past, present, and future) that constitute the structure of temporality require further elucidation. The past, present, and future in the temporality of world experience are pregnant with vectorial radiations mutually penetrating one another. The past is a removed present and a former future, the present is a recent future and an imminent past, the future is an impending present and an arriving past. The values of each interpenetrate as the values of all. The past as removed present is the present that has been, but the "having been" character of the present as past does not cancel its existential bearing on the experienced now. The past "has been" but it is not "gone by," as one might speak of the going by of representational nows. The past has not lapsed out of the range of existential meaning. It continues to nourish the present, hold its destiny, and provide it with repeatable possibilities. Heidegger has elaborated the distinction between *Gewesenheit* and *Vergangenheit* for the purpose of clarifying the modality of the past in existential time as distinct from the modality of the past in chronological time. Only in chronological time can one properly speak of the past as having "gone by" (*vergangen*). The past in the ecstatic time of human existence "has been" (*ist gewesen*), but it has not vanished from the scene of the present. It continues to bite into the present and plays a role in man's life decisions. With equal power the past radiates into the future. The experienced past is a former future, a future that was once.

The past is a future become historical. But the historicality of the future as past is not an item of "dead history." It is rich with possibilities for repetition. It can be reclaimed and projected again as an anticipatory goal, posited as a lure for creative action. The past continues to slip into the future and witnesses to the experiential fact that what was once can be again.

The present is an imminent past, a past that will quickly come to be. The present already holds within it the past. The experience of presence is infected with the awareness of its *pass-ing* character. This is displayed in the experience of the urgency of choice, in the experience of the present as the "right time" or the opportune moment for the actualization of personal and practical projects. In the experience of the urgency of choice the transiency of the present is most poignantly revealed. The present is there to be chosen, it contains possibilities ripe for actualization. But it also has the character of slipping away, and over the experiencer hover the saddest words "of tongue or pen" —the words "It might have been!" In existential-phenomeno-logical time, the present appears as a *lived* present, best described as the moment of choice or decision. This apprehension of the present as "the moment" distinguishes the present in exis-tential time from the present in chronological time, where it is represented as an instant within a series. In this apprehension of the present as the "moment of choice," the insertion of the past in the present and the insertion of the present in the past can be clearly discerned. The present is on its way, and the possibilities which it holds can be regretfully and remorsefully neglected or hopefully affirmed. Concomitantly disclosed with this interpene-tration of past and present in the "hour of decision" is the interpenetration of present and future. The present is a recent future, a recent future now presented. More precisely expressed, *the present is future possibility now presented*. In thus appre-hending the present, the experiencer grasps the present with respect to its source. The present *comes from* the future. The future occasions the present, in a noncausal sense, and provides a horizon of anticipated possibilities which can be concretely chosen when the future comes-to-presence. So the present con-tains within it both the character of slipping away or becoming past and the character of having arrived. Herein resides the *thickness* of the lived present. It is situated not as a knife-edge but as a bridge with its girders rooted both in the banks of the past and in the banks of the future. The present is situated as imminent past and as recent future. This is the situationality of the present—to merge into the past and into the future—and it is this which defines the present as the moment of choice.

Our phenomenology of the future discloses the same vectorial expansiveness that we discerned in our phenomenology of the past and the present. The future is an impending present, a present which is about to be, and an arriving past, a past which eventually is to come. Although one cannot view the present from the future, insofar as in one's viewing one is already situated in the present, one can in one's experience of presence apprehend the future in the mode of *anticipatory* presence. The future in existential or lived time is not a series of successive nows which will fall into reality at some later date; it is an anticipated region of experience which already infects and colors life-experiences. The future in chronological time is simply an item of calculative awaiting; the future in existential time is experienced as an anticipatory goal of human existence.[6] The future as an impending present invades the now of world experience. Without the future, the present would become sedimented or collapse because it would have no horizon. The very experience of being present in the world requires the solicitations of the future. As the future has a bearing on the present, ever rescuing the present from the fate of sedimentation, so the future provides support for the past. As an arriving past, the future projects the possibilities that will come to define that which has been. The future prefigures the past. It projects the figures of possible choice, which can either be taken over in the moment and given a place in the destiny of chosen possibilities, or be neglected and sacrificed as nonchosen possibilities and enter the past in another mode. The future is something for the past; it makes a difference for the past, projecting the possibilities of how the past might come to be determinate in a specific

6. Heidegger has contributed the distinction between "awaiting" (*Erwarten*) and "anticipation" (*Vorlaufen*) to indicate the two basic attitudes toward the future. (See *Sein und Zeit*, pp. 336 ff.) The former is the attitude present in the vulgar view of time; the latter is the attitude characterizing the understanding of the future in the ecstatic temporality of *Dasein*.

way. The future inserts itself into the present and the past, supports them with its anticipatory possibilities, and coexists with them in a gestaltist temporality.

We have sought to elucidate what we understand by the gestaltism of time as a horizon-form of experience. World experience is temporalized as a retentional-presentational-protentional structure, vitalized by the living interpenetration of the values of past, present, and future. Our task now is to elucidate the gestaltism of space as the other horizon-form of experience. World experience is spatialized as well as temporalized. It has its existential source in the spatial experience of here as well as in the temporal experience of now. We have discerned the thickness and expansiveness of the now, so we will look for a similar texture in the experience of here.

Every event or occasion of experience is spatially situated. The experiencer inhabits space while he inhabits time, and the figures and background of experience assume a variety of spatial reliefs in the act of experiencing. In the world of pure experience, as James would call it, the world is forcefully disclosed as *being here*, with ourselves as an aspect of it. It is in this experience of the being here of self and world that space as a horizon-form becomes manifest. The mode of manifestation is itself varied, although the originary presentation of the being here of self and world would seem to be one in which the determinant of existential mood or sentience plays a rather significant role. One is bored with one's being here, or one is enthused about it. One despairs or rejoices over the fact that one is here. One is astonished because of it, or it becomes a matter of indifference. But whatever the mode of manifestation or disclosure that might be at work, the presence of world is experienced as a being here to which values and attitudes are already attached.

The experience of here is as structurally complex and vectorially expansive as is the experience of now. Just as the now of primordial experience is not an abstracted time-instant, so the here of primordial experience is not an abstracted space-point. The here is itself encompassed within the totality of world as global presence. This totality, within its spatial expression, includes the distinction between here and there as correlative determinations of what it means to have space. The originary experience of the spatiality of world moves within the dialectical interplay of here and there. The two are related not with reference to fixed coordinates, but with reference to world perspectives and world projects that vary with existence itself. The there is a possible here. I can move from here to there, and after I have moved the here becomes a there and the there becomes a here. The same variance occurs in one's apprehension of the place of utensils and perceptual objects. My pen is here but now I place it there, and my ashtray which previously was there has now been brought here. No fixed coordinates obtain between here and there. They vary with the circumstantiality of human existence.

Here and there constitute the root phenomena in the primary apprehension of space. They are not, as we have seen, self-referentially enclosed, but rather intend one another within the variability of human existence, and through their interplay they open up a wider spatial horizon. Here and there vectorially expand into a wider horizon which encompasses them, a horizon structured by vertical and horizontal axes. The vertical axis is present to experience as the span between up and down; the horizontal axis is present as the span between right and left and between front and back. World experience is situated along these two axes and is presented as a holistic, living complex (experiencing-figure-with-background) because the space which it inhabits is itself holistic or gestaltist in character. This space is a space in which projects are actualized by moving up or down, front or back, to the right or to the left. Lived space is not an empty continuum, as is abstract representational space. Its axes and dimensions are not mathematical constructs; up and down, front and back, right and left are not loci of points filling in a vacuous extensive continuum. They are the paths that we follow and the corridors through which we pass as we stylize and frame our existence. Space, thus understood, comprises the dwelling place for world experience. It is the abode in which the world-experiencer lives and moves and searches for meaning.

One of the major and more striking features of lived space as the dwelling of world experience is that it is centered in a being who is himself mobile—the embodied experiencer. Through his bodily movement the experiencer situates himself in a lived space and determines the variable values of the vertical and horizontal axes. There are no fixed points of reference and no predetermined values assigned to the up and down of the vertical axis, or to the front and back and right and left of the horizontal axis. This accounts for the anisotropic character of lived space. There are no measurable properties which can be uniformly attributed to the dimensions of space as in the isotropism of representational space. The values of space vary with the bodily movements of the experiencer. The vertical axis is granted a greater value because of its relative permanence in comparison with the horizontal axis. Although right and left and front and back are readily interchangeable, up and down has a more abiding and constant value. The latter would thus seem to be the most basic axis of world experience. The embodied experiencer is able to turn about and thus interchange right and left, but the upward-downward reference poles remain constant. To be sure he can be turned "upside-down," but this position is itself defined by the abiding value assigned to the vertical axis. Likewise the frontal direction on the horizontal axis enjoys a priority over the other three. The experiencer inhabits space in such a way that life is lived primarily forward. In walking it is the front, rather than the back or the two sides, which solicits bodily movement. In working we face the front, for it is there that our project lies; we face our work. In talking with others we meet them "face to face," and again the frontal direction is primary. It is thus that the directions of space receive different values in accordance with the projects and behavior of the embodied and mobile center of space.

The horizon-form of space as the intersection of the vertical and horizontal axes in the mobile embodied experiencer is a complex of places and directions. One might speak of place and direction as the main modalities of space. Again, it is necessary to proceed beyond the meaning of place and direction as representational concepts. Place, in our understanding of it, is not an isolable segment, boundary, or part of the vertical and horizontal axes. Place is not in the axes in the way that parts of an object could be said to be in that object. At this level the language of physical or logical relations does not appropriately apply, for what is at issue is neither a physical object nor a logical entity. Distance also takes on a peculiar and distinctive character in experienced space. It is not an objectively measurable dimensional length between two points. Place and distance as modes of lived space are inseparable from the human projects through which they become manifest. The significance of place resides in the accessibility or inaccessibility of utensils to be used in the execution of a task, in the perspectival terminus of the perceptual vision, in the encountering of the presence of another self. Distance, before it is represented *ad geometrico*, indicates the range of perceptual objects and manipulable utensils and marks out the path to the social other. Distance, as it is immediately experienced, signifies the reach of one's concerns and structures the world of care. As so aptly expressed by Minkowski, distance measures the scope of one's life at every moment.[7]

Place, in its alliance with my concerns and projects, is where utensils are situated. The pen, the knife, and the hammer have their place. They are within reach or they are beyond reach. They are close enough or too far away. Their place either facilitates or impedes the actualization of a project. Place is where the other self is situated, where he is to be met, where one is to shake his hand. Place is where the embodied experiencer is situated, whence the projects and concerns that link him to the place of a utensil and the place of the other take their origin. Distance is the connective tissue in the concerns that reach toward utensils, objects, and other selves. The distance of lived space, like the distance of representational space, can be said to be a measure of something; however, what is measured is not metrical length but the reach and range of human concern. Near and far, before they are expressed in numerical notations, are sentient valences of concern. A close friend, although distant in meters and miles, is nearer than a mere acquaintance next door who has entered only the periphery of one's concerns.

The places and distances of world experience embody sentient tones and intentionalities of purpose. This provides the gestalt structure of space with a teleological texture. Place is where my purposes reside. Distance is that which is traversed to actualize these purposes. The world-experiencer inhabits space by assigning values to places which figure either decisively or peripherally in his lived experience. Space thus becomes a horizon of existence itself. It is a horizon to be conquered, defended, explored, utilized, and mastered in such a way as to be made concordant with human purposes. It is only through an awareness of the sentient tones of this teleological texture of lived space that one can penetrate to the meanings of "neighbor-

7. Eugene Minkowski, *Le Temps vécu* (Paris: d'Artrey, 1933), chap. 7.

hood space," "national space," "aesthetic space," and "psychological space."

Neighborhood space is space defined through the interests and purposive designs of the community. It indicates the range of communal concerns by marking off those who are neighbors ("close by"). But the proximity of the neighbor cannot be determined by yardsticks and mileage charts. This would leave him shorn of his neighbor qualities and reduced to an object positioned somewhere in representational space. There is no metrical circumference to neighborhood space. It is not a perimetrical setting in which objects are juxtaposed. Perimetrical representations yield only an abstract juxtaposition of abstract objects and abstract points. The neighbor does not live within such a representation. He inhabits his space by penetrating the distance between himself and the other with concern and singularity of purpose.[8]

National space illustrates the same nonperimetrical texture. Although it may be externalized in the demarcation of geographical boundaries, the national space that is inhabited by the world-experiencer has no geometry. It is neither measured by rods nor marked off by rivers and oceans. Its center resides in the capital city rather than in a geocentric locus. It is never an empty receptacle but is always filled with historic memories. Its frontiers are indices of the self-actualization of spirit rather than chunks of acquired land. Shrines, monuments, and battlefields are the peculiar markings which provide national space with its living communal memories and its present vitality. National space is a living reality which houses the concerned experiencer as he projects his sociopolitical destiny. It provides him with the *Lebensraum* requisite for the actualization of his political existence.

Architectural space affords another instance of the spatialization of world experience as this spatialization is imbued with purpose. The space between the garage and the entrance way, the distance from the foyer to the living room, and the place for the stairway and the patio are not apprehended as divisible geometrical points and parts, each external to the other; rather, they indicate the utilization of space, pointing to the regions

8. Cf. Martin Heidegger, *Unterwegs zur Sprache,* 3d ed. (Pfullingen: Günther Neske, 1965), p. 210.

where human concern and purpose are manifest. Architectural space is the spatiality of life in its practical and everyday expression. It is a perspective of space as a dwelling, as a horizon-form of world experience.

Another perspective of lived space is "psychological space." The psychological moods of happiness and hope, regret and remorse, grief and despair, exude their peculiar tones of spatiality. In moments of happiness and hope, space is full and expanded. The experiencer is not bound to an isolated here; his bodily movements are not restricted; he can move uninhibitedly in the directions where his varied concerns lie. In the experiences of regret and remorse, space becomes restrictive and confines the movements of thought and action alike. Concern for the use of utensils as well as concern for other people, the concern through which one spatializes one's world, loses its vitality and significance. In grief and despair the very structure of lived space appears to be threatened. Lived space shrinks and withers; there is no place for the experiencer to move because there are no vital projects to be undertaken and no vital concerns to be realized. Nothing satisfies and spatiality itself is threatened with meaninglessness.

Psychiatric phenomenology has contributed interesting and revealing studies on the nature of psychological space and psychological time in their pathological expressions. Ludwig Binswanger, Eugene Minkowski, and Erwin Straus have provided clinical materials on the pathological distortions of lived space and time.[9] They have shown how the psychotic loses the consistency and plenitude of lived space and time. The shrinkage of his space deprives him of the room for movement which is necessary to actualize his finite freedom. It is precisely from this

9. The reader is referred particularly to Binswanger, "Das Raumproblem in der Psychopathologie," in *Ausgewählte Vorträge und Aufsätze* (Bern: Francke, 1955), II, 174–225; Minkowski, *Le Temps vécu;* Erwin Straus, "Die Formen des Räumlichen: Ihre Bedeutung für die Motorik und die Wahrnehmung," *Der Nervenarzt,* III (1930), 633–56; and Straus, "Chronognosy and Chronopathy." For an introductory summary of the understanding of time and space in psychiatric phenomenology, the reader would do well to consult the essay by Henri F. Ellenberger, "A Clinical Introduction to Psychiatric Phenomenology and Existential Analysis," in *Existence: A New Dimension in Psychiatry and Psychology,* ed. Rollo May, Ernest Angel, and Henri F. Ellenberger (New York: Basic Books, 1958).

freedom that he flees, so this constricted and shrunken space provides a convenient refuge. Accompanying the shrinkage of the psychotic's lived space is the voiding and stagnating of his lived time. The future is blocked and rendered inaccessible, as in severe depression; or it becomes vacuous, as in mania. And with the loss of the future the present and past become impoverished. No longer can the individual look upon the future as a way of retrieving or redeeming the past and crossing the present. The very structure and vitality of his lived time is put into jeopardy. Now what is lost in the shrinkage of space and the impoverishment of time in the life of the psychotic is not a numerical sum of elemental quanta which have been subtracted from an aggregate. There was no such aggregate of atomistic units or quanta of time and space to begin with. What is lost in the disoriented spatial and temporal existence of the psychotic is a manner of comportment, a style of world orientation. The values of spatial movement and temporal projection have lost their original meaning for the psychotic. Both the psychotic and the sane man apprehend time and space as horizon-forms, as dwellings which are to be inhabited, but they inhabit these dwellings in different ways. The delineation of these different ways of inhabiting time and space—the psychotic way and the sane way—remains the specific task for phenomenological and existential psychiatry. What interests the philosopher in the above elucidations is the evidence which psychiatry furnishes for a validation of the gestaltist character of lived time and space.

[3] THE LIVED COORDINATES OF TIME AND SPACE

THE PRINCIPLE of a spatio-temporal coordinate, either implicitly or explicitly stated, is virtually as old as the history of philosophy. The paradoxes of Zeno, formulated in the interests of denying the reality of change and plurality, were occasioned by reflections presupposing some species of coordination between temporal nows and spatial points. Although denying the reality of both time and change, Zeno's arguments presuppose that one cannot talk about time without also talking about the movement of objects across a series of points. It was left to Aristotle to refute the dialectical arguments of Zeno, justify the reality and intelligibility of time, and render more explicit the type of coordination that obtains between time and space. Although Aristotle had no category of space, he did have a category of place, and his justification of the reality and intelligibility of time requires the use of the categorial determination of place as the locus of movement or motion. Time, in one of Aristotle's less obscure definitions, is the enumeration of motion with respect to before and after.[10] In this definition the principle of a spatio-temporal coordinate receives its first decisive expression. There seems, however, to be a problem in this definition, even within Aristotle's framework of presuppositions. The definition unduly limits the meaning of time, restricting it to the measurement of only one form of change. (Along with motion, Aristotle specifies qualitative alteration and quantitative change as the forms of *kinesis.*) It becomes apparent, however, that Aristotle considers motion, understood as the movement of objects across determinate loci, to provide the *standard* for the measurement of time. Hence motion, and more specifically celestial motion because of its alleged uniformity and perfection, becomes the paradigm for the change which time measures. Time with its "before," "now," and "after" is the element in this motion which makes it "enumerable" or measurable. Hence time becomes, for Aristotle, "a kind of number." [11] Time is the enumeration of the passage of objects moving through determinate positions. The enumeration of the passage of celestial bodies as they move across their celestial loci provides us with the standard for measuring all forms of terrestrial change and makes possible the time reckoning of clocks and calendars. According to Aristotle there can be no time without objects moving in space. Time is represented as a coordinate of moving bodies. Indeed it is through a coordination with bodies moving across space that the representation of time becomes possible. The temporal nows are coordinated with the spatial points traversed by the moving bodies, and intervals are coordinated with the metrical distances between spatial points. According to Aristotle the movement characteristic of moving bodies is continuous in nature. Hence, time must also be viewed as continuous, properly understood as an "attribute of that which is continuous." [12]

10. Aristotle, *Physics*, IV. 11. 219b.
11. *Ibid.*
12. *Ibid.*, 220a.

Representational time thus becomes a continuum of nows, correlated with the continuous movement of objects in space. Aristotle, in a rather decisive way, laid the foundation for a spatio-temporal coordinate and marked out the destiny of representational views of time and space in the Western tradition.

We must now investigate to see whether a coordinate obtains in the time and space of lived experience, without as such minimizing the contribution of Aristotle toward a possible theory of the foundation of objective clock and calendrical time. Aristotle's definition of time as the enumeration of motion with respect to before and after may retain its natural justification. Yet it becomes evident that his definition is restricted in its scope, applicable only to the realm of external, objectively presentable bodies whose movement can be calculated and measured. Appropriately, Aristotle's examples are taken from moving celestial and terrestrial objects. What remains unquestioned in Aristotle's philosophy of time is the primordial time of world experience which precedes not only the objective representation of time as an attribute of continuous motion but also the subjective time of inner experience. Augustine's interest in subjective time came as a needed corrective to Aristotle's objective view, and although Augustine may have touched more closely the time of world experience, like Aristotle he failed to penetrate to the more primordial time which functions as a condition for both objective, or representational, time and time subjectively apprehended. Bergson, in his study of the time of immediate consciousness, followed along the path opened up by Augustine but removed himself even further from the time of world experience by *interiorizing* time as a datum of inner consciousness. The only access to this subjective time that remains for Bergson is provided by the insights of intuition. Intellect is unable to grasp the *duré* of consciousness because the intellect, with its analytical and abstractive manner of knowing, pulverizes and stabilizes everything within its scope. The intellect fractures time, brings it to a halt, and in this way loses the very data under consideration. Time thus remains unintelligible. Bergson inverts Aristotle. For Aristotle time is intelligible, within the range of reason; for Bergson time is unintelligible, grasped only in the immediacy of intuition. There follows from this inversion and alleged dualism between intellect and intuition a rather emphatic rejection of a spatio-temporal coordinate. Space, as the proper object of the intellect, is, according to Bergson, *objective, static, divisible, quantitative, homogeneous, discontinuous,* and *geometrical.* Time, on the other hand, is *subjective, dynamic, qualitative, heterogeneous, continuous,* and *nongeometrical.* Space is space and time is time and never the twain shall meet. When the intellect seeks to know time it inevitably spatializes it and falsifies its distinctive character by reducing it to a series of discontinuous and discrete instants. Time and space for Bergson must thus be held in separation.

Our investigation into time and space as the horizon-forms of world experience seeks to avoid the limitations and difficulties in both the Aristotelian and Bergsonian views. Aristotle offered an account only of external and objective time; Bergson offered an account only of internal and subjective time. How is the dilemma to be overcome? The root problem in Aristotle is that he does not give sufficient consideration to the temporalized character of world experience itself, which precedes any measurement of time lapses and sequences in the movement of external bodies. The root problem in Bergson is that he interiorizes time in an encapsulated subject of consciousness, exteriorizes space as an abstractive continuum, and remains unable to recognize the phenomena of lived space which is copresently given with lived time. Our claim is that the time of world experience is not accessible as an object, nor is it originatively present as an attribute of the movement of objects. But neither is time simply present in the continuous *duré* of consciousness. External as well as internal time is secondary and derivative. The world experience of "experiencing-figure-with-background" is already infected with a temporality that first provides the horizon along which distinctions between subject and object, interior and exterior, are rendered possible. The determination of subjectivity as well as objectivity can occur only with the horizon-form of temporality. This horizon-form, with its interpenetration of past and future, is that which determines *presence;* and from this primordial experience of presence the distinguishing qualities of the "presence of a subject" or the "presence of an object" can be derived. It is this primordial time of world experience that both Aristotle and Bergson neglect. Edmund Husserl, in his lectures on time, has suggested a fresh approach to the age-old problem of the status and meaning of time.[13] Pursuing the issue with the tools of phenomenology, Husserl is able to free the discussion from the stalemate of objective and subjective counterattacks. Phenomenological time "shows itself" prior to the determination of an objective, cosmic time and precedes the internalization of time as a counterpart of objective time. Internalized time remains determined by external, objective time. It is introduced because of the inherent limitations of objective time. Objective time is unable to measure the movements of consciousness, thus subjective time is brought in to account for that which cannot be accounted for by objective time. Subjective time is "pieced on," so to speak, to the predefined objective time so as to provide a temporal structure for both subject and object. But suppose that the subject-object distinction itself becomes problematic in a phenomenological description of primordial experience, experience in its immediate presentation not yet being differentiated into subjective and objective poles; then the temporality of this primordial experience will lie beyond the very distinction which gave rise to the piecemeal character of objective and subjective time. One of the abiding contributions of Husserl's lectures on time-consciousness is the delineation of the path which leads to a phenomenological understanding of temporality. It was left to Husserl's most illustrious student to follow this path in his elucidation of primordial temporality as the ground and meaning of Dasein.[14]

Husserl and Heidegger have offered profound suggestions

13. *Vorlesungen zur Phänomenologie des inneren Zeitbewusstseins*, ed. Martin Heidegger (Halle: Max Niemeyer, 1928); English translation, *The Phenomenology of Internal Time-Consciousness*, by James S. Churchill (Bloomington: Indiana University Press, 1964).

14. In *Sein und Zeit*, Heidegger sets for his task the delineation of a phenomenological ontology which takes its point of departure from an analysis of the structural constitution of *Dasein*. At the basis of this structural constitution is what Heidegger calls "ecstatic temporality," occasioning the formulation "*Der Sinn des Daseins ist die Zeitlichkeit*" (p. 331). The temporality that constitutes *Dasein* and confers upon it its distinctive meaning is *ecstatic* in character. Future, present, and past are coexisting and interpenetrating *ecstases*, each standing out from its own background like a projected beam of light, mutually illuminating one another. Heidegger's analysis constitutes an indictment against the representational view of time as three juxtaposed phases following each other in a serial order. He suggests an approach to the problem which avoids the Scylla of

and have developed seminal insights for surmounting the Aristo-
telian-Bergsonian controversy with respect to the character of
time. But what remains unsaid in Husserl and Heidegger is the
manner in which the primordial temporality accessible to phenomenological inspection is coordinated with primordial spatiality. Primordial temporality is never separable from primordial
spatiality. The now of world experience is coordinated with a
here of world experience, and lived time is associated with movement in space. Thus far the implied Aristotelian spatio-temporal
coordinate must be accepted. However, the movement and the
spatiality with which primordial time is coordinated has a non-
Aristotelian (i.e., nonobjective) character. That which is coordinated with primordial temporality is space as a horizon-form
of existence in which the "standard of motion" is the movement
of the lived body. Bergson was clearly correct in denying that the
duré of consciousness could be coordinated with objective space,
but he neglected to consider the more fundamental coordination
on the level of lived experience in which primordial time is coordinated with the spatiality of the lived body.[15] To be sure, we
cannot speak of this *lived* coordinate as quantitative and measurable, for the lived body, whose movements determine place
and distance, is not an object among objects. The lived body is
not open to the investigative procedures of quantitative analysis.
It is the center of world engagement, the center of concern,
radiating into a world in which subjectivity and objectivity are
results of later construction.

----

subjectivizing time on the one hand and the Charybdis of objectivizing it on the other.
  15. Merleau-Ponty, in *Phenomenology of Perception*, formulates
a criticism of Bergson similar to the one that we are here suggesting:
"In order to arrive at authentic time, it is neither necessary nor
sufficient to condemn the spatialization of time as does Bergson. It is
not necessary, since time is exclusive of space only if we consider
space as objectified in advance, and ignore that primordial spatiality
which we have tried to describe, and which is the abstract form of
our presence in the world. It is not sufficient since, even when the
systematic translation of time into spatial terms has been duly stig-
matized, we may still fall very far short of an authentic intuition of
time. This is what happened to Bergson. When he says that duration
'snowballs upon itself,' and when he postulates memories in themselves accumulating in the unconscious, he makes time out of a pre-
served present, and evolution out of what is evolved" (p. 415 n.).

The difference between the movement of the embodied experiencer and the movement abstracted from the change of loci by external bodies is a qualitative difference. The lived body is not "in" movement as one might speak of a trajectory being in movement. Movement itself is a mode of bodily existence. The movement of the body is a mode of gaining access to the world, a manner of orientation, a comportment through which other people, tools, and objects are first able to announce their presence and enter the various regions of concerned existence. It is by virtue of this movement that the body is able to inhabit space, to dwell in the world in such a manner that spatiality characterizes its existence. The space of the body is not a collection of juxtaposed points. It does not occupy space in the sense that one would speak of an ashtray taking up room and hence possessing the attribute of extension. Correspondingly, bodily movement cannot be defined as the *abstract* movement across points. It is the *concrete* movement of manipulating tools, placing objects, clearing one's vision, grasping the hand of one's fellow man, and achieving a general structure of orientation as one makes one's way about in the world. It is with this concrete bodily movement that time is coordinated, and not with the abstract movement of external objects across adjacent points. The body inhabits time and space as horizon-forms. The lived coordinate of time and space is thus a coordination of inhabited horizons.

The lived body moves along vertical and horizontal axes. The movement along these axes is already infected with temporality, not in the sense that time is an "attribute" of a moving body, but in the sense that time and space are copresent in the projects of the lived body. The vertical-horizontal axial complex is interlaced with a retentional-presentational-protentional complex. Up and down are coordinated with the experience of temporal presence. The continuation of presence, the experience of presence-to-the-world which characterizes the life of the embodied experiencer as long as he exists, is linked with the relative permanence of existing in the midst of upward and downward directions. The now of world experience has its here; it is lodged between that which is up and that which is down. But the now and here of world experience, as we have seen, are not self-enclosed. They are vectorially expansive. The now reaches into the future and remains tied to the past. The here intends a there, which is in front or in back, to the right or to the left, above or

below. Forward movement contains within it a temporal orientation. In moving forward, the lived body faces the future. It
moves in the direction and to the places where its concerns lie,
where the projects yet to be actualized reside. In ordinary language we speak of moving forward in time as well as in space,
indicating that at the source of world experience there is a
coordination of forward with future. We also say that the past is
behind one, it has already been lived through. That which is
behind or in back indicates places where projects have already
been actualized, tasks already accomplished, undertakings already begun and either finished or left unfinished. We have
already noted that the frontal direction on the horizontal axis
enjoys a priority over the backward direction. Life is lived primarily forwards, in both time and space. As the frontal direction of
lived space enjoys a priority over the backward direction so the
future enjoys a priority over the past. In the world experience of
spatial presence, the front marks out the primary path of movement; in the world experience of temporal presence, the future
enjoys a corresponding priority. The temporal significance of
right and left needs to be understood in connection with movement forward and backward. By virtue of their variability, right
and left exist as possibilities of becoming front or back. I can
turn to the right, face that which elicits my attention, and
convert left to back. Or I can turn left and convert right to back.
The temporal values of right and left are thus contingent upon
their possibilities of becoming front or back.

The chief existential import of the lived coordinate of time
and space is that it provides the context in which the relatedness
among the figures of experience occurs. The coordinate provides
the connective tissues between the events of the life-world. Time
and space enable the experiencer to be related to tools, objects,
and persons. By virtue of the lived spatio-temporal coordinate I
am connected with the various figures of my world, and access to
them is rendered possible. It is also within this coordinate that I
experience unification with myself. I experience unity with what
I have been and with what I hope to be, with my possibilities that
are strung along my vertical and horizontal axes. But this synthesis rendered possible by the coordination of time and space is
never given as a *permanent* synthesis. Only an abstract coordinate is able to share in the permanence and universality of
logical relations. The connective tissues between persons and

things and between persons and persons can be severed. The life-world affords disjunctions in experience as well as connections. Space connects, but it also separates. It provides the access to my neighbor but it is also the occasion of my estrangement from him. By virtue of spatiality, tools are at hand for the realization of concerns, but it is also by virtue of spatiality that tools are too far away, out of reach, and hence existentially remote. My experience can be temporally unified in such a way that past and future are synthesized with the present, but time can also separate me from what has been and what is yet to be. The synthesis between time and space as well as the syntheses within time and space are not fixed determinates. They are syntheses which, in the words of Merleau-Ponty, constitute tasks that always need to be performed afresh. They are never given beforehand; they never precede the act. The temporality and spatiality of world experience are characterized by contingency, which invites both connections and disjunctions. This contingency provides the most impressive expression of the irrevocable finitude of lived time and space.

[4] THE FINITUDE OF TIME AND SPACE

TIME AND SPACE, as the horizon-forms of world experience, are *forms of finitude*. The dwellings of world experience are themselves finite, and this confers upon the structure of world experience the indelible stamp of finitude. This finitude of time and space, and the experience which they house, is most decisively disclosed by the contingency which characterizes the project of synthesis in the lived coordinate of time and space. As we have seen, the syntheses within time and space, as well as the coordinate unity of time with space, are *achieved* syntheses, occasioned by the projects and tasks of the world experiencer. The syntheses exhibit no abiding permanence. They need to be achieved again and again. This contingency subjects time and space to the possibility of disjunctions or discontinuities. The discontinuity of experience needs to be acknowledged as a fact of world experience. Discontinuities are as forcefully presented in the life-world as is any undivided and continuous portion of experience. World experience with its inherent dynamism and

vitality manifests a fluidity in which both the drive for unification and the display of disjunctions receive expression. The
positive and the negative, the creative and the destructive, are
both children of experience, given birth in the primordial upsurge of world encounter. This is to say that the ontological
structure of experience is such that being and non-being intermingle dialectically, and it is this which provides the formal
definition of finitude. World experience is finite in that it is
occasioned as a mixture of being and non-being.

In speaking of connections and disjunctions, unities and
disunities, positivities and negativities, the question as to the
priority of the one over the other inevitably arises. Is the positivity of the value-laden connections of temporalized and spatialized world experience prior to its negativity, or is it the other way
around? It is at this point that both extreme essentialism and
extreme existentialism remain impoverished in coming to grips
with the phenomena as experienced. Extreme essentialism as-
cribes an uncontested primacy to unity and positivity. Being is
construed in such a manner that it becomes identical with the
fixity and completed unification of ideas or moments in the life
of Absolute Spirit. Being is a harmonic unity of ideas and ideals
ontologically prior to the negativity of non-being. As we shall see
later, it is precisely this traditional "metaphysical" view of being
and non-being which will need to be placed into question and
transvalued. In the present context, however, it renders intelligible the metaphysical source of the claims of essentialism. In
extreme existentialism—particularly in that of Sartre, who does
little more than invert the traditional metaphysical scheme—the
negativities of non-being are granted a priority and the basic
reality becomes that of existential estrangement. To say, however, that Sartre still remains enslaved to traditional metaphysics is not to minimize the incisive character of his elucidations of
estrangement. The point we want to make clear is that in our
philosophy of world experience there can be no talk of the
ontological priority of either the connections or disjunctions of
experience, of either its positive or negative expression. Primordial experience is an occasioning and a dynamic upsurge
that lies beyond the positive and the negative. It is, in the words
of Nietzsche, veritably "beyond good and evil." The connections
and disjunctions of experience are first posited in the comport-

ment which drives experience to its actualization. Time and space as the horizon-forms of experience are not definable by a metaphysically prior network of necessary connections, nor are they somehow subject by their own nature to the destiny of fractionated existence. Our notion of finite experience is thus rescued from both its possible essentialist and existentialist distortions. Finitude is not an ideal essence which precedes experience, nor is it a determination of experience as necessarily estranged. It is that contingent character that makes the horizon-forms of world experience subject to variance and ambiguity.

Time contains both positive and negative elements. It is a condition for both creativity and destructivity. Temporalized experience (and there is no experience that is not temporalized) is threatened with the dissolution of its achieved value. The creative character of time is threatened by various modes of anxious concern (principally boredom, loneliness, guilt, despair, and death). Anxiety is the awareness of finitude, and through this awareness the finite or contingent temporality of world experience is disclosed. The modes of anxiety in their varied intensities reveal the nonfulfillment of past and future in the experience of presence. The primordial experience of being-present-with-the-world is threatened with respect to its achieved essentiality. The structure of meaning that accompanies the lived present is threatened with annihilation. The emptiness of boredom and melancholy bespeaks the inability of one's present projects to provide ultimate and abiding meaning. That which is tried and accomplished fails to afford final satisfaction. The present becomes empty, falls into a vacuity of value, because it is nourished neither by a past nor by a future. The disquietude of loneliness also has its temporal texture. The experiencer stands anxiously alone in a present in such a way that he is separated from enriching communal memories and hopes. Guilt discloses the unfulfilled potentialities of one's past and defines the present as bereft of a positivity that might have been. Despair, which involves a higher intensification of the negativity of time, is the awareness of future nonfulfillment, the veritable loss of hope, in which the privileged ecstasy of time is shorn of its life-giving quality. The anxiety of death reveals the finitude of time with respect to its implied transitoriness. Death finishes the time of world experience.[16] Not only is the act of dwelling *in* time subject to negative valuations but the temporalized dwelling of world experience is itself infected with an annihilating power because of death. The anxiety of having to die provides the experiencer with the most poignant index of the negative element in time. His concerns here lie not simply with the factuality of ceasing to be. Biological cessation is certainly an element in the anxiety of death, but it is not that which constitutes its decisive existential sting. Death is the loss of expansive presence, the possibility of the loss of possibilities, the negativity of no longer being able to affirm the creative moment. Death is the irrevocable limit to fulfillment in temporalized experience.

Space, as the horizon-form coordinated with time, is susceptible to the same negativities as is time. Boredom and melancholy flatten the terrain of lived space. The axes and directions of space are leveled and lose their value. Space is deprived of its vitalizing and enriching character. The places to which my body might move no longer elicit interest. All places are equally boring. The here and there where projects might be actualized do not afford any possibilities for creative actualization. Space becomes the place where one is bored. In loneliness the experienced isolation is the isolation from the place of the other. Guilt discloses the unfulfilled space of the past, the places where creative projects might have been realized but which through freedom and destiny have remained unoccupied. Despair, as the extreme limit in the boundary situations of world experience, indicates a more violent form of displacement. In despair the

16. In what sense a cosmic time, both antedating and postdating the time of world experience, occurs independently of experience, and the character that such a time would have, cannot be discussed here. It may be sufficient to remark that no claim is made either for or against its "existence." Knowledge of such time, clearly, would be the result of an inference rather than the result of phenomenological description and analysis. Pre- and post-human cosmic time, being the result of an inference, would be layered at a second remove from lived reality. Its association with lived reality need not, however, be entirely severed. The "knowability" of pre- and post-human cosmic time, if it is not to evaporate into the dizzy heights of pure speculation, would still require the horizon-forms of world experience in which the knower is situated and from which he makes his inferences.

value of being here is, as such, threatened. The here-now of existence, the lived coordinate of space and time on its primordial level, is rendered problematic in such a way that an "exit" from existence itself would seem to provide the only solution. In despair the consistency of lived space is interrupted. Death not only finishes one's time, but it occasions the ultimate displacement. Death threatens one's having space in a radical and decisive way. It is thus that the various modes of anxiety—boredom, loneliness, guilt, despair, and death—threaten the structure and value of lived space as we have already seen that they threaten lived time.

Through the revelatory character of anxiety the discontinuities or negativities in the various modalities of lived space become manifest, and the finitude of these modalities is brought into focus. The space of my neighborhood is finite; it can become an insecure place in which to live, no longer offering support for my projects. The security of my national space is subject to threats. It can be disrupted and I can lose my place in history. Discontinuities can enter my aesthetic space and fissures can appear in my psychological space, producing profound disjunctions in my bodily orientations. Anxiety forcefully discloses that man cannot totally rely on space. There is no final spatial security, as there is no final temporal security. Herein resides the telling testimony of the finite character of time and space.

But there are also positive forces at work in the finite forms of time and space, enabling the unification of lived experience. These positive forces are most readily discernible in the phenomenon of decision, which functions as the existential ground of unity and continuity. Anxiety makes manifest the negativity of experience; decision occasions its positivity. It needs to be remembered, however, that decision is not an isolated act of will. Decision requires a world, a context of vectors and lived intentionalities, which enter into the constituting process of making choices. The unification of experience is not based on a voluntaristic act, traditionally understood. The achievement of unity requires energies and contexts that go beyond the traditional isolation of a willing faculty.

The positive factors in the finite form of temporality center around the presentation of time as the *opportune time for decision*. Aristotle, in his *Nicomachean Ethics*, already apprehended the significance of the "good in the category of time" (*kairos*), and with this concept of ethical time he was able to define the special moments of moral realization. Time apprehended as the right or opportune moment for the realization of a project or the fulfillment of a concern provides us with the positive feature of finite temporality. The main problem that Aristotle bequeathed to his successors was that of relating the good in the category of time to lived historical experience. It would appear that his cosmologically oriented metaphysics remained inadequate for the task. What is significant, however, is that in spite of his metaphysics Aristotle was able to acknowledge a form of ethical time. In its positivity finite time is present as the opportune time for decisions in the exercise of finite freedom. Time can be affirmed in the creative moment, uniting the past and the future with the present in the resoluteness of committed thought and action. The experience of presence can be the experience of the creative moment as well as the experience of an impoverished now.

The experience of the creative moment has been given a literary exemplification by Proust in his idea of the *"moment privilège,"* by Camus in his discussion of the "hour of consciousness" in his existentialized version of the myth of Sisyphus, and by Dostoevsky in his depiction of Kirilov's experience of the "moments of eternal harmony." Kierkegaard, Jaspers, and Heidegger have elucidated the phenomenon in question in their discussions of the "moment" (*Augenblick*) as the authentic time for resolute choice. Authentic existence apprehends the moment in choice and commitment. But what is lacking in the above-mentioned literary and philosophical elucidations is an explicated view of the dynamics and structure of experience whereby the creative moment is seen in its proper role as the source of unity and continuity within the finite temporal-horizon of world experience.

The acknowledgment and affirmation of the creative moment does not place the experiencer beyond the determinations of finitude. The finitude of time may be transcended, but it cannot be annulled. The dynamics of experience contains the power of transcendence, making possible the freedom required for authentic choice, but this transcendence does not entail a removal of finitude. Even in the experience of the "presence of eternity," eternity is experienced as being present in finite time. The experience of the creative moment, whether religiously or nonreligiously defined, occurs only within an "experiencing-fig-ure-with-background" context in which both experiencer and world are qualified by the finite form of time. World experience, even when intensified by the ecstasy of aesthetic or religious experience, remains under the conditions of finitude.

The unity of temporalized experience needs to be seen as coordinated with the unity of spatialized experience. Decision centralizes and unifies lived space as well as lived time. The discontinuities and insecurities of lived space can be combated by commitment and resolve. I can affirm value-bearing qualities in the various modalities of the horizon-form of space. Neighbor-hood space, creatively affirmed, is the space for creative interac-tion with my neighbor. The space of the one who is "nearby" is no longer apprehended as a threat, no longer presents itself as a "coefficient of adversity" (in the language of Sartre's negativistic existentialism), but rather becomes the place where the other can be acknowledged and addressed. In the creative expression of neighborhood space, the neighbor is no longer the possible threat for my displacement; he is the one with whom I achieve mutual fulfillment through dialogue and shared experience. The positive expression of national space discloses the world in such a manner that the experiencer and the other become open to the experience of their place within a national history. The figures of national space—the place of the capital city, historical monu-ments, markers, and shrines—take on significance within the wider context of a common national destiny. The solidarity in the experience of national destiny counters the various threats of national displacement. Space in its aesthetic orientation can be unified and continuous as well as fractionated. Through the various forms of art, man is able to order and organize space so that it fulfills his yearning for beauty and aesthetic harmony. Psychological space can be broadened and deepened to provide places for the creative actualization of the embodied person. The shrinkage and restriction of psychological space that character-izes experience under the conditions of estrangement can be combated through the apprehension and affirmation of the axes of lived space as horizons of purposive activity.

The threats to one's spatially oriented existence can be countered by various movements of spatial affirmation. Experi-ence resists the threat of not having creative space and seeks to expand and enrich the horizon-form of space in such a manner that its various modalities can achieve a purposive expression. As there are creative or opportune moments, occasioning the drive for temporal unification, so there are creative or opportune places and directions providing the pivots for spatial unification. The spatiality of experience can be accepted and affirmed, appropriated as a context for valuation and meaning-laden decisions. But in the creative affirmation of space its finitude is not removed. The negative expression of space can be attacked and successfully combated but the possibilities of estrangement remain. This means that space, as well as time, remains ambiguous with respect to the polarity of positivity and negativity. This constitutes the telling and persisting evidence of their irremovable finitude.

3 / The Intentional Structure of Experience

*All perceptions and experiences of a self, as they
relate themselves to a particular time, hang
together by virtue of their intentional objects. Likewise all of the self's perceptions and experiences
of being-with-others hang together by virtue of their
intentional objects—hanging together in such a
manner that subjective time is constitutive of an
objective time and an objective world.*
      —Edmund Husserl, *Erfahrung und Urteil*

[1] VECTOR AND MEANING

THE QUESTION ABOUT INTENTIONALITY is at bottom a
question about meaning. An intentional structure is a structure
of meaning. To speak of an intentional act is to speak of an act
which reaches toward or gropes for a meaningful content. To
speak of an intentional datum is to speak of a datum-as-meant.
An exploration of intentionality and an elucidation of its operations and objects will thus provide a clarification of the meaning
of meaning in its diversified modalities. In this chapter we will
make an effort to show how the dynamism of world experience,
occurring always within the horizon-forms of lived time and
space, is imbued with and structured by intentionality. Intentional or meaning-bearing connectives pervade the whole of
experience and underlie its varied affective, volitional, and conceptual permutations. Intentionality, we will see, is a structural
component of affective and volitional as well as noetic acts. One

[82]

thus needs to acknowledge *felt* and *willed* meanings as well as noetic meanings. Intentionality infuses the total fabric of experience.

Intentionality, generically understood as the pervasive vectorial connections within experience that occasion the emergence of meaning or sense, carries with it neither a doctrine of a timeless ego nor a doctrine of intended eternal essences. Admittedly such doctrines have often accompanied the use of intentionality as a phenomenological concept, but it is one of our contentions that the notion can be pruned of these particular metaphysical accompaniments without sacrificing anything in our account of the structure of experience. Intentionality develops in the world of dynamic and streaming experience. Intentional structures are not imposed on a chaotic dynamism. Structure develops with the dynamic flow of experience. There is a much greater kinship between structure and dynamics, between form and vitality, than traditional philosophies have been willing to allow. In discussing the dynamics of experience we find ourselves already speaking about structure, and any talk about structure remains vacuous unless the dynamic development of that which is being structured is kept in view. Intentional structures, as the bearers of meaning, are thus not separable from the dynamic flow of the experienced world. Meaning does not come to experience from the outside. It has its source neither in a timeless ego which functions as a logical condition for the experience of world, nor in a region of eternal essences which transcend the world.

If intentionality is neither rooted in a timeless ego nor borne by eternal essences, how is it occasioned and what traces lead to the discernment of it? Where does one look to see it operate? Our answer here, as always, is to experience itself. Intentionality is embedded within the vectorial texture of world experience. It resides in the vectorial pathways and connecting tissues within the experienced life-world. Experience in its dynamic unfolding shows itself an as organic complex of vectors which bind together its world-manifesting constituents. The constitutents of world experience (experiencer-experiencing-figure-with-background) achieve their connections and conjunctions in a vectorial flow which binds the constituents together into meaningful configurations. When a particular content of experience is focused upon, consciousness is directed toward an attended figure, and the figure itself reaches out toward a background, differentiated into multiple regions. These vectors of experience which forge the pathways from experiencer to figure, and from figure to background, are the bearers of intentionality. They occasion the meanings which the world-experiencer articulates through his speech and his bodily bearing. They provide the basis for affective styles, volitional tendencies, and noetic forms. By virtue of them felt, willed, and noetic meanings surge up in the world.

The vectors within this world experience, which houses a manifold of meanings, move along the horizon-forms of time and space. More precisely, time and space are themselves vectorial. The experience of temporal presence has embedded within it vectorial associations with past and future. Presentation is vectorially linked with retention and protention. The three modes of time, as we have already observed, are ecstatic; they interpenetrate and intermingle. Likewise the experience of spatial presence is imbued with vectorial references to right and left, above and below, front and back. The very forms in which experience lives evince a vectorial character and provide the primordial basis for meaning. Meaning can never be severed from its temporal and spatial horizon. It undergoes an ontogenetic development within time and space. Thus it will be necessary in the following discussion to illuminate the intentional structure of felt, willed, and noetic meaning vis-à-vis their intrinsic temporality and intrinsic spatiality.

The vectorial character of experience becomes discernible in its sharpest relief through an investigation of its mosaic patterning in the everyday, workaday world. Experience as that which is *lived through* is never closed off or self-contained within interior boundaries. Lived-through experience is lodged in situations in such a manner that it connects the ingredients of the situation. Using the ordinary language of the workaday world we speak of experiences *in* a situation or *in* a state of affairs. There are the experiences of being *in* the army, *in* love, *in* a predicament, *in* the proceedings of a court case, and *in* a state of anxiety. One also speaks of experiences *of* something—*of* an impending catastrophe, *of* an emerging social evil, *of* a colored object. Again, the lived-through experience may involve the presence of other selves as in our experience of being *with* a friend, *with* a loved one, or *with* a fellow patriot. The vectors of sympathy, fellow-feeling, devotion, loyalty, and respect reach out toward the other self and make him encounterable. We also make use of the prepositions "on" and "over" and speak of experiences *on* the battlefield, and *over* a cup of coffee. These are but some of the ways in which the indefinite and dynamic development of world experience is situated. But in all cases the prepositions are indices that experience *is situated,* situated with respect to lived time and lived space, situated in such a manner that things, artifacts, moods, other selves, and events are focused and become topics of attention in the progression of experience. These items, it should be pointed out, are not brought into focus as terminations of an inference. On the primordial level of world experience there is no inference from an isolated point of consciousness to an inferred object or event. Vectorial bonds precede inferential claims. This is not to reject the utility of the language of inference or theories supported by inferential evidence. What is at stake is a disclosure of the vectorial character of experience on the basis of which talk about inferences first becomes meaningful. The language of inference is applicable only on the level of abstraction and objectification, the level on which those regions of world experience susceptible to quantification and measurement properly become the focus of attention. Inferential claims find their field and their origin in experience-charged vectorial bonds.

One might elaborate further the vectorial character of experience by viewing the vectors of which we speak as *tendencies* and *dispositions*. Every occasion of experience exhibits certain tendencies which mark out the direction and possible configurations which experience can assume. In the act of experiencing, consciousness tends toward its world-enveloped figures. Experience is tendential. Describing experience as dispositional provides a still sharper delineation of what is at issue. A disposition has to do with an arranging or setting in order (*disponere*). So when we speak of experience as being disposed toward its attended content, the suggestion of an arranging and interlacing of experiencer, figure, and background is already offered. This tendential or dispositional movement of experience must not be construed as a simple pointing, referring, or indicating. It is a more fundamental type of relating or connecting. Every occasion of experience "takes over" or appropriates its content, not by internalizing it but rather by determining the content as content for me in my lived world. The figures of experience are disclosed as figures experienced by me as experiencer, not as figures defined by a detached observer or contrived according to textbook analogies. Only under such conditions can meaning occur. Experienced objects, events, and persons are objects, events, and persons *as meant*. Meaning is always meaning for an experiencer even though the conditions for meaning are not all supplied by the experiencer. An object or event "in-and-for-itself" remains a theoretical limit. Such an object remains outside the intentional structure and never enters the fabric of world experience.[1]

After our discussion of the field notion of world experience in Chapter 1 it should come as no surprise that when the question of meaning is raised we talk about vectors, tendencies, and dispositions. The central thrust of our previous discussion was aimed at a displacement of the granular theory with its pulverization of experience into self-contained atomistic units. In such

1. Whitehead has recognized the vectorial and tendential character of experience and has provided a formal clarification of it with his category of *prehension*. The term, prehension, would seem to be peculiarly appropriate because it suggests the function of grasping, taking over, making one's own. According to Whitehead any occasion of experience can be analyzed into three interrelated modes of functioning which structure its process of becoming. There is the act of occasioning, the datum which provokes the act, and the subjective form or the manner in which the datum is taken over. These three modes constitute a prehension. What is of particular interest to us in Whitehead's theory of experience is what he calls the *subjective form*. It is this that binds the occasion with its datum. This conjunctive binding is not at all an abstracted logical relation of subject and object but rather a conjunction charged with sentience. Experience for Whitehead has an indelible sentient quality. It is permeated with enjoyments, feelings, and valuations which reach out toward their environment and appropriate their contents. At one point Whitehead speaks of "concern" as the manner in which an occasion prehends its datum. "The occasion as subject has 'a concern' for the object. And the 'concern' at once places the object as a component in the experience of the subject, with an affective tone drawn from this object and directed towards it" (*Adventures of Ideas* [London: Macmillan, 1933], p. 226). An intentionality of concern operates at the basis of experience. Occasions are intentionally tied to their data in the mode of concern. Experience as a knowledge-relation is undercut and is given a wider range of signification. The knowing subject and the known object are derivative distinctions. They are late emergents in the creative advance of actual occasions. Primordial experience exhibits a nexus of vectorial concerns.

a theory, experience is dissected into subjects (isolated know-
ers) and objects (atomistically discrete knowns), and the question of the epistemological commerce between the two becomes
the main investigative problem. We proposed, instead, that experience be approached in its world-horizon and viewed as a configuration of "experiencer-experiencing-figure-with-background."
Now we have been required to explicate the connective tissues
within this configurative structure of experience and have been
led to speak of vectors, tendencies, and dispositions. These
connective bonds account for the noncausal, preinferential
structure of experience. They constitute the basis for the intentional structure of experience, and suggest once again that
meaning can be found in a direct investigation of experience
itself. Experience is ready to give up its secrets when directly
confronted.

In seeking to make our notion of the vectorial-intentional
structure of experience clear, it is important that we avoid some
of the well-worn and inviting misinterpretations. It is by choice
rather than by chance that we have spoken of the vectorial
rather than relational character of experience. Assuredly one
might argue with some persuasiveness that a vector is a "kind" of
relation. We have no quarrel with this so long as the term
"relation" is divested of the accumulated metaphysical and epistemological underpinnings that have traditionally defined the
"problem of relations." It is this "problem" that needs to be
reexamined in light of our proposed view of experience. The
language of relations, like the language of subject and object, is
applicable in a discussion of the dynamics and structure of
world experience only in a secondary and derivative manner.
Strictly speaking, the problem of relations becomes a problem
only when the subject-object distinction is made normative. If
the basis of experience is the subject-object structure then
clearly the question of the nature of the relation of subjects to
objects is unavoidable. Traditionally, the solution to this problem
has tended in one of two directions—either toward a doctrine of
internal relations or a doctrine of external relations. The former,
the way of idealism, lays out the claim that entities and items of
experience are related in such a manner that they are mutually
constitutive one of another. Everything is what it is because it is
related to something else. The epistemological basis for the doctrine of internal relations is the coherence criterion of truth; its

metaphysical implication leads to a rejection of self-constituting individuality. The proponents of the doctrine of external relations take another path. They hold to a correspondence theory of truth and maintain that everything in the world is what it is independently of its relation to anything else, and thus they opt for a metaphysics of real, self-identical and enduring individuals. Now if the question is asked: "Is a vectorial relation internal or external?" the answer must be that it is neither. It is not a relation in the traditional sense at all. Primordial experience antedates the distinction between "internal" and "external" because it has neither an interior nor an exterior. The interiority of a constituting subject is a late arrival, as is the exteriority of a constituted object. Primordial experience is occasioned *with* the world. The world has already settled in when experience awakens.

Our preference for the language of vectors over the language of relations is thus not simply a matter of semantical preference. It involves a disavowal of the implicit metaphysical ruminations which have accompanied traditional doctrines of relation. Relation, in the history of philosophy from Aristotle to Kant and beyond, has suffered the destiny of becoming a metaphysical category. To be sure, the logical and empirical relations of positivism had their metaphysical filaments trimmed by Occam's razor, but the ghost of metaphysics—specifically, of an idealistic variety—continued to lurk in the background. Hence, we wish to underscore our distinction between an existential vector and a categorial relation. Categorial relations are abstract and derived; existential vectors are concrete and primitive. Vectors are the connective tissues that accompany experience; they are *with* experience rather than derived *from* experience. Embedded within the stream of experience vectors occasion the growing together or *concretion* of experience. A vector is a world-fact within the phenomenal field, that which James has aptly called the "fact of coalescence of next with next in concrete experience." [2] The necessity of importing a categorial construct, supplied by a transcendental ego, to account for the conjunctions in experience is obviated. Likewise the task of juxtaposing isolated sense data by equally isolated relata is displaced. Vectors

2. *A Pluralistic Universe* (New York: Longmans, Green, 1909), p. 326.

are neither brought to nor deduced from experience. They are the immediate and concrete connections which are present within the flowing stream of experience.

The significance of the recognition and elucidation of the vectorial-intentional structure of experience for any future theory of knowledge is far-reaching. What is required is a relentless reappraisal of the genesis and status of the categorial scheme in traditional epistemology. Our new approach to the dynamics and structure of experience carries with it a fresh approach to the problem of knowledge. We intend to show that the umbrella of knowledge covers more than the range of conceptualization. Feelings and volitions already have their cognitive import. They are essentially intentional in character, disclosing various regions of reality through their organizing tendencies and dispositions. They reveal a sentient and value-charged world with its distinctive figures and backgrounds. The elucidation of this is the task of Sections 2 and 3 of this chapter. In the concluding section, the genesis and status of concepts and categories will be investigated with the purpose of expliciting their anchorage in the stream of world experience. It will be shown that the concepts and categories of predicative judgments have their genealogy in the operating intentionality of world experience. The structure of thought is already anticipated by the structure of experience, from which it receives its figure-ground correlation. The categorial scheme, instead of being deduced from a predelineated table of judgments, lies embedded in perception. Both thought and perception are world oriented. Noetic meaning, no less than felt and willed meaning, is grounded in world experience.

[2] Felt Meaning

In the preceding section we proposed the general thesis that experience is imbued with vectors, tendencies, or dispositions. These vectors provide the connective tissues in the gestaltism of world experience. As vectors and tendencies which disclose various levels and aspects of the experienced world these vectors and tendencies are bearers of meaning. Thus we come to speak of the intentional structure of experience.

We need now to determine with some precision the varieties

of meaning that are disclosed within the intentional structure of experience. We have discussed in an earlier chapter the distinction between the prereflective and the reflective posturing of experience. Our analysis of meaning will need to proceed with this distinction in mind. Meaning emerges both in a prereflective and a reflective manner. It is an appropriation of nonthematic as well as thematic contents. And along the prereflective-non-thematic–reflective-thematic continuum (and it needs to be underscored that this *is* a continuum rather than a juxtaposition of separable moments) there are numerous intentional complexes. Meaning has multitudinous modalities. We will attempt to elucidate some of these varied expressions of meaning through a delineation of *types* of meaning, specifically *felt* meaning, *willed* meaning, and *noetic* meaning. This typology of meaning needs to be elucidated with some care because of the possible misunderstandings that such a division invites. To speak of such a division would seem to presuppose a psychic tripartism, reminiscent of the traditional and problematic faculty psychology. Such a presupposition, however, does not seem to be warranted by the data. The doctrine of a tripartite self, endowed with separate faculties containing distinct powers, raises more difficulties than it solves. Our view of world experience, and more specifically our analysis of the contextualized experiencer in Part II, admits of no such separation. Felt, willed, and conceptual meanings mix and mingle in primordial world experience. Feelings vitalize concepts, concepts organize feelings, and both feelings and concepts are colored with volitional dispositions. It is not as though there were three separate sources of meaning, emanating from three separate psychic powers, but rather there is one source, world experience, contextually differentiated, expressing meaning in three interrelated modes. Each of these modes is situated squarely within the stream of world experience. Felt, willed, and noetic meanings emanate from a common center of experience and partake of the common intentional structure that is embedded in the vectorial bonds that connect experiencer-experiencing-figure-with-background. Feelings, volitions, and concepts intend figures against a background. They are differentiated not with respect to a separation of faculties but by the particular focus of attention which each assumes.

It is necessary, however, to proceed a step further. Not only must we reject faculty psychology, we must reject a mere psychological interpretation of feeling, willing, and conceiving. Indeed, before a psychological interpretation of these modes of world experience can be formulated, their ontological significance —i.e., their genealogy and development in world experience— needs to be grasped. Although feeling and willing in particular seem to carry an unavoidable psychological connotation, we must press the point of their ontological significance. In the writings of both classical and contemporary philosophers, the ontological significance of these modes has at times been suggested. Aristotle, for example, discusses fear not in his *De Anima* but in his *Rhetoric,* thus suggesting that fear is not simply a psychological state but also performs the more basic function of disclosing a dimension of human reality. Fear is an intentional disclosure of world experience. Heidegger, in *Being and Time,* explicates the phenomenon of mood (*Stimmung*) in such a manner that its ontological significance becomes apparent. Mood, according to Heidegger, is not simply a psychological feature of the self; it reveals fundamental facts about the human condition. In *Adventures of Ideas* Whitehead informs the reader that "the basis of experience is emotional." [3] But Whitehead's doctrine of sentience has little to do with psychic states. Sentience is that component in the phenomenon of prehension which makes possible the appropriation of a datum by an experiencer. It is a connective tissue in world experience. It is evident to the reader of Nietzsche's philosophy that his use of will is quite different from the employment of it as a psychological category. "Will-to-power" is neither will in the psychological sense nor power in the sociological sense. Will-to-power characterizes the movement of the self-affirmation of life, the resource and resolve by virtue of which man can say "yes" to life and circumvent the stultification of convention. It is well known that Husserl, both in his *Logische Untersuchungen* and his *Formale und transzendentale Logik,* undertook a penetrating critique of the psychologism of concepts and purged logic of its psychological admixtures. Concepts and judgments, as he showed in his later work, *Erfahrung und Urteil,* find their genesis in a more primordial experience than that of which the psychologist speaks.

To grasp the intentional structure of felt-meaning it will be necessary to approach feeling as a *basic* phenomenon. Feeling

3. P. 226.

cannot be derived from a more elementary stock of psychic data. Anger, shame, hate, love, and anxiety are not psychic facts hidden in the cellar of consciousness. They are styles of behavior or types of comportment and are inserted into behavioral configurations which are already pregnant with meaning. Feelings manifest meanings, sometimes obscurely and at other times rather clearly. It is a mistake to relegate feelings to the limbo of the nonessential, to the nether regions of dim and confused knowledge. Feelings deploy their own field of cognition. They disclose concomitantly the determinants of the situation and the situated experiencer. Feelings are bearers of intentionality; they manifest a behavior style and disclose a world. Paul Ricoeur is profoundly aware of the thesis here set forth when he writes: "Feeling . . . is the manifestation of a relation to the world which constantly restores our complicity with it." [4]

What initially strikes the student of feelings is the virtually inexhaustible variety of forms of feeling, which would seem to saddle a general phenomenology of feeling with an impossible task. What Wittgenstein said about phenomenology in a wider sense would seem to apply particularly to a phenomenology of feeling: "The description of the phenomena by means of the hypothesis of a corporeal world, by virtue of its simplicity, is easily accessible; as compared with the inconceivably complicated phenomenological description." [5] The description of the phenomena of feeling, if not inconceivably complicated, is at least extraordinarily complicated. It is difficult to discern where a cataloguing of the various types and forms of feeling would end. Pain, pleasure, comfort, discomfort, fatigue, zest, boredom, melancholy, disgust, aversion, repulsion, fascination, resentment, spite, admiration, distrust, trust, confidence, self-worthiness, self-negation, remorse, regret, sorrow, grief, anger, fear, fright, tremor, horror, shock, anxiety, despair, awe, shame, sympathy, bliss, rapture, hope, and love are assuredly candidates for forms of feeling; and many others could be listed. And in every possible inventory of feeling one might be able to discern varieties of feeling-tones, degrees of specificity, distinctions as to bodily involvement, and levels of self-transcendence. Assuredly

4. *Fallible Man*, trans. Charles Kelbley (Chicago: Henry Regnery, n.d.), p. 129.
5. *Philosophische Bemerkungen* (Oxford: Basil Blackwell, 1964), #230, p. 286.

having a pain is a different behavior form than feeling remorse. The former lends itself to a bodily localization in a way in which the latter does not, although a general bodily comportment is expressive of both. One can meaningfully answer the question "Where does it hurt?" but it would be odd to ask "Where do you feel remorse?" The feelings of fatigue and zest exhibit a different intentional background than do the feelings of sympathy and love. The latter are more explicitly social in character. Fear differs significantly from anxiety. The intended figures in the feeling of fear are definite and specific. Anxiety has no definite object. The feelings of shame and hope have stronger moral tones than do the feelings of comfort and discomfort. This perplexing variety of feelings is the bane of all systematizers of feeling and gives pause to all those who seek a neat typology and simple hierarchical scale of feelings. Criteria for selecting some feelings as more basic, more value-laden, or more spiritual than others are peculiarly precarious.[6] Each feeling is a mode of entry into the world, and a phenomenological investigation of this mode of entry needs to remain intentionally neutral to specific ethical determinations, which inevitably rest upon other considerations. Each feeling must be approached as a basic phenomenon in a world, comprehended within its spatio-temporal horizon, and assessed with respect to its power of intentional disclosure. In our analysis we will select two feelings for investigation, anxiety and hope, and seek to elucidate the intentional structure which they exhibit. With these examples we trust that the tools and procedures for the investigation of any other feelings will be provided.

6. It is for this reason that we harbor certain reservations about Max Scheler's otherwise illuminating discussion of feeling in Part II of his book, *Der Formalismus und der Ethik und die materiale Wertethik* (Halle: Max Niemeyer, 1916). Scheler's hierarchical stratification of feelings into sensory, vital, mental, and spiritual feelings is both too simplified and too arbitrary. To maintain, as Scheler does, that sensory feelings are purely bodily in character and spiritual feelings purely nonbodily is to import a false dichotomy and conceal the prominent role of the lived body in the organization of all world experience (see Chapter 4). Likewise to define sensory feeling as exclusively a phenomenon of the present moment, as Scheler also does, is to overlook the ecstatic unity of the horizon-form of lived time which pervades the configurative complex of experience-with-background (see Chapter 2).

Anxiety and hope manifest through their intentional tendencies and dispositions a fabric of felt-meanings which vibrate through the affective life of man. Anxiety "withdraws from . . . ," "succumbs over . . . ," or "fights against. . . ." Hope "moves toward . . . ," reaches into . . . ," or "expands beyond. . . ." By following the leads of these prepositional connectives (from, over, against, toward, into, and beyond) the vectorial and intentional character of these forms of feeling can be discerned. Anxiety withdraws from that which is uncanny, it succumbs over an alienated existence, it fights against that which threatens; hope moves toward that which offers liberation, reaches into resources for self-affirmation, and expands beyond a confining temporal and spatial presence. Through these affective movements levels and regions of the life-world are disclosed. The world is revealed as uncanny, alienated, and threatening, or as enriching and laden with creative possibilities. Anxiety and hope are not isolated and encapsulated psychic states. They occur *with* the world. They are tendential in character, oriented toward a nonthematic and indeterminate background, conveying immediately felt and prereflective meanings. Through anxiety and hope dimensions of the world *as I exist in it* are uncovered and brought to light. Herein resides the cognitive quality of feeling. In anxiety and hope the world is *known*—known not through representational and objectifying knowledge but through the knowledge that accompanies intentional disclosure.

Much is made in existentialist writings about the distinction between fear and anxiety. Fear and anxiety are both modalities of mood but they are differentiated by virtue of their attentive directionalities. Fear intends a specific object or event—a plane crash, a death in the family, an illness, a criminal attack. The vectors of fear move toward something determinable and specifiable. Anxiety knows no such determinable object or event. Its vectors intend the indefinite range of alienating possibilities that encroach upon existence. When anxiety overcomes us in the workaday world we express our experience of it by saying that there is nothing determinate that threatens. What is at issue is a pervading mood of uncanniness in which the trustworthy supports of everyday existence are shaken and the security and contentment of our routine life is called into question. Anxiety reveals the *existential non-being* that infects our being-in-the-world. Brought to the fore is the not-yet of future existential actualization which might lead to this or might lead to that, as well as the already actualized possibilities of the past which confer upon one an alienated destiny. It is thus that anxiety, as numerous existentialist thinkers have pointed out, is associated with non-being and the ineradicable finitude of the human condition.[7] Yet both anxiety and fear are revelatory phenomena, which make manifest prereflective felt meanings and, in different ways, provide entry into the experienced world.

Hope, like anxiety, resists all reduction to an objectively determinable psychic state. Granted, like all affective modes, hope is bound up with the neurological-psychological functioning of an organism, but hope, *as experienced,* patterns itself within a wider context of situational deployment. Hope is lodged in the world as a type of behavior impregnated with meaning. The objectively determined schemes of a neurological mechanics and a quantitative sociology are unable to account for the upsurge of meaning in the experiential act. They fail to account for the manner in which neurological-psychological functioning and social conditioning are incorporated into a world-oriented existential bearing. Hope is never riveted to an objective-empirical state of affairs. Indeed it is an inalienable feature of hope to transcend the objectively given and deploy itself, if need be, in spite of it. Hope can be experienced in situations in which all enumerable objective factors count against it. There is ample evidence for this in memoirs of concentration camp experiences, where hope continued to nourish itself in the presence of insuperable, objectively calculable odds against the possibility of liberation. Hope displays the movement of transcendence, the power to project itself beyond the objectively given. In this transcending and projecting character resides its intrinsic felt meaning, a meaning which is appropriated and reappropriated in the concrete immediacy of the experience. A post-mortem of the experience, or a reconstruction of the experience by analogy, can at best yield only a serial juxtaposition of its abstracted elements.

A further clarification of the intentional structure of anxiety

7. See particularly Sören Kierkegaard, *The Concept of Dread,* trans. Walter Lowrie (Princeton: Princeton University Press, 1946); Martin Heidegger, *Sein und Zeit,* 7th ed. (Tübingen: Max Niemeyer, 1953), pt. I, chap. 6; and Paul Tillich, *The Courage to Be* (New Haven: Yale University Press, 1952), chap. 2.

and hope requires a consideration of the relevance of the horizon-forms of time and space for the organization of affective experience. Our discussion of time and space in Chapter 2 has already established the thematic clarification of the temporality and spatiality of world experience. It is now our task to render explicit the spatio-temporal foundation of anxiety and hope and thus indicate how the intentionality of felt meaning operates within spatial and temporal horizon-forms.

Intentionality is particularly grounded in time. Meaning in its manifold variety is imbued with time. Felt, willed, and noetic meanings grow and develop within the temporal horizon-form of past-present-future. Kant, in his first *Critique,* recognized the temporal conditionedness of meaning and knowledge when he observed that schemata, which project the organizational field for intuition and understanding, are in the final analysis to be understood as "transcendental determinations of time." [8] Yet the autonomy of felt meanings is submerged in Kant's analysis because of his contemplative view of experience and his *a priori* deduction of the categories. Hence, it is the temporal foundation of felt meaning which needs to be accentuated and brought to light. Anxiety and hope will again provide the examples for this task.

The upsurge of anxiety occurs within a temporal present. To say that someone is anxious means that he is *now* living through a phase or condition of disquieting existence. But this temporal present is not an isolated instant, chopped off from the rest of time; the present is not an instantaneous now, riveted to a space-time point and enclosed within itself. The temporal present in the experience of anxiety is a present with *fringes.* These fringes intermingle and interweave with a future and a past. Indeed, the temporally decisive feature of anxiety is that it projects and anticipates a future. The vectors of anxiety reach into a future, and the intentionality of anxiety resides most specifically in its disclosure of the indeterminate possibilities of what might yet occur. Anxiety has a protentional cast. It is peculiarly occasioned by that which is not yet, but might be. Anxiety confronts the future and shrinks back from the possibilities that line the future horizon. It is thus that the future assumes a

8. *Critique of Pure Reason,* trans. Norman Kemp Smith (London: Macmillan, 1953), p. 181.

privileged role in the temporalization of anxiety, as Heidegger correctly maintained in *Being and Time*. Without a future, anxiety would have no occasion to arise. In all this we see an illustration of the general point that we developed earlier concerning the ecstatic interpenetration of the future with the present. The present needs be understood in light of the future. But also we saw that in the configurative synthesis of time, the bearing of the past remained in force. This also is illustrated by a phenomenology of anxiety. Anxiety is structured by retentional as well as protentional vectors. In the experience of anxiety there is a continuing recollection of the past through the intending of past discontinuities and disturbances which *could* be repeated, which *could* be rendered present. Anxiety continually reopens the past, translates it into possibility, and keeps alive its disturbing relevance for the present. The intentionality of anxiety is thus rooted in a temporality which synthesizes past, present, and future in its structural development.

The felt meaning in the experience of hope is embedded in a similar temporal structure. Hope announces the future, not as a horizon of alienating possibilities, but as a time for well-being and creative actualization. In the experience of hope the present is lived in light of what the future might bring. In the deepest depths of despair hope can be nourished and kept alive through an envisagement of the transcending and redeeming power of the future. Hope, like anxiety, is protentional in character, occasioned by the vectorial reach of the present into the future. Hope is a feeling of temporal directionality in which the value of the future contributes to the meaning of the present. In this protentional reach toward the future the retentional vector is not left behind. In part, one hopes for that for which our past has conditioned us to hope. The facticity of the past is taken over in the project of hope. The past contributes the limits and the repeatable possibilities which enter the charter of one's future being. A hope that rejects the facticity of its past stands in danger of losing part of its foundational support. As hope finds its meaning in the future, so also it finds its meaning in the past. Without memory of the past hope dissolves into a fantasy of volatile possibilities and loses its sense and significance. The intentional structure of anxiety and hope alike requires the interpenetrating ecstasies of the horizon-form of time.

In a similar manner the horizon-form of space invades the

experience of these moods. Felt meanings occur in world experience as deployed within an existential nexus of lived time and lived space. Anxiety is spatialized as well as temporalized. It is informed by an oriented space, a spatiality of situation which marks out the places where tasks are to be assumed and projects executed. In the experience of anxiety this oriented space is revealed in its ineradicable contingency. The space of anxiety is the abode of adversity, subject to the loss of a value-laden orientation. Space can be deprived of its existential value, lose its places for decisive action, and constrict the movements of the lived body. Man is subject to displacement—relatively through the breakdown of purpose, absolutely through death. This is the texture of space that anxiety manifests. Space is disclosed as the place where threats occur.

Hope has its spatiality as does anxiety. However in the experience of hope the texture of oriented space which is disclosed is different. Although both anxiety and hope are intentional in character and are inserted into the horizon-form of space, their intentionality discloses distinguishable configurations of experience. We have already observed that lived or oriented space is anisotropic rather than isotropic in character. It exhibits a manifold of significations that vary with existence itself. The consistency of the lived space that surrounds hope is expansive rather than constrictive. Hope assigns to space a liberating character. The here and there of space mark out places for creative actualization in which the threats of existence can be courageously faced. Through hope space is secured from the threats of value privation and dissolution. The man of hope affirms his space as the opportune place for creative action and self-fulfillment. Space becomes the "promised land" in which alienation is to be overcome.

The purpose of this discussion of the intentionality of feeling has been to elucidate the role and status of felt meaning in the dynamism of world experience. Making use of anxiety and hope as illustrations of intentional feeling modes, we have explicated their revelatory function and indicated their relevance to the horizon-forms of time and space which lie at the foundation of world experience. The task that remains in this section is to anticipate the following chapters by relating the intentionality of feeling to the question of the contextualized experiencer. The intentionality of feeling is in one of its expressions an intentionality of self-reference, functioning as a *lumen naturale* with respect to the experiencer himself. The intentional vectors of anxiety and hope reveal the sense of anxious and hopeful situations in such a manner that the experiencer himself becomes an issue and possible thematic topic. The intentionality of feeling discloses the sentient experiencer. However, the sentient experiencer is disclosed *with* the situation and *within* the horizon-forms of time and space. He is never disclosed in isolation as a timeless encapsulated subject or substance. He is disclosed as present-with-a-sentient world. Hence we find it appropriate to speak of the *contextualized* experiencer. In the experience of anxiety it is the personal selfness of the experiencer that is at stake. It is *his* purposes which are threatened, it is *his* everyday world that is about to lose its security and contentment, it is *his* being that is confronted with an inevitable having to die. Likewise in the experience of hope a self-referentiality is operative whereby a hopeful self is individuated as the center of a continuous portion of world experience. The intentional vectors of feeling radiate into a world and concomitantly reveal an embodied, speaking, and communal experiencer who lives in an oriented time and space. The elucidation of this contextualized experiencer remains the task of Part II of this study.

[3] WILLED MEANING

WE HAVE SEEN that a feeling is a network of intentionalities, embedded in the horizon-forms of time and space, through which a complicity with the world is established. The intentional vectors that operate within the various forms of feeling are bearers of meaning, disclosing the sense of the situation in which the experiencer lives. Thus we are able to speak of felt meaning. We will now explore a related type of meaning—*willed* meaning. We will attempt to explicate what is at issue in speaking of willed meaning from the perspective of a phenomenology of willing. The concept of will, as is well known, has undergone a tortuous development in the history of philosophy. For the most part, philosophies of will have suffered the fate of being impaled on the proverbial horns of a dilemma. The inquiry-standpoint which has directed the pursuit of the issue has largely been a search for confirming evidence for either a free will on the one hand or a determined will on the other. The basic presupposition of this inquiry-standpoint—namely that the will is an entity possessing a quality, either the quality of being free or the quality of being determined—has cunningly escaped questioning. The free-willist views the will as an entity possessing the quality of freedom, and appeals to the confirmation of subjectivity in his search for internal evidence. The determinist likewise views the will as an entity, but turns his attention to the canons of objectivity (either empirical or intellectualistic) as he collects a ledger of external evidence. The discussion of will, proceeding from such an inquiry-standpoint remains interminable and unproductive, for the one party latches on to an internal evidence and a private seeing while the other stakes out a region circumscribed by external evidence and public seeing. What is required is the relocation of the traditional inquiry-standpoint and the displacement of a postulated entitative will so as to permit the phenomenon of willing to show itself. Made aware of the notorious impasses in the traditional discussions of the problem of the will, it may indeed be wise to dispense with the term entirely. However, insofar as everyday usage seems to have found a relatively permanent place for will, an effort needs to be made to rescue it from its traditional distortions and indicate its role in our new approach to experience.[9]

The difficult task of a phenomenology of willing is to relocate volition in the stream of temporalized and spatialized experience and to study its development and advance. To describe, analyze, and interpret the phenomenon of willing in its lived concreteness and existential deployment is the formidable task which confronts the phenomenologist of the will. A reminder that every such description, analysis, and interpretation is incurably partial may be in order. In focusing the phenomenon of willing one finds that the wealth of proliferating meanings is so vast that total comprehension can at best be a regulative ideal. The finitude of world experience affords no privileged standpoint above the world from which a God-like survey might be conducted.

9. A remarkably successful venture in such a rescue effort has been undertaken by Paul Ricoeur in his three-volume work, *Le Volontaire et l'involontaire* (Paris: Aubier Editions Montaigne, 1950). The first volume of this work has been translated by Erazim V. Kohák under the title: *Freedom and Nature: The Voluntary and the Involuntary* (Evanston: Northwestern University Press, 1966).

The phenomenon of willing is a complex in which various fibers run to and fro, connecting constituents which figure in some manner or another in the birth and development of the volitional life of man. As in feeling, so in willing there are vectorial threads which link will and world. Willing does not occur in a void. Willing is a project that reaches toward figures (that which is willed) outlined against a background. Willing, on its most primoridial level, is lodged in the interstices of an experiencing-figure-with-background complex, which formally designates our phenomenological notion of world. The self in its volitional activity assumes a decision-making stance and inserts itself into a plan of action. It becomes committed *to* . . . something; it responds *to* . . . some prior action upon it; it assumes an obligation *for* . . . some existential project. An intentional correlate—something to be done—accompanies every projection of will. In all this the intentional structure of willing becomes apparent. Willing exhibits a centrifugal movement whereby intentional vectors reach out toward the world and reveal it as the time and place for decision and action. An analysis of the constitutive elements in the phenomenon of willing needs to proceed with a firm grasp of the intentional structure of world experience. If this structure is forgotten, then the contextual background, which supplies the framework for willed meanings, is concealed, and will retires into itself as an encapsulated entity. As a result, willing as a phenomenon that one *lives through* is lost.

The constituents of willing are phenomenologically diverse. Yet a basic polarity of constituting elements shows itself in the life of will. This is the polarity of decision and action. Decision is not yet action. One can decide on a project to be done and hesitate in the execution of the project, and one might engage in an action without being explicitly aware of a definite decision which projects the action. Yet, the two are not entirely separable. Decision already entertains action in the mode of possibility. Decision places the will face to face with action, action which is yet to be executed but which nonetheless is within range and in some sense determines the form for the enactment of decision. Correspondingly, prereflective tendencies are already at work in nonpremeditated action and can later be explicated as the decisive factors involved in the execution of the action. Decision and action thus develop in the phenomenon of willing through a dialectical interplay and comprise the basic polar structure of the phenomenon.

This polar structure of decision and action, which lies at the base of the phenomenon of willing, is itself an intricate complex of constituting elements. It incorporates a field of possibilities, motives, powers, judgments, needs, desires, inclinations, and wishes. In the act of deciding one decides not only *to* do something, but one decides *because* of something. One bases one's decision on this or that. This accounts for the motivation of decision. Without motives decisions cannot be properly understood as decisions. Nor does the meaning of motives become transparent without the act of deciding that accompanies them. Motives have to do with the *motility* which lies at the basis of decision and contributes to its genesis. Motives however must not be confused with causes. The language of causality is applicable only on a level of abstraction and objectification which emerges later in the constellation of world experience. Closely allied with the phenomenon of motive is the phenomenon of power. A decision projects a future action to be occasioned by me. The action resides *within my power*. To carry through a decision is *to be able* to execute a plan of action. But this power that resides in the deciding self is finite and conditioned. No action is absolutely within my power. It is conditioned by my personal and social past, by the demands of my present environment, and by my limited perception of future possibilities. The exercise of power in decisions is always in some sense a response to powers already acting upon me. The power of decision is not hermetically sealed in a self-enclosed subject functioning as a dynamo of self-determination. The very notion of self-determination is problematic, because there is no pure, unlimited power possessed by the self by virtue of which such determination might proceed. The power in decision is shared by the world. The interplay of conditionals in world experience conspires to give and take away power. This confers upon the power of decision an irremediable finitude as well as an unavoidable ambiguity. Freedom itself needs to be understood in light of this finitude and ambiguity. Freedom is the power to respond in situational contexts in which there is at the same time an acting and a being acted upon. In freedom the contributions of initiation (originating the action) and facticity (prior action upon one) remain ambiguously intertwined.

The constituting elements of judgments, needs, desires, inclinations, and wishes also must be given a place in a phenomenology of willing. Each of these elements could become a topic for extensive phenomenological description. Our present task, however, is not so encompassing. We simply wish to indicate their general relevance for the intentional structure of will. Decision is linked with judgment. In deciding to take up the study of medicine I gather up a complex of practical judgments about the worthiness of the profession, about "goods" delivered in terms of services, about the consequences for self-fulfillment, and the like. These practical judgments are neither based on a paradigm of theoretical judgments, nor are they separable from the conceptualization at work in the formulation of theoretical judgments. This is to say that will as the germination-bed of decision remains in league with the intellectual-theoretical posturing of world experience. To the extent that this is the case the rationalistic tradition, with its tendency to intellectualize the will contributes an important insight. But decision is also linked with need, passion, desire, inclination, and wish. By virtue of this linkage will maintains a liaison with sentient world-experience, and romanticism is partially vindicated. Yet will is not simply the mediating principle between sentience and intellect. One does not return to the phenomenon of will through an eclecticism of the isolated insights of the rationalist and romantic traditions. Willing, like feeling, needs to be approached as a basic phenomenon. It is neither primarily intellectual nor primarily emotive; nor is it half of each. Will stakes out its own region of deployment and becomes manifest as a continuous development of behavior with its peculiar intentional field and distinctive meaning. It was one of the noteworthy contributions of Nietzsche to centralize the notion of will, liberate it not only from psychologistic distortions but from its rationalistic and romantic servitude as well. Nietzsche was able to understand will as the movement of self-affirmation in life, particularly as life comes to grips with its existence-problem. Will, according to Nietzsche, is not a faculty among other faculties; it is rather a style of life that the *Übermensch* assumes in his battle with herd morality in a noble effort to become himself. The error in Nietzsche's philosophy of the will resides not in his description of its character and movement, but in the tendency to absolutize the will and to confer upon it a metaphysical supremacy. In the end Nietzsche succeeds only in inverting Plato. Will-to-power replaces The Good as the category of the ultimate.

As in the intentional structure of felt meaning so in the intentional structure of willed meaning existential time and space provide the horizons along which the meaning-laden vectors proceed. Willed meanings are both temporalized and spatialized. Decision and action have their time and place. In the projection of will the horizon-form of temporality becomes manifest in the voluntaristic perspective of *time for decision*. The committed will apprehends time as a horizon for its decisive action and engagement. The present is the *opportune moment* for the shouldering of a responsibility, for the actualization of a purpose, for the grasping of a live option. Present time is *time for* commitments and actions. It should be evident that there can be no talk of the present as an isolated, atomistic, serially successive now. The present as manifest in the movement of will has an existential breadth. It is protentionally and retentionally expansive. The present as the appropriate or opportune time for decision and action is at once anticipative and commemorative. In decision the future is anticipated, possibilities of what might be are envisaged, and goals and purposes are entertained. Decision has a forward-looking character, and it is precisely this character that contributes the basis for the operation of willed meaning. The atomization of time and the isolation of the present as an instant lies behind the devitalization of will and the dissolution of willed-meaning. A meaningless life is correctly characterized as a life lived as a succession of discontinuous nows with no projection into a future. For such a life there is nothing to be decided, nothing to be done, nothing for which to hope. When the future is cut away decision itself and its intentional meanings are destroyed. Meaning is commemorative as well as anticipative. Decision and action have their past as well as their future. Not only is there the prereflective motivation in decision which has an anchorage in past experience, there is the reflective assessment of the past as repeatable or avoidable in light of future possibilities. The past provides both limits and leverages for decision. The conspiring of the past limits the choices that remain open, and defines the temporal finitude of will. But the past also provides repeatable possibilities which can be brought into the range of an existential freedom. The past thus continues to gnaw into the present, and in remembering the past the decided self continues to grow in wisdom and stature, cognizant both of its finitude and transcendence.[10]

This temporalized willed meaning is intersticed along a spatial horizon as well. The will orients the experiencer in lived space. Its intentionalities run along the vertical and horizontal axes and circumscribe the embodied situationality of the deciding and acting self. Without space, decision would be severed from a concrete body and action would have no arena for its existential deployment. Will is inseparable from the bodily comportment in which oriented space is anchored. The intended figures of the will (such as promises, loyalties, obligations, duties, and purposes) are positioned in an existential spatial texture of the world. In making a promise, the promise-maker is brought into existential proximity with the one to whom the promise has been made. The breaking of a promise or the abrogation of a pledge of loyalty "distances" the other party and makes him existentially remote. Obligations and duties require a place as well as a time. There is a place where they are to be carried out, and they may be of such a nature that they are projected as binding in all situations or relative to a possible reorientation in space and time. Purposes and ends are projected not only into a future "when" but also into a spatial "where." Purposes and ends which remain relevant to world experience require a place to be realized—a neighborhood or a nation in which embodied wills strive and struggle. The various expres-

10. It will not do to restrict finitude to the past and place all of the burden of transcendence on the future, as is the case in Sartre's phenomenological ontology. Sartre oversimplifies the relation of facticity and freedom as simple products of the dialectical interplay of past and future. By ascribing a privileged status to the present, Sartre is unable to account for the reopening and transformation of the past through the projection of the past as future. If one acknowledges the future as the privileged ecstasy then one is able to account for the continuing penetration of future possibilities into the past. Projective existence is able to translate the past into repeatable possibilities and deliver it from the threat of sedimentation. And insofar as the future cannot be without a past, the conditioning factors of the past enter into the constitution of the future. Precisely formulated, the past always partakes of a borrowed transcendence, and the future is saddled with an inherited finitude; the past is subject to an open finitude and the future occasions conditional transcendence.

sions of lived space (such as neighborhood, national, aesthetic, and psychological space) take on distinctive features through the orientation of promises, loyalties, duties and purposes.

The above-discussed deployment of willed meanings in existential time and space is not to be confused with an ethic of the will. A phenomenology of willing does not supply any normative basis for decision. If traditional ethics is permitted to define the program of ethics as a discipline then it must be said that a phenomenology of the will is meta-ethical in character. Implied in this endeavor is an attempt to think beyond the subject-object structure of experience which has plagued the traditional ethicist and has impaled him either on the horn of emotivism and relativism or on that of a pretentious absolutism. The impasse in traditional ethics seems to result from a predilection to consider the ethical in terms of the possession of moral *qualities,* either generated within the subject and hence subjectivistic, or somehow read off an objective state of affairs. A phenomenology of willing, which moves along the lines of our reconstructed view of experience, seeks another foundation for ethical inquiry. It seeks to elucidate the world of will as a field of moral activity in which various styles of life can be assumed, arising out of the possible configurations of experience. It strives to explicate an ontology of world experience which will make it possible to approach the problem of ethics as one of life-styles emerging from experience as one lives through it. The search for a pivotal moral subject on the one hand, or objectively valid propositions about moral qualities on the other, is, if not displaced, at least seen as being secondary and derivative.

Thus far in our exploration of the intentional structure of will, we have focused our attention on the centrifugal movement of the intentional vectors. The vectors in willing find their intentional correlates in projects (the "figures" of willed meaning) which stand out from a wider background. The intentionality of decision and of action thus discloses the figure-ground structure of the phenomenon of willing. This is to say that intentionality reveals the *world* of will as it makes its appearance through the horizon-forms of time and space. But copresent with this centrifugal movement of intentionality is a centripetal movement which at the same time reveals the deciding self and the acting agent. In deciding and in acting the one who decides and acts is already implicated, although principally in a prereflective manner. As in sentient experience so in volitional experience there is a self-referential intentionality which is prereflective in character. I commit myself in my decision, I involve myself in the design of my projected action. But I become committed and involved without predicative knowledge of a reflectively observable self. This is what Paul Ricoeur has in mind when he speaks of the "prereflexive imputation of myself." [11] In the earliest stages of decision and in the initiation of projects there are discreet references to myself as the one who . . . is about to commit himself, shoulder responsibility, or effectuate a plan of action. Ricoeur interestingly points out that in both the French and German languages, and to a lesser degree in English, the double, copresent relation to self and project is indicated. In French one says "*Je me decide.*" The form in German is similar: "*Ich entscheide mich.*" To explicate the same point in English one would need to make use of the circumlocution: "I make up my mind." In these pronominal and transitive constructions an active and self-referential operation is made explicit.

The contemporaneity of this prereflective self-referentiality with the project and the action needs to be underscored. In the birth and development of a decision and in the execution of an action, the one who decides and acts is inserted in the project and action. There is a symbiosis of decider and decision, actor and action. The self is *bound to* its project and its plan of action in a bond of commitment, and only in this bond, in this span of transitivity, does reference to the self germinate and develop. The self is not given prior to its projects. It does not antedate its action. It emerges with its projects and its actions and first discovers itself in them. "I meet myself in my project." [12] The phenomenon of willing, like the phenomenon of feeling, announces its resident self. Until man has decided, he does not apprehend

11. "The task of our analysis is to elaborate an aspect of the project which we might call the prereflexive imputation of myself. This implies a self-reference which is not yet self-observation, but rather a certain way of relating oneself or of behaving with respect to oneself, a non-speculative or, better, non-observant, way. It is an implication of the self rigorously contemporaneous with the very act of decision which in some sense is an act with reference to the self. This implication of the self must contain the germ of the possibility of reflection, contain the willing available to the *judgment* of responsibility, 'it is I who . . .' " (*Freedom and Nature*, p. 58).

12. *Ibid.*, p. 60.

himself as a deciding self. It is only through the historical advance of the decision-making process that the self comes to a stand, constitutes itself, and finds itself within its commitment. Any explicit reflection on the character and existential posturing of the self is consequent upon this prereflective self-imputation that occurs with the project. Hence, again we are able to anticipate the following chapter in which the contextualized experiencer becomes the focal theme.

[4] NOETIC MEANING

NOETIC MEANING is the third type of meaning displayed by the intentional structure of world experience. There are connective tissues of thought as well as of sentience and volition. Thought is experience determined by reflection. Through reflection a distinctive network of meanings is disclosed, thus rendering explicit yet another phase and feature of the general intentional structure of world experience. What needs to be underscored at the outset of our discussion of noetic meaning is that thought itself is allied with experience. Thought is world experience infused with reflection. From this there follow two noteworthy implications. First, thought is lodged in the "experiencing-figure-with-background" constellation which defines our phenomenological notion of world. There is no thought without figure, without an intentional correlate, without a *meant* object. Thinking as reflective consciousness is present in world experience as consciousness *of* something. Further, these figures or intentional correlates never appear in isolation but only in relief against some indeterminate background. This placing of thought within the figure-background complex confers upon it an intentional structure, formally similar to that which we discovered in our elucidation of felt and willed meaning. This leads to the second implication, that thought shares with sentience and volition the power of intentional disclosure and conspires with them in the elucidation of meaning and the achievement of knowledge. Although meanings can, and should, be differentiated for purposes of analysis, in the streaming flow of experience they fraternize and depend upon the support of each other. Felt, willed, and noetic meanings are not discrete entities, fixed in a self-enclosed relational scheme. Thought occurs in a world in which sentience has already marked out its paths, and the deciding will borrows from the mind as well as the emotions. Feeling, will, and thought interdependently mark out multidimensional meanings and contribute to a disclosure of world. It is for this reason that it will not do to saddle thought with the exclusive function of providing knowledge, and banish sentience and volition from the kingdom of cognition. This has constituted the peculiar bias of the traditional approach to "theory of knowledge," which might be understood as a working out of the destiny of Plato's bifurcation of "worldly" *doxa* and "super-worldly" *epistēmē*. What is required is a new ontology of knowledge, which takes its point of departure from an elucidation of world experience, intentional in character and ready to yield up its secrets through a discriminating analysis. We have already seen that feeling and will have *cognitive* significance in that they disclose intended figures and styles of behavior within an encompassing background. Knowing as a *process of intentional disclosure* is already operative in sentient and volitional experience. The prejudice of traditional epistemology, with its absolutization of representational knowledge (*adequatio rei et intellectus*) needs to be uprooted, and a theory of knowledge more consonant with the solicitations and intentionalities of lived experience developed.

A phenomenology of thinking is confronted with the same disturbing proliferation of data as is a phenomenology of feeling and a phenomenology of willing. There is no one operation which defines the movement of thought. Thought is such a multifaceted phenomenon that any attempted answer to the question "What is thought?" would seem to be fated with oversimplification. Indeed the phenomenon seems to be so elusive that the very formulation of the question concerning its character is beset with extraordinary difficulties. To ask "What is thought?" is already to prejudge the phenomenon in question by suggesting that one is searching for an "essence" or "nature." It may indeed be that thought is more like a *how* than like a *what*, more like an achievement than like a determinable result. To minimize the risk of prejudging the phenomenon one might choose circumlocutions such as the following: "How does thinking proceed?" "In what manner does thinking come to expression?" or "How does one discern the operational development of thinking?" [13]

Perplexity results when one becomes aware that there is no single object, event, or process which answers to the above questions. Thinking knits up within its fabric a manifold of threads, interwoven and interlaced. Thinking can involve conceiving, judging, comparing, abstracting, generalizing, calculating, inferring, deducing, understanding, introspecting, meditating, and deliberating. Thinking encompasses all of these operations—and more. What then is one to make of the phenomenon of thinking and the noetic meanings to which reflection attests? To develop an inventory of the various modes of thought might provide helpful information, but it would provide little in the way of clarifying the issue with respect to the origin or genealogy of thinking in world experience. Likewise it would be fruitful to analyze the specific conditions and criteria in concept-formation, forms of judgment, rules of inference, calculi of probability, generalization, and abstraction. Many technical studies on these, and related, topics are extant, and their results are not irrelevant to an exploration of the phenomenon of thinking. Yet, our basic concern moves out from a different inquiry-standpoint. How does thinking, in any or all of its modalities, show itself or come to presence in the phenomenal world? What configurative occasioning of world experience postures experience as reflected (or more precisely *reflecting*) experience? Now when we ask about the origin or genealogy of thinking we ask not about its psychological and anthropological origin. Rather we seek the ground of thought in world experience. Our concern is ontological rather than psychological or anthropological. We wish to elucidate the development and expression of thought within the context of the structural constitution of the world as experienced.

The genealogy of one particular modality of thinking—the predicative thought of modal logic—has already been traced

13. Martin Heidegger addresses himself to this perplexing issue of proper *Fragestellung* as concerns the phenomenon of thinking in his book *Was heisst Denken?* (Tübingen: Max Niemeyer, 1954). The title of the book seems to be intentionally ambiguous, suggesting on the one hand the question "What does thinking mean?" and on the other hand "What does thinking name?" Thinking, according to Heidegger, is a matter of both meaning and naming, through which preobjective being is manifested.

with remarkable insight by Edmund Husserl in his book *Erfahrung und Urteil: Untersuchungen zur Genealogie der Logik*. This work, along with the *Krisis,* marks a decisive turning point in the philosophy of Husserl—the turn from transcendental idealism to genetic phenomenology. In this work Husserl follows the genealogy of logic back to its source in the evidence of world experience (*Welterfahrung*) as this experience conspires and advances in a life-world (*Lebenswelt*) which precedes the idealization of logic and the exact sciences. The order of predicative judgment has its source in "prepredicative experience" (*vorprädikative Erfahrung*). The judgmental activity of categorial operations is founded on perceptual appearance. The active genesis of explicit judgment yields priority to the passive genesis of living perception.[14]

Not only do the predicative, deductive, inferential, and calculative modes of scientific thinking find their genealogy in world experience; the other modes are rooted in experience as well. The deliberations, self-understanding, and conceptual meanings that are given expression in ethics, aesthetics, and religion are anchored in the same life-world. Nor will it do to separate the traditional value disciplines from the logico-scientific ones in terms of the assignment of squatters rights to clear and distinct modes of thought. Religious experience requires predicative judgments for its expression, and science cannot remain immune to considerations of value. The much discussed bifurcation of the "two cultures" conceals more than it reveals. Yet, within the welter of world-encompassing modes of thought two general directions show themselves in the pulsating profusion of world experience.

We shall name these two directions *representational thinking* and *hermeneutical thinking*. Our task will be to elucidate both of these directions, indicate in what manner they are both bearers of noetic meaning, and explicate their anchorage in world experience vis-à-vis their development within the horizon-forms of time and space.

Representational thinking is *objectifying* thinking. The in-

14. See *Erfahrung und Urteil,* ed. Ludwig Landgrebe following Husserl's instructions (Hamburg: Claassen, 1964), pt. I: "Die Vorprädikative (Rezeptive) Erfahrung"; and, more specifically, chap. 3: "Die Beziehungserfassung und ihre Grundlagen in der Passivität."

tentionality of representational thinking isolates its figures as *objects* which exist for a *subject* and which can be controlled by the subject. Representational thinking picks out those features of world experience which are objectifiable and in some manner lend themselves to quantification and measurement. The mathematical and empirical sciences, although different with respect to methodological orientation, seem to provide relatively clear and distinct examples of the operation of representational thought. Integers, fractions, sets, lines, points, surfaces are mathematical conceptual-objects, amenable to quantification and calculation. Electrons, protons, and DNA are empirical conceptual-objects, constructed in the interests of measurement and control. What is of philosophical interest in the conceptual schemes and the calculating and controlling procedures in representational thinking is the assumption of a subject-object relationship. This is indeed unavoidable given the very project of mathematical and scientific thought. Objectification is required to fulfill the aims of controlling knowledge. What remains to be investigated, however, is the conditions that make objectification possible, and for this one will need to turn one's attention to the contributions of time and space.

Hermeneutical thinking is *nonobjectifying* thinking. This characterization, however, does not carry the implication that hermeneutical thinking is therefore *subjectivistic*. It is neither objectifying nor subjectifying in character. The subject-object structure of thought is suspended in a drive to grasp the experiencer-figure-ground complex in its originary presentment. The subject as a constituted ego is a late arrival for hermeneutical thought. The experiencer apprehends himself not as an isolable subject, standing over against an object to be manipulated and controlled; rather he apprehends himself as a way of being installed in the world. Correspondingly, the figures intended by hermeneutical thought are not denotable facts or objective conditions but rather situational possibilities through which existence can move. Hermeneutical thought opens up a world region which is not susceptible to measurement, control, and prediction. Representational thinking is a thinking that controls; hermeneutical thinking is a thinking which "lets things be." Heidegger has captured this aspect of the character of hermeneutical thought in the word *"Gelassenheit,"* which he has used as the title for one of his books, and which has appropriately been rendered into English as "releasement." [15] *Gelassenheit* is the condition for philosophical thinking, according to Heidegger. It is the opening of the path of thought toward being by releasing thought from the compulsion for control and permitting meanings to present themselves in the phenomena. Hermeneutical thinking frees one from the urge to dominate and goes the way of disclosure and understanding.

Hermeneutical thinking discloses the world as a dwelling in which various styles of behavior can occur. Hermeneutical thinking is a *path* or a *way* to an understanding of the world as a region of involvements. It uncovers not denotable objects, although assuredly such denotation may accompany it, but rather the historical self-understanding of the experiencer as he is lodged in the world, advancing his projects amidst a welter of existential possibilities. Whereas representational thinking disengages itself from the experiencer and prescinds from his existentiality, bracketing him as a mere subject-pole so as to attend discriminately to the objective state of affairs, hermeneutical thinking attends to the existentiality of the experiencer and the historicality of the life-world. In hermeneutical thinking the historicality of life-forms remains an issue, indeed *the* issue, for it apprehends the horizon-form of time as historicized, housing a unique, personal, decision-making, unrepeatable historical self. Hermeneutical thinking is thought *with* a thinker, embodied and historicized.

The intentionality of representational thinking, grounded in the subject-object correlation, furnishes *informative* meaning. The noetic meanings in representational thinking are vehicles of information. To be meaningful the intended object must function as the terminus of an objective signification, tested, classified, quantified, or in some sense funded. The criterion of meaning is coextensive with the validation of information. The

15. *Gelassenheit* (Pfullingen: Gunther Neske, 1959); English translation, *Discourse on Thinking*, by John M. Anderson and E. Hans Freund (New York: Harper and Row, 1966). The reader may be interested in pursuing other aspects of Heidegger's reflections on thinking, for example, his distinction between "commemorative thinking" (*andenkendes Denken*) and "representational thinking" (*vorstellendes Denken*), which he develops in the introduction to the fifth printing of his essay "What is Metaphysics?" For a translation of this introduction, see Walter Kaufmann, *Existentialism from Dostoevsky to Sartre* (Cleveland: Meridian Books, 1956), pp. 206–21.

intentionality of hermeneutical thinking, grounded in a historical life-world, furnishes *interpretive* meaning. Hermeneutics is an interpretive grasping, whereby the experiencer is *placed between* (*inter-pretre*) the data and thus insinuated into the world. Meaning is borne by this interpretation, and its fruits are self-understanding and world-comprehension. Informative meaning is delivered through a speaking *about* . . . numerical progressions, solubility of substances, phylogenetic developments of species, etc; interpretive meaning is expressed through a speaking *of* . . . lived experiences and life styles.

We must now attempt a more concrete elucidation of interpretive meaning through the method of illustration. For our illustration we will take one of the purer forms of interpretive meaning—poetic interpretation. We will use as our illustrative example Robert Frost's well-known poem "The Road Not Taken":

> Two roads diverged in a yellow wood,
> And sorry I could not travel both
> And be one traveler, long I stood
> And looked down one as far as I could
> To where it bent in the undergrowth;
>
> Then took the other, as just as fair,
> And having perhaps the better claim,
> Because it was grassy and wanted wear;
> Though as for that the passing there
> Had worn them really about the same,
>
> And both that morning equally lay
> In leaves no step had trodden black.
> Oh, I kept the first for another day!
> Yet knowing how way leads on to way,
> I doubted if I should ever come back.
>
> I shall be telling this with a sigh
> Somewhere ages and ages hence:
> Two roads diverged in a wood, and I—
> I took the one less traveled by,
> And that has made all the difference.

What sort of meaning is illustrated by this poem? How does one proceed in interpreting it? One needs to be careful at the outset not to prejudge the meaning of the poem by asking a "what . . ." question. The phenomenon at issue requires rather a "how . . ." question. We ask "How does the poem mean?" rather than "What does the poem mean?" Proceeding from this inquiry-standpoint, the peculiar path of poetic interpretation begins to open up. We are not moving in the direction of informative meaning. The poem provides neither direct information about objects nor about a subject. To be sure, objectifiable figures are named—roads, woods, undergrowth, grass, and leaves—but the intentionality of poetic thinking does not isolate these figures as items within an information scheme. To discover information about roads, woods, and trees, one would consult the objectifying thinking of geology, engineering, and horticulture. Admittedly some bare and general information travels with the meaning of the poem, but this is at best incidental to the insinuation of interpretive meaning. Likewise it will hardly do to retrench the information scheme so as to include inner or emotive meanings residing in a subject. We have already observed that the distinction between the inner and outer, internal and external, remains problematic on the level of primordial experience, and, while this distinction is employed with a relative justification in the interests of achieving psychological information, we find that its relevance for poetic meaning is minimal. It is superficially evident that certain psychic conditions are operative in the construction, speaking, and hearing of a poem, but these conditions do not provide the foundations for interpretive meaning. Only incidentally does a poem provide information about the adventitious psychic experiences of the poet. Only a psychoanalysis of the poet could unearth such information. An interpretation of the meaning of the poem must simply leave this question open.

It thus becomes evident that the information scheme is not applicable to interpretive poetic meaning. But we still need to address ourselves specifically to the question "How does a poem mean?" A poem means by calling up memories and evoking anticipations, by suggesting life styles, by disclosing possible ways for man to be. A poem is an occurrence or an event of a peculiar kind. It is an event that invites a participation, a placing of the interpreter into the figure-background complex that structures the poem. A poem means by disclosing a world perspective in which certain bearings and behavior styles become manifest. Frost's poem discloses a world perspective in which there is a moment of choice, in which there is facticity and freedom, in which there is regret and fulfillment.

Our example from poetic interpretation could be supplemented with examples from the interpretation of political and religious writings. Hermeneutics originally developed as a method of Biblical interpretation, a method whereby the text was to be permitted to speak for itself, to show its meaning without reductive explanations. And although examples of textual interpretation (literary, political, or religious) may be of extraordinary value in elucidating the character of hermeneutical thinking and interpretive meaning, the primary philosophical relevance of hermeneutics can be seen only by focusing its relevance for issues concerning human existence and the life-world. Principally through the efforts of Heidegger and Gadamer (to a lesser degree, also, Dilthey), hermeneutics has been expanded to encompass a hermeneutic of existence as well as a hermeneutic of textual interpretation. Indeed, it is the former which ultimately provides the foundation for the latter. It is in a hermeneutic of existence that the distinction between informative and interpretive meaning comes to the fore. The interpretive meanings in Heidegger's analysis of *Dasein*'s being-in-the-world are not the end product of representational thinking, although representational concepts may emerge obliquely. His analysis does not provide information about serially isolable objects in the world, nor does it provide a classification of the traits of an empirical self. Rather his analysis and interpretation projects a way of dwelling in the world that opens up paths to self-understanding.

The importance of the relevance of hermeneutical thinking for the methodological foundations of phenomenology can hardly be overemphasized. The very stance of the phenomenologist is already colored by interpretation. Merleau-Ponty has shown us that no complete phenomenological reduction is possible. The students of hermeneutics have shown us that no pure phenomenological description is possible. This becomes particularly evident when phenomenology turns its attention to existential reality, when phenomenology becomes *existential* phenomenology. In this turn the experiencer as embodied, as capable of speech, and as a social and historical being, becomes the reflective focus of attention. This shift in attention, which is not to be confused with a reversal of standpoint, is already discernible in the writings of the philosophical father of phenomenology,

Edmund Husserl. As one compares the idealism of the *Cartesian Meditations* with the later writings (*Erfahrung und Urteil, Krisis,* and the *Nachlass*) one notices a methodological restructuring of phenomenology whereby it becomes a return to the phenomena by way of the *Lebenswelt* rather than by way of a monadic ego. In Husserl's shift to the antepredicative evidence of a life-world, which is historicized from the bottom up, there is a concomitant awareness of the role of hermeneutical thinking and interpretive meaning. Thus when phenomenology becomes existential phenomenology, it becomes hermeneutical phenomenology at the same time. When the phenomenologist philosophizes, he is already embedded in the solicitations and projects of a historical life-world.

We must now carry our investigations another step along the way and elucidate the peculiar bearing of the horizon-forms of time and space on the structural development of representational and hermeneutical thinking. Both types of thinking display a network of intentionalities whereby the act of thought, figure, and background are synthesized in the achievement of noetic meaning. This synthesis is not the result of the constituting activity of a transcendental ego. Herein resides our rejection of idealism. As we have seen, such a synthesis is already operative in the intentionality of feeling and will, an intentionality which is primarily prereflective in character and as much passive as active. Now the reflective synthesis of thought is not another kind of synthesis, somehow added or attached to the operating prereflective synthesis; it mixes and mingles with the prereflective synthesis in a drive toward meaning. The two syntheses are properly understood as complementary tendencies and moments in the deployment of meaning. Each, so to speak, feeds on the other. They can be separated for purposes of analysis, but they remain bonded in the upsurge of world experience. The interweaving of reflection and feeling, thought and action, conception and perception constitutes a world-fact of lived experience. Time and space intercalate in a determinate way the reflective and prereflective syntheses which are at work in this process of interweaving.

The reflective synthesis of intentional consciousness is an offspring of time. Thought is borne by the ecstatic temporality in which the thinker is lodged. Merleau-Ponty speaks straight to the point when he says, "Time and thought are mutually entangled." [16] Thinking is a process of temporalization, an in-gathering of presentation, protention, and retention. The manifold forms of thinking intend figures which come to presence in the midst of protentional and retentional pulls and pushes. Thought runs forwards and backwards. It anticipates the future while it recollects the past. It runs ahead toward possible configurations (whether they be those of representational or those of hermeneutical thinking) and takes over the collocations of past experience in light of the present. In this operating synthesis of thought, the future assumes a priority over the other ecstasies of time. The future is the way to noetic meaning. Thought anticipates future possibilities through which the recurring contents of the past and the present can be organized. Thought brings the future to bear upon the past and the present. This is why the traditional British empiricist notion of thought—as a recording of copies of present sense-impressions—is unable to approach the phenomenon of thinking in its world engagement. Without the future, thinking could never be an *operating* synthesis; it could only be an achieved state, a static result riveted in an atomistic present, without fringes and without intentionality.

It was the genius of Kant to perceive the temporality of thought in the achievement of the unity of apperception. The unity of apperception is the triadic unification of a synthesis of apprehension in perception (presentation of the present); reproduction in the imagination (retention of the past); and recognition in conception (protention of the future). Kant made explicit both the operating synthesis of thought and its temporal condition. But Kant's chief concern was with temporality as a condition for objectification, preoccupied as he was with the investigation of representational thought. He offered little in the way of an elucidation of the historical temporality which underlies interpretive meaning.

Time and space as the horizon-forms of world experience are ingredients of both nature and history. Time informs the natural world of objects and things as well as the historical world of personal and social existence. In the former, time insinuates itself as a condition for the appearance of figures as objects. Time determines the *ob-ject* character of reality, the possible

16. *Signs*, trans. Richard C. McCleary (Evanston: Northwestern University Press, 1964), p. 15.

appearance of things and events as *standing-over-against*. Time contributes the succession and simultaneity by virtue of which figures are marked off from each other, thus rendering possible their appearance as objects. As Kant had already discerned, this objectification under the conditions of temporality requires a doctrine of finitude. There could be no objects for infinite thought, no congealing of reality as something given to consciousness as standing over against it. Infinite thought would have the privilege of viewing reality as nontemporal e-ject rather than temporalized ob-ject.

Space also conditions the objectification of representational thought. Figures of experience can appear as objects because of the contribution of space. Specifically, space makes possible the discrimination of the subject-pole from the object-pole, as well as the discrimination of distance between objects. Whenever, for example, a figure is perceived against a background, it is marked off both from other figures and from the perceiver. Representational thought grasps this perceptual fact through the discrimination of subject and object, and in this discrimination thought already finds itself working with the form of space. This contribution of space, in conjunction with the contribution of time in its determination of succession and simultaneity, is that which provides the condition for the appearance of objects. The objectification of representational thought thus finds its genealogy in time and space as the basic horizon-forms of world experience.

But time and space assume another posturing and provide another way of trenching meanings. Time has a historical as well as a natural dimension. And although it is important to fix the foundations of both dimensions in world experience, the distinction needs to be maintained so as to avoid any reductivism, either of a naturalist or historicist variety. Time as a condition for nature contributes succession and simultaneity as the temporal matrix for objectification; time as a condition for historical experience contributes the existential matrix of beginning and end. It is within this matrix of beginning and end that all interpretive meanings find their source. It is the matrix not only for the cultural history of the race but it is within this expression of time that the self-understanding within finite personal existence emerges. It is this expression of time that makes possible the hermeneutic of an existence in transit from birth to death, determined by a beginning and an end. The synthesis of figure and background in the occasioning of interpretive meaning has its foundation in this historical expression of time. The figures of hermeneutical thinking are not disengaged from the historical experiencer; they do not stand over against him, objectified through the coordination of succession and simultaneity with separability in space. There is a spatio-temporal coordinate operative in historical meaning, but it is the coordination of *lived through* time with *lived through* space. Hermeneutical thinking grasps its intended figures (such as freedom, purpose, and justice) not as objects or entities but as ingredients in a situation which is lived through in finite existential time and space. The meanings of freedom, purpose, and justice become transparent to finite existence as it is suspended between beginning and end and struggles to preserve and enrich its lived time and lived space. This suspension between beginning and end and this movement within oriented space, subject to devaluation or loss, constitutes the coordinated temporal-spatial horizon-forms which lie embedded in hermeneutical thinking and ground its intentional structure.

In concluding our discussion of noetic meaning as it is borne by these two fundamental types of thinking we are in position to state an implicatory issue to be taken up in the following chapter. The implicatory issue is precisely the same that emerged in our discussion of felt and willed meaning. All the paths in our exploration of thought, as already in our exploration of sentience and volition, lead back to a contextualized experiencer. Thinking implicates a thinker. The virtuosity of thought extends to a self-reflexive ability to comprehend the thinker. There is a self-referential intentionality which carries all noetic meaning back to a common center. Noetic intentionality, like sentient and volitional intentionality, is centripetal as well as centrifugal. It reaches "back" to a centered experiencer as it reaches "out" toward figure and background. The terminus of this self-referential, centripetal intentionality, quite clearly, cannot be a representational object or entity. What is at issue is, among other things, that which makes objectification possible. This does not constitute a denial that certain levels of human reality are accessible through the tools of the anthropological, sociological, and psychological sciences, which cannot avoid objectifying procedures. But what remains unasked in the projects of the behavioral sciences is the question about the being who is thus able to objectify himself. It is for this reason that the notion of "behavior" has to be broadened with respect to its range of signification, and liberated from the reductive and metaphysical strictures which accrued through the proliferation of *behaviorisms* in the various social and psychological sciences.[17] The behavior of man reaches beyond the arbitrary limits of objective knowledge. It drives to a more originative questioning, a questioning about the limits and possibilities of the objectification of behavior. Although the scientist may define himself as an object of investigation and derive significant information about predictable personality traits, his existential stance as concerned researcher and inquirer is not itself an investigable object.

We do not score appreciably better in our search for the source of thought by turning our attention from man as a representational object to man as a transcendental ego. Although a notable advance has been made by Kant and Husserl through their respective transcendental turns, particularly in their explication of the conditions for objectification, the fact remains that the notion of the transcendental ego has at best limited applicability in our search for the self-referential terminus of thought. The transcendental ego may be a useful concept for clarifying the operating synthesis of representational thinking, but it remains incurably poverty-stricken in providing a grounding of hermeneutical thought. The transcendental ego has neither life nor history, and hence it is a postulation which has little relevance to the engaged thinker who is seeking to understand himself in his life and history. To account for the genealogy of hermeneutical thinking, the transcendental ego—if indeed one is to make use of it at all—needs to be historicized and placed into a wider context of solicitations. Only in this wider context can the presence of the thinker be approached. So again we are led to ask the question about the *contextualized* experiencer, in an effort to become clear about the character and context of the experiencer implicated in the intentionality of feeling, willing, and thinking.

17. One of the singular merits of Merleau-Ponty's book, *The Structure of Behavior*, trans. Alden Fischer (Boston: Beacon Press, 1963), is the broadening of what is meant by behavior and the consequent overcoming of the imperialism of scientific behaviorism with its confining and concealing stimulus-response models.

PART II

The Contextualized Experiencer

4 / The Embodied Experiencer

My body is my body just in so far as I do not con-
sider it in this detached fashion, do not put a gap
between myself and it. To put this point in another
way, my body is mine in so far as for me my body
is not an object but, rather, I am my body.
—Gabriel Marcel, *The Mystery of Being*

[1] BEYOND MONISM AND DUALISM

OUR PRECEDING DISCUSSION has placed on us the
necessity of exploring the life-distinguishing character of the
experiencer who stands implicated by the centripetal intentional
vectors of feeling, willing, and thinking. It is not accidental that
our inquiry into the posture and bearing of the experiencer
follows rather than precedes our discussion of the dynamics and
structure of experience. A philosophy that remains true to the
configurative development of world-experience cannot *begin*
with a doctrine of the experiencer without risk of isolating the
experiencer as an *a priori solus ipse*. The experiencer needs to be
understood and elucidated *contextually*. The various modes of
intentionality already implicate the experiencer as the existential center of world experience, and this center is never presented independently of the vectorial radiations which emanate
from it. The experiencer is the *center* of world experience. Now

[125]

speaking of a center in this connection is not at all analogous, for example, to the case of a cabbage, various layers of which can be peeled away one by one, disclosing a relatively permanent core. No matter how carefully one peels away the layers of experience, no such fixed and identifiable core shows itself. If one were pressed for a metaphorical analogy, it would appear that an onion would be more suitable, for with an onion the peeling of layers proceeds without ever arriving at a core. However, in elucidating the meaning of center as applied to the experiencer, any analogy drawn from the realm of objects or nonhuman living matter remains suspect. The center at issue is more like a base of operations from which things are perceived and valued, projects entertained, and decisions enacted. The "position" of this base of operations is always relative to the intended figures and background which surround it. Thus it is that one is required to speak of a *contextualized* experiencer.

The objective and subjective approaches to the experiencer would seem to have at least one thing in common—their search for an entity, act, or condition that could provide a stable support for a theory of human nature and human knowledge. The theories of experience that have flourished since the beginning of modern philosophy have found their focal point in epistemological concerns. This tendency already became well established in the philosophy of Descartes with the turn to the *res cogitans* in the hope of securing the foundation of knowledge. In British empiricism this tendency reached its zenith. One needs only to recall Locke's effort to found all knowledge, without exception, on experience (sensation and reflection), which then reached its apotheosis in Hume's sense-impression theory. The advance of Kant beyond Hume left untouched both the epistemological design and the view as to what constitutes experience. Experience, which remained in bondage to theory, continued to be understood as a succession and accumulation of sensations and reflections. Admittedly, in Kant's philosophy the transcendental subject replaces the thin-skinned and evasive sensing subject of British empiricism, but the servitude of experience to theoretically oriented knowledge remains in force. In this servile condition, experience inherits a confining subject-object structure in which the subject is neatly identified with the knower and the object becomes convertible with the known.

In spite of Kant's inability to extricate himself from the view of experience proposed by British empiricism, the critical results of his philosophy with respect to the status of the experiencer were decisive. His demonstration, in the "Transcendental Dialectic" of his *Critique of Pure Reason,* that the self can never apprehend itself as object provided a well-designed sheet anchor against any pretentious and dogmatic scientific behaviorism. But the avenue to any positive knowledge of the self remained closed for Kant because of his acceptance of the subject-object structure of experience. There are indications, however, as Jaspers in particular points out, that Kant did not accept the subject-object dichotomy as being normative for all experience and that he struggled to think himself out of the dichotomy.[1] But a more fruitful pursuit of the issue had to wait until the philosophies of the later Husserl, Heidegger, and Merleau-Ponty with their call to return not to a monadic epistemological subject but to a prepredicative life-world.

In every reflective turn this prepredicative life-world has already announced its presence. The experiencer, reflecting upon himself as experiencer, is already housed in this life-world, which is not yet determined by the objectification of representational thought. Meaning is indeed already operative, borne by the prereflective intentionality of feeling and volition, but this is all in advance of the bare and abstracted relation of subject as knower to object as known. An existential knowledge through involvement is already operating in the world when the subject-object distinction is put into play by representational thought. This knowledge through involvement, secreted in the prereflective projects of the engaged experiencer, provides the foundation for the specification of that which is subjective and that which is objective. Heidegger, Sartre, and Merleau-Ponty have in various ways contributed to a clarification of this existential knowing. Heidegger speaks of knowing as a mode of *Dasein* grounded in his being-in-the-world; Sartre elucidates knowing as a mode of the *pour-soi;* and Merleau-Ponty finds the genesis of knowledge in a perception which is itself a manner of being-to-the-world (*être-au-monde*). In all of these thinkers the traditional subject-object epistemological scheme comes under rather severe indictment, and world experience is liberated from its servitude to representational thought.

1. Karl Jaspers, *The Great Philosophers,* trans. Ralph Manheim (New York: Harcourt, Brace & World, 1962), pp. 244–45.

But the dethronement of the subject-object schema as absolute monarch need not entail its expulsion from the kingdom. The subject-object distinction can be undercut, but it cannot be annihilated. After giving way to prereflective intentionality so that it might deploy its peculiar and varied meanings, the subject-object distinction returns to buttress and direct representational thought. Although Sartre's criticism of the transcendental ego as the foundation of knowledge is trenchant and defensible, he fails to grasp the role that it plays in the development of thetic consciousness. Without the transcendental ego, Sartre is unable to account for the unification that is operative in representational thinking as well as for the continuing identity of the knower.[2] Granted that the transcendental ego is an emergent rather than an ontological prius, the acknowledgment of its achieved status may be required to account for the conditions of one genre of noetic meaning. A persisting weakness in existential philosophy generally, and the existentialism of Sartre in particular, is a neglect of the conditions and world basis of representational thought. Such conditions could indeed be clarified through an appeal to a transcendental ego, but if this is done it must be remembered that the ego is a bloodless abstraction from a wider context of world-attuned experiencing. The transcendental ego needs to be integrated with the existential deployment of an experiencer who is always already situated in the world in his prereflective life.

It is this contextualism and situationality of the experiencer that becomes our topic of attention in Part II. We will seek to elucidate the contextualism of the experiencer through an investigation of his *embodiment, speech,* and *sociality.* To exist as experiencer is to exist within these three contextual structures. The multiple intentionalities of feeling, willing, and thinking (both representational and hermeneutical) implicate an expe-

2. See particularly his essay, *The Transcendence of the Ego: An Existentialist Theory of Consciousness,* trans. Forrest Williams and Robert Kirkpatrick (New York: Noonday Press, 1957). For an incisive criticism of Sartre's theory of the ego the reader is referred to Maurice Natanson's article, "Phenomenology and Existentialism: Husserl and Sartre on Intentionality," *The Modern Schoolman,* XXXVII (1958), 1–10; reprinted in *Phenomenology: The Philosophy of Edmund Husserl and Its Interpretation,* ed. Joseph J. Kockelmans (New York: Doubleday Anchor, 1967), pp. 338–48.

riencer who is at the same time embodied, speaking, and social. Our investigation will yield not a distillation of a timeless essence of man but rather an elucidation of man in his finite human condition. Embodiment, speech, and sociality provide the contextual structures in which and through which the sentience, volition, and thought of the engaged experiencer become manifest.

In this chapter our topic of investigation is the experiencer as embodied. Our discussion will begin with a delineation of a new inquiry-standpoint whereby the traditional dilemma of dualism and monism with respect to the mind-body issue can be surmounted, and it will then proceed to an examination of three related themes—bodily comprehension, embodied spirit, and the body-as-myself.

The history of the conventionally classified "problem of the self" has been pretty much the story of recurring tendencies in the direction of a dualism of mind and body on the one hand and a reductive monism on the other. In its most pronounced variety, accredited principally to Descartes, dualism sets forth a framework in which mind and body appear as distinct and separable substances. Admittedly even for Descartes these substances were related, but with respect to their essential determinations they remained "entirely and absolutely distinct." [3] Monism takes the other path and seeks to locate one within the other. Monistic theories of the self are legion, but generally they tend either toward a reductive materialism or a species of panpsychism. The history of the problem of the self has become defined within these alternative frameworks, all of which move out from an inquiry-standpoint that prejudges in advance the phenomena under investigation. Here again phenomenological investigation must begin with the foundation work of investigating and reassessing presupposed standpoints. The various theoretical alternatives on the relation of mind and body must be placed in moratorium, and the phenomena examined as they show themselves. Merleau-Ponty speaks directly to the issue at hand when he says: "In the last analysis, phenomenology is neither a materialism nor a philosophy of mind. Its proper work is to unveil the

3. *Meditations on First Philosophy*, VI; *The Philosophical Works of Descartes*, trans. E. S. Haldane and G. R. T. Ross (New York: Dover, 1955), I, 190.

pre-theoretical layer on which both of these idealizations find their relative justification and are gone beyond." [4]

There are two interrelated presuppositions within the inquiry-standpoint of traditional theories of the self which contribute more to a veiling than a revealing of the phenomena. The first, at least covertly metaphysical in character, concerns the pre-delineation of mind and body as determinable entities, as figures appearing in the mode of objective being, or what Heidegger has appropriately called the mode of *Vorhandensein*. The mind, it is assumed, is some kind of entity to which attributes can be assigned and in which processes or activities occur. The mind is pictured as a container or receptacle into and out of which a train of sensations and reflections pass. This picture remains suspect from a phenomenological point of view, for mind as it appears in world experience is a *developing* or *streaming* consciousness, never catching up with itself and congealing into an entity. The entitative status of mind must therefore be questioned. Correspondingly, the entitative status of the body needs to be reexamined. One of the most deeply ingrained habits of traditional philosophy, due primarily to its representational mode of thought, is the rendering of the figures of experience into entities. Everything in heaven and earth becomes an entity, some species of *object* for thought. But we have seen that it is only representational thinking that gives a franchise to the subject-object structure of thought, and representational thinking does not exhaust the reach and range of world-experiencing intentionality. The body as an experienced phenomenon is primordially presented not as a representable object but in the immediacy of its lived concreteness. The experienced body is not an object for the abstractive gaze; it is the body as lived, as lodged in the world as a base of operations from which attitudes are assumed and projects deployed. The body as object, which has its limited natural justification in the anatomical and physiological sciences, is the body excerpted from its living involvements and quoted out of context. The anatomist and the physiologist view the body in the perspective of its *dissectibility* whereby the body becomes a potential corpse. The body is *represented* by objectifying thought, instead of being apprehended in its *presentational* immediacy. In no sense is this an indictment against the

4. *Signs*, trans. Richard C. McCleary (Evanston: Northwestern University Press, 1964), p. 165.

study of the body with respect to its physiological systems and chemical constitution. What is required is an awareness that the entity hypothesis, whereby the body is a material *thing* composed of parts, has a limited applicability. The phenomenal or lived body does not surge up in the world as a thing in the midst of other things.

The second presupposition within the inquiry-standpoint of traditional theories of the self pertains to a more specifically semantical issue. In dealing with the nature of the body, theorists have been misled by the tempting analogy of ownership when speaking about the body. The mind or the self, it is said, *possesses* or *has* a body. The propriety of such a locution becomes problematic when the seeing of the phenomenon is at stake. My pipe has a stem. The book which I am reading has 250 pages. The mountain top has a cap of snow. A square has four sides. In all of these cases a relationship of having or possessing obtains. But when one proceeds from these cases to speak of myself as having a body one falls into a mistake of description. To be sure I can say, without misleading the hearer, that by virtue of my embodied existence I am able to have and possess tools for the execution of certain tasks, but then my body is understood as a condition for having rather than itself something which is possessed. The lived body is neither an object among other objects, nor is it properly speaking an instrument used by the self. To speak of the body as an instrument which I use is to externalize the body from myself in a way which is not warranted by the data. The lived body does not belong to me any more than I belong to it. The lived body *is* myself in my manifold concretions. This is why Marcel has correctly insisted on the locution "I am my body" rather than the misleading expression "I have a body." [5] The body makes use of instruments and utensils as it inhabits the world but it is itself not an instrument. Neither is it a substance which is attached to me, nor is it a composition of properties which I possess. The body is myself in my lived concreteness. My body is *who I am*. I exist in the world as embodied.

We thus reject the governing presuppositions in the traditional formulation of the mind-body problem, presuppositions which already legislate in advance what is to be discovered. A

5. *The Metaphysical Journal*, trans. Bernard Wall (London: Rockliff, 1952), pp. 332–33.

phenomenological investigation of the body will proceed beyond the restricting alternatives of monism and dualism. There is neither one entity nor are there two entities. What shows itself is an embodied existence which anchors the manifold intentionalities of world experience. Entities, whether mental or physical, are not phenomenal realities directly presented within experience. Entities are the peculiar postulates of representational thinking, designed for the convenient classification of objectifiable reality. Mind and body are not the result of postulatory thought. They are already at work when thought in any of its expressions begins.

The contribution of William James to the surmounting of the monism-dualism controversy is often overlooked. In his "Essays on Radical Empiricism" he rejects both the entitative status of consciousness and the entitative status of the body. Consciousness and body are functions or operations in the "world of pure experience." They are neither "subjects" nor "objects." They are ways in which pure experience is occasioned. Consciousness is a streaming present on the fringes of a past and a future, projecting a perceptual and conceptual grasp on the world. The body is inseparable from this consciousness for this consciousness is always centered in its embodiment. "The world experienced," writes James, "comes at all times with our body as its centre, centre of vision, centre of action, centre of interest." [6] The body is where perception and vision happen, where desires and interests are occasioned, where action takes place. The body is an *incarnated project* that feels, wills, and thinks. It is the common center of the manifold intentionalities that we discussed in the previous chapter, and thus provides, as Merleau-Ponty has expressed it, "our anchorage in a world." [7] The remarkable similarity between James's radical empiricism of the body and recent studies in the phenomenology of the lived body (by Marcel, Sartre, and Merleau-Ponty in particular) should not be overlooked. Although James's discussion of the body remains sketchy and more on the level of suggestion than explicit formulation, when he speaks of the body as our center of vision, action, and interest he assuredly anticipates Marcel's formulation "I *am* my

6. *Essays in Radical Empiricism* (New York: Longmans, Green, 1942), p. 170 n.
7. *Phenomenology of Perception*, trans. Colin Smith (New York: Humanities Press, 1962), p. 144.

body," Sartre's observation that the body is a "synthetic totality of life and action," and Merleau-Ponty's insight that "my body is wherever there is something to be done." [8]

In this section we have sought to clarify the inquiry-standpoint which we assume when we ask about the embodiment of the contextualized experiencer. We have found it necessary to reject certain traditional concepts and frames of reference in marking out our path of inquiry. The body as experienced is not a material thing, nor is the mind or consciousness a mental thing. Materialism, mentalism, and psycho-physical dualism are hollow alternatives to a phenomenology of the experienced body. They prejudice the phenomena in advance with their objectivism. The phenomenon of body, we have suggested, is less like the appearance of a thing and more like the presentment of an incarnated behavioral project in which our perceptions, feelings, decisions, and actions are centered. It is along these lines that our further elucidation must move, describing the body as a behavioral project with its distinctive comprehension, determination of spirit, and power of individuation. Only then will we be on the way to understanding the experiencer within the context of his embodiment.

[2] BODILY COMPREHENSION

IT IS BY VIRTUE OF HIS EMBODIMENT that the experiencer is exposed to the world. This exposition is not that of simple contact with objects, tools, and other selves, but the more fundamental exposition through which the world is opened and made available as experienced. The body in its concrete motility plays a decisive role in the comprehension of world. To understand the body as incarnated project is to understand it as a project of world comprehension. It is *with* his body that the experiencer achieves access to the tools and utensils which he uses, to the objects which he handles and manipulates, to the other selves whom he experiences in the handshake and the embrace. It is by virtue of the body that objects are there to be inspected, touched, and perceived in a variety of changing perspectives.

8. Marcel, *Metaphysical Journal*, pp. 332–33; Sartre, *Being and Nothingness*, trans. Hazel Barnes (New York: Philosophical Library, 1956), p. 346; Merleau-Ponty, *Phenomenology of Perception*, p. 250.

The body furrows paths to the perception of things, to the performance of tasks, to the place of encounter with other selves. But the body in its experiencing of the world is not itself a thing touched or an object observed. An observable object is always *there,* somehow positioned over against me and seen from different perspectives; but my body is always *here,* present with my perceiving and observing, accompanying my every perspective or point of view. Objects can be made to disappear. I can escape from them. But I cannot escape from my body. The body is thus present for experience in a distinctive manner. It is present as a condition for there being objects without itself being an object. It is indeed, as James had already discerned, the center of vision and action without being an object for vision and action.

We thus begin to understand how the body opens and comprehends the world. It brings the world into reach, opens possibilities for perception, marks out the ranges of one's activities, and mediates felt, willed, and noetic meanings. Ricoeur has expressed it well by saying that the body is the "mediator of the intentional consciousness." [9] The intentionality of feeling, will, and thought are borne by a bodily engagement or comportment. My body marks out the situations in which the threat of anxiety is felt and in which hope is entertained and nurtured. I am a sentient creature insofar as I am embodied. Further, the body is the locus of my action. Through my body I appropriate the world as a field of activity. My body is wherever there is a task to be performed or a project to be carried through. The experiencer is embodied as an "I can" as well as an "I feel." The intentionality of thought is also borne by a bodily engagement. Thinking and the lived body intermesh. Thought, even that of the loftiest abstraction, remains the thought of an embodied thinker. Thought can transcend toward the infinite, but even in this transcending flight it remains the thinking of a finite, embodied being. Hence, although the body opens one to the world, it also defines one's limits within the world. It is by virtue of the lived body that there are objects, objects of perception and conception

9. "It is always *upon* the world and beginning from the manifestation of the world as perceived, threatening and accessible, that I apprehend the openness of my body, mediator of the intentional consciousness" (*Fallible Man,* trans. Charles Kelbley [Chicago: Henry Regnery, n.d.], p. 30).

alike, for it is from perception that conception takes its rise. Embodiment thus infects thought as it infects sentience and volition. The lived body is the center or operating base for the varied intentionalities of world experience. Hence, it can be properly understood as the mediator and bearer of intentional consciousness.

The hand achieves a privileged role in this bodily comprehension. Of all the primates it is man who relies most heavily on his hands for survival and cultural progress. The hand is at the same time a vehicle of sensory and motor meanings. It is with the hand that one touches and discriminates textures. This tactile experience is not simply a matter of receiving inert sense-impressions. Even touch has its background, its context of associates, its anticipations and perspectives. Furthermore it is in league with the other senses, particularly sight, with which it corroborates its findings in concert. But the hand leads the way in matters of touch and is the more proximate sense in comparison with sight and hearing. That with which it deals is "at hand," the inspection which it executes is direct and immediate. Coupled with this sensory function of the hand is a motor function. The hand "handles" its experienced objects, it gropes and grasps, it pushes and pulls, it strikes and strokes. The hand is the handler of tools, and through the making and use of tools an environment is at the same time created and made known. Through the use of his hands man is disclosed to himself as a *homo faber* who can fashion new environments and rethread the old. It is for this reason that Erwin Straus correctly maintains that the hand has "an insight of its own." [10] Through its sensory and motor operations the hand comprehends the world and invests it with pretheoretical significance.

10. "The Upright Posture," in *Essays in Phenomenology*, ed. Maurice Natanson (The Hague: Martinus Nijhoff, 1966), p. 179. Phenomenologists of the lived body have tended to overlook Karl Jaspers' suggestive discussion of the hand in *Von der Wahrheit* (Munich: Piper, 1947). In the relevant passage of this work he supplements the abstract definition of man as a rational animal with the concrete characterization of him as that being who makes use of his hands, and shows how the manipulative activity of the hand is already an expression of thought, uniting body and mind in a synthetic project of existence. "Wie sehr alles Tun mit der Hand schon ein Denken in sich schliesst, ist daran zu bemerken, das Denktätigkeiten durch Handtätigkeiten ausgedrückt werden" (p. 329).

Through the use of the hand, various attitudes toward the world are assumed and different styles or modes of being-in-the-world are achieved. Two such definite attitudes are disclosed by the operations of grasping and pointing. With the grasp, objects are *incorporated* into the proximate space of my lived body. The grasp brings and keeps things within reach, accessible for the execution of projects through which I organize my lived space. I grasp the pen to be used in the writing of my letter. I grasp the hammer in my project of hammering. I grasp my pipe and my golf club and with this grasp appropriate my world and live it in a certain way. Pointing expands my world to include the other. The meanings conveyed by pointing have an explicit social signi-fication. I do not point for myself. I point so as to elicit a region of attentiveness for someone else. In pointing, a world and a space shared by the other become manifest. Pointing is a more distant gesture than is grasping. I can point to that which is beyond reach, beyond the incorporation range of my lived body. Pointing marks out the distance of tools and objects from the embodied center of perception and action. Pointing and grasping thus illustrate two ways in which the hand comprehends tools and objects, two ways of being-in-the-world.

This sensory and manual comprehension of the world by the hand takes place within the wider context of a bodily-anchored orientation of space. In our discussion of the horizon-form of space in Part I, we observed the relevance of the concrete move-ments of the lived body for the experience of the world as spatialized. The body provides the place from which the direc-tional axes of existential space are viewed and valued, and it provides the vantage point for the measurement of existential distance. By virtue of its concrete movements, whereby the stances and stations within a given surrounding region are de-ployed, the lived body provides the "standard of motion" in the existential coordination of time and space. When one speaks of the time of world experience, the movement by which it is meas-ured is not the abstract movement of objects traversing an abstract loci of points, but rather the concrete movement of em-bodied existence. The question of the connection of embodiment and spatiality arises again when we ask about the contextualized experiencer, as indeed it must, for the experiencer in the con-text of his embodiment is destined to the fortunes and mis-fortunes of being spatialized.

The lived body as the center of vision, action, and interest organizes its perceptions and projects to accord with its orientation in space. In seeing, feeling, willing, and thinking, the embodied experiencer *lives* his space in a variety of manners. We have already observed how the hand in its grasping and pointing achieves two types of orientation in space. But the lived body comports itself not only through the use of the hands; embodiment is a postural complex in which legs, thorax, and head also contribute to the marking out and opening up of lived space. The alignment of hands, legs, thorax and head to form an upright posture establishes a definite mode of coping with space, inhabiting it in a particular manner. The body marks out a surrounding territorial space over which it maintains a relative sovereignty. Not only the space that I incorporate with my grasp, but also the space in which I stamp my foot in anger, the space in which I kneel in prayer, the space for my feet when I walk, the space oriented in the act of reclining when I am tired—these all mark out my territorial claims and define the places and directions in which I achieve a certain world orientation. This space is my own. Inhabiting it I achieve my identity; it becomes conditioned and attuned to my intentionalities of feeling, willing, and thinking. Yet this identity has not the character of an unchanging substance or of a set of fixed relations. It is subject to the variance of existence itself. The vectors of despair mark out my territorial space as a confining space. My space becomes a space in which my body is constricted and confined, with shoulders slumped, head lowered and movements slackened. Hope expands my territorial space and revitalizes the movements of the body. The intentionality of will prepares space for the execution of a plan of action. My territorial space becomes the place for something to be done. The consistency of lived space is not given once and for all, and the self-identity borne by the orientation within space moves along a spectrum polarized by achievement and loss. Self-identity can be lost, as in the case of schizophrenia, and this loss of self-identity is inseparable from the dissolution of the consistency of one's lived space. The spatiality of embodiment thus carries with it factors of negativity as well as conditions for the unification of experience.

There is another element in the territorial space surrounding my lived body which determines my sovereignty as only relative. My territorial space, explored and claimed by the posturing and movement of my lived body, is not an indisputable possession; for already in the handshake and the slap, in the nod and the shrug, the other is prereflectively acknowledged as a codweller in the horizon-form of space. I do not create the other through my spatializing of the world as I might create or fashion a utensil. The other is congenially confronted in my space, as in the handshake; or present as a threat to my space by virtue of his stare and his shaking fist. My embodied space mediates between the other and me, it defines my "spatiality of situation" as a spatiality of *social* situation. The other is present to my space. I cannot avoid taking him into consideration. I must assume some kind of attitude toward him. I join him in such a manner that we share each other's territorial space; I fortify my space in an attitude of defense; I assume the offensive and seek to penetrate his space; I place him on the periphery of my concerns and remain indifferent. All of the vectors of feeling that inform one's concrete relations with others—love, hate, anger, shame, spite, disgust, and so forth—operate within the context of acceptance or rejection of the integrity of the other's territorial space. In accepting the other I must accept his lived space, for the manner in which he embodies his space is inseparable from his manner of existing.

The bodily comprehension of the contextualized experiencer, exposing the experiencer to a world of objects and tools, marking out places and directions of his inhabited space and opening paths and relations to the territorial space of the other, reveals another dimension of incarnated consciousness which is, for the most part, neglected in traditional theories of the self. This is the dimension of sexuality. Sexuality is itself a mode of world comprehension. The enduring embarrassment of the transcendental ego is that it is unable to apprehend itself in its sexual embodiment. It is neither male nor female. It allows no distinctions of masculine and feminine behavior, for it "exists" only in abstraction from the world, disembodied and hence sexless. It is at this juncture that transcendental phenomenology, with its return to a monadic transcendental ego, suffers one of its most severe shortcomings. A phenomenology which is geared to an elucidation of world experience should not neglect the role that sexuality plays in self and world awareness. Hence, one is required to go beyond the transcendental postulates of representational thought and return to the embodied experiencer, always already contextualized by virtue of his or her sexual differentiation.

Sexual consciousness has figured significantly in the literature of mythology, both ancient and modern. In the Hebrew myth of creation and fall, the emergence of self-consciousness and the drive to self-actualization is accompanied by sexual awareness. Adam and Eve, yielding to the temptation of knowledge, are disclosed to themselves and to each other in their embodied sexuality. They enter a world with a sexual background, against which styles of feminine and masculine behavior are projected. Delivered over to an unavoidable estrangement through their loss of innocence, Adam and Eve fall before each other's gaze and face each other in the experience of bodily shame. The insights expressed in this and other myths concerning the awareness of one's sexual embodiment and the experience of bodily shame are phenomenologically relevant. They point to the phenomenon of sexuality and the phenomenon of shame which are conditioning factors in the contextualism of the world-experiencer. A whole legion of psychological, sociological, and metaphysical theories, many of them conflicting, have ushered from the fact of sexual self and world awareness. Aristotle ascribed to the female nature a natural passivity and a natural defectiveness. According to Augustine, womanhood implies indecision and inconstancy. Aquinas defined woman as an imperfect man. Schopenhauer and Nietzsche found little in the feminine principle that might commend it (for Nietzsche the great art of women is deception). Montaigne, Diderot, and John Stuart Mill rallied in different ways to the feminist defense. In recent times a kind of *summa feminologico* has been attempted by Simone de Beauvoir in her book *The Second Sex*, in which biological, psychological, sociological, and philosophical discoveries and insights are brought to bear in a herculean effort to understand the role and destiny of the feminine point of view.[11]

There may be little positive that one can directly glean from this ancient and modern accelerated theorizing about the nature of male and female, but it points obliquely to the bodily comprehension which is at work in the consciousness of self and world. One may not be able to distill the "eternal feminine" or the

11. Trans. H. M. Parshley (New York: Alfred A. Knopf, 1952).

"masculine archetype" from such investigations, but the destiny of one's sexual embodiment is brought to the fore. The situation of the experiencer is such that the standpoint from which one comprehends the world is either masculine or feminine. The categories of representational thought may be the same for male and female, but the interpretation, the manner in which the experiencer installs himself in a world, varies with sexual embodiment. This provides the phenomenological foundation upon which all theories about the masculine and feminine rest. Before the masculine and feminine become *principles* or explanatory categories, they are modes of embodiment which register the meanings of world experience in a definite manner.

Sexual embodiment figures in the phenomenon of bodily comprehension not only with respect to the provision of masculine and feminine standpoints and backgrounds within world experience, but also with respect to the "knowledge" of sexual union. The knowledge component of sexuality has been concealed in most traditional views because the body is prejudged as a sexual mechanism of interacting physiological drives and psychic states. The sexual act is then construed as a series of local stimulations, accompanied by physiological-psychic reactions. What is lacking in such an explanation is the specification of the sexual act as a mode of behavior or as a libidinal project which comports its own intentionality. Sexuality exhibits what Merleau-Ponty has called an "erotic comprehension." [12] Physiological and psychic stimulation are components of this intentional mode of behavior rather than the atomistic foundation of it. It is by virtue of this sexual intentionality that the sexual partner is "known" or comprehended, clearly not in terms of the subsumptive function of representational thought but in terms of an appropriation of the world as lined with sexual meanings that can be shared. The sexual bond which unites the lover and the beloved is an intentional vector that follows the movements of existence along a world-horizon. The body of the other is apprehended as a nonobjective figure, with its own territorial space, projected against a background of sexual meanings. The world is disclosed, in the sexual act, as encompassing a field of sexual possibilities.

The libidinal project in the sexual mode of behavior never

12. *Phenomenology of Perception*, p. 157.

makes its appearance in a pure or isolated form. Intentionalities of willing and thinking interpenetrate the libidinal project and stand in a relationship of reciprocal expression. To use the Freudian terminology, the superego and the ego are already operative in the libidinal project. We must, however, avoid the Freudian tendency of viewing the id, ego, and superego as compartmentalized psychic facts. Rather they delineate possible modes of existence. The experiencer exists as id, ego, and superego. They define possible directions into which one's life can be projected. The sensualist and the moralist do not possess different psychic facts. They orient themselves in terms of different life styles—and in the choice of one or the other of these life styles, the structure of world comprehension is already present, as Kierkegaard has incisively shown in his book *Either/Or*. In the realization of the libidinal project, attention is focused upon a particular constellation of world experience, but all of the constitutive elements of personality remain in force. The whole existence of the embodied experiencer participates in the sexual act. This includes the participation of unconscious as well as conscious elements. The conscious and the unconscious, feeling, will, and thought, conspire in the sexual act and determine its structure of comprehension. Sexuality does not reduce existence to the sensual. Sexuality achieves a libidinal comprehension of the world through the medium of existence. There can be no talk of a pan-sexual reductivism. It is rather that existence, with its manifold intentionalities, provides the setting for the libidinal project as it opens up definite movements, directions, styles, and meanings for the embodied experiencer and makes possible the comprehension of world in a specific manner.

[3] Embodied Consciousness

THE THEME OF EMBODIED CONSCIOUSNESS has been implicit throughout the preceding section. In our discussion of bodily comprehension we were able to discern how the embodied experiencer exposes or opens himself to the world through bodily posturing, handling objects and utensils, grasping, pointing, incorporating lived space, and sexuality. Consciousness is already at work in this operation of bodily comprehension. The phenomenon of embodiment as a mode of existence is precisely the compenetration of consciousness and body in the projection of styles of behavior. What is required at this juncture in our continuing elucidation of the contextualized experiencer is a thematic focus on that consciousness which is always already at work in the comportment of the lived body, so as to explicate the history of its structural development. We would choose to make use of the terminology of "spirit" and speak of embodied spirit instead of embodied consciousness, were it not for the accumulated distortions which have become attached to the term "spirit." Also, there is the general tendency in contemporary philosophy to substitute consciousness for spirit. What must be kept in mind is that this substitution is beset with certain perils. The term consciousness in modern and contemporary epistemological theories has been made virtually synonymous with "mental activity" or "mind" and has thus not only suffered a narrowing of the range of meanings that attach to a proper use of the term "spirit," but has also fallen heir to the objectivistic prejudice. Contemporary philosophy sorely needs a new "phenomenology of spirit," a phenomenology of *embodied* spirit, in which spirit, as Nietzsche would have it, remains "true to the earth" and cognizant of its bodily bearing. It is in the direction of such a new phenomenology of embodied spirit that the explorations of the present section are geared, although for the most part we will make use of the more familiar language of consciousness.

The phenomenology of spirit achieved its most profound expression and suffered its most grievous distortion in the movement of German classical idealism. Hegel, not only in his *Phenomenology of Spirit* but even in his *Youthful Writings*, exhibited a seminal comprehension of the life of spirit in its dynamic advance. The chief merit of Hegel's explorations in these early works was that he extricated the meaning of spirit from its subordination to the classical concept of substance and invested it with a projective intentionality. Spirit for Hegel stands-out-of-itself, is tendential in character, temporally and historically projective, ever reaching beyond itself in a compulsive drive for world comprehension. Hegel replaces the classical doctrine of substance, whereby reality is viewed as standing-in-itself, with a fecund subjectivity, always on the move, in tension with itself and its environment, seeking to attain self-consciousness and actualize itself as freedom in the hard struggle for self-fulfillment. The phenomenon of spirit, according to Hegel, appears initially in the mode of *subjective* spirit, and is saddled with the task of working its way beyond the merely subjective to the fulfillment of dialectical unity of subject and object. In this dynamic-dialectical struggle, spirit passes through a painful process of self-actualization. Subjective spirit is posited in the form of negativity and first exists in the condition of servitude. In this condition spirit is infected with alienation from its environment and from itself; but already in this stage that power of self-reflection which enables it to penetrate its servitude with consciousness is at work. Subjective spirit becomes aware of its "servant" character and drives beyond its present state to the purity of consciousness and self-mastery. Spirit is thus able to master itself and exist in the pure idea of itself. The dialectic of spirit culminates in the absorption of self-existence into the purity of ideal essence, in the state of transfigured and peaceful coexistence of subject and object.

The influence of Hegel's concept of spirit was so far-reaching that even those who attacked it (for example, Kierkegaard, Feuerbach, and Marx) did so only by making use of some of the insights that undergirded its formulation. They were placed in the peculiar position of using Hegel's insights against him. They appropriated Hegel's notions of "subjectivity" and "alienated consciousness" and used them in elucidating various perspectives on the philosophy of existence. Kierkegaard sought to place spirit back into the perspective of man's concrete ethico-religious existence; Feuerbach rooted the movement of subjectivity in man's concrete sensory-biological development; and Marx took over Hegel's analysis of spirit in charting man's concrete socioeconomic history. The indictment against Hegel, which accounted for their "anti-Hegelianism," pivoted around their opposition to the idealizing and essentializing of spirit. Hegelianism culminates in essentialism. The anti-Hegelianism of Kierkegaard, Feuerbach, and Marx gave birth to existentialism. For the latter the freedom of spirit remains an existential freedom, limited by its finitude and pervaded by the ambiguities of man's personal, social, and religious history.

The advent of the anti-Hegelian protest marks a turning point and will play its role in any prolegomenon for a future phenomenology of spirit or consciousness. It is primarily through the acknowledgment of the relevance of the anti-Hegelian protest that phenomenology is summoned to reassess its transcendental idealism and redefine itself as existential phenomenology. Husserl's "transcendental consciousness," in the idealistic stage of his phenomenology, is threatened with irrelevancy when lived experience becomes an issue. His transcendental consciousness is insulated from misfortune, unable to apprehend itself in the unhappiness of its alienation. Hegel made room for the "unhappy consciousness," but, as Kierkegaard poignantly put it, "he beheld the kingdom from afar." [13] It is questionable whether Husserl in his stage of transcendental idealism even makes room for an alienated consciousness; however, the later philosophy of Husserl moves in the direction of correcting the earlier deficiency. Husserl inverts the history of Hegel's own philosophical development. Hegel proceeds from the phenomenology of concrete consciousness to the system of a science of logic; Husserl begins with logic and ends with concrete and loosely systematized explorations of the life-world.

A new phenomenology of spirit must be designed so as to avoid the abstract anonymity of reified consciousness which has neither life nor history and so as to restore the full sense of existence with its tragic resonance and joyous fulfillment. To achieve this goal a notion of "embodied spirit" or "incarnated consciousness" is required. Consciousness is always contextualized in the deployments of the lived body, and embodiment always provides the *vicinity* for consciousness. Semantically, the terms "embodied spirit" and "incarnated consciousness" have a convertible form. One might, without loss of meaning, speak of "spiritual embodiment" or "conscious incarnateness." Consciousness and body interpenetrate at the source of existence and conspire in a consummate reciprocity to anchor the intentional vectors which produce a world. Spirit or consciousness manifests or shows itself in a *Gestalt* of living intentionalities, borne by the sentience, volition, and thought which are already at work within world experience. Spirit and body remain united within an existential dialectic (as contrasted with the quantitative dialectic of Hegel), interlaced in such a manner that the contributions of body and spirit are indistinguishable and yet not objectively reducible one to the other. The movement of consciousness can

13. *Either/Or*, trans. David and Lillian Swenson (Princeton: Princeton University Press, 1949), I, 181.

be elucidated only within the context of its incarnation, and the body by virtue of that which makes it a *lived* and *intentional* body already shares in the determinations of consciousness.

Embodied spirit or consciousness exists under various forms of negativity. In its embodiment consciousness comes to grips with its personal guilt, the threat of despair, and the possibility of death. Alienation, in its multiple guises, infects the forms of life assumed by incarnated consciousness. There is the alienation of incarnated consciousness with the surrounding world of objects and things, with the social world of the other, and with its own project of self-actualization. Alienation is present when the world of objective nature becomes an overpowering reality no longer subject to man's calculation and control; when technology develops into technocracy and the tools which man has fashioned by virtue of his embodiment rise up to enslave him; when the incarnated other gazes at one's body and seeks to remove it in an effort to achieve undisputed sovereignty over one's lived space; when consciousness is threatened with personal guilt, personal death, and the loss of personal meaning. The feature which is common to all of these forms of alienation is the context of embodiment which envelops them. Alienation is the threat of the loss of embodied space and embodied time—the supporting horizon-forms of world experience. Objective nature, tools, and the other self threaten the territorial space of my lived body and the existential time which I need to actualize my projects. Likewise, in self-alienation it is my spatial and temporal embodiment which is at stake. Personal guilt convicts me of the neglected possibilities in my past embodied orientation, meaninglessness threatens by removing the proper and opportune times for creative actualization, and death confronts me with the dissolution of embodied existence itself. The environmental world and the social world play their vital roles in the phenomenon of self-alienation. Embodied spirit does not become alienated from itself in isolation. Self-alienation is not the solipsistic movement of an encapsulated subject in a facile turning back upon itself. The experience of alienation is an implication within a wider context of operating world-intentionality. The contextualized experiencer already exists *with* his surrounding environment when he becomes alienated from himself, taking over aspects of the surrounding world in the process; he shares a world *with* the other whose gaze and whose responsive actions

first make the emergence of self-consciousness and self-alienation possible. The gaze of the other is a contributing factor not
only in the experience of shame and bodily embarrassment; also
in the anxieties of guilt, meaninglessness, and despair, the presence of the other is felt. My being guilty arises through the
interplay of action and response-to-action in my dealings with
the other. The meanings which are threatened through the intentional disclosure of anxiety have an indelible social character.
The boundary-situation of despair involves the loss of hope
which I might share with others. Self-alienation is inseparable
from social alienation. Jean-Paul Sartre, in one of the more
illuminating passages in *Being and Nothingness*, discusses the
phenomenon of alienation in connection with the "look" (*le
regard*). By virtue of the look, the other affirms his self-mastery
by "stealing" my world, threatening the subjectivity of my lived
body by transforming it into the objectified mode of *en-soi*. The
other seeks to make my body appear as an object. He reveals my
body as an object to be gazed at, and through his gaze elicits my
experience of shame. What is absent, however, in Sartre's otherwise incisive phenomenological description is a clear distinction
between authentic and unauthentic objectification. The objectification which occasions self and social alienation is of a peculiar
type. It is not the objectification necessitated by the intentionality of representational thought in its drive for calculating and
controlling knowledge. The objectification carried through by
biology, psychology, and sociology remains a legitimate project
of science. The objectification which alienates is the misdirected
objectification of primordial world experience which transforms
the existing and historical experiencer into a metaphysical object. Predications about human behavior in which man functions as a logical and empirical object are unavoidable in the
scientific enterprise. This type of objectification is authentic and
is not at issue in the elucidation of alienation. The objectification
which produces alienation is of a metaphysical sort, geared to a
transformation of incarnated consciousness into a reality other
than itself.

Embodied consciousness, as it appears under the form of
negativity, is constantly reminded of its ineradicable finitude. A
phenomenology of embodied consciousness stands in the service
of a philosophy of human finitude. This was foretold in our
discussion of the finite character of existential time and space in

Chapter 2. Consciousness is finite because of its insertion in temporal and spatial horizon-forms which are themselves finite and in turn determine the finite structure of world experience. We are now required to elucidate with more precision the peculiar character of this finitude of embodied consciousness, particularly in light of our foregoing description of alienation. The meaning and use of the term itself needs to be rendered clear. This can best be achieved by first distinguishing it from alienation. Alienation, or consciousness existing under the form of negativity, implies finitude. Wherever there is alienation there is finitude, but finitude does not by virtue of necessity (neither logical nor ontological) imply alienation. Although not separable they remain distinct moments of consciousness. Alienation provides a determinate qualification of finite consciousness. Through alienation a mode of behavior is introduced which thrusts the actualization of consciousness into peculiar figure-background constellations. In both Sartre's existentialism and Heidegger's ontology of existence the distinction between alienation and finitude is removed. According to Heidegger, *Dasein's* being-in-the-world is always already fallen (*verfallen*), sacrificed to the alienation of objectified presence. Likewise, Sartre's *poursoi*, in the moment of its upsurge in the world, falls to the alienating gaze of the other. The other is an irreducible facticity in the finite constitution of consciousness and places finite consciousness under the conditions of alienation in the moment of its upsurge. Kierkegaard in his *Concept of Dread* labored to maintain a distinction between finitude and alienation with his use of the notion of "dreaming innocence," which "precedes" the determination of guilt; but his labors were not wholly successful. In the end, temporality is viewed as subject to the conditions of alienation and is understood as a sign of sin-consciousness.[14] What is required is a more consistent distinction between alienation and finitude and an elucidation of them as manifest styles of behavior endowed with distinguishing significations.

What then characterizes the moment of finite consciousness and wherein resides its genealogy? Finitude as it determines finite consciousness can be characterized phenomenologically as the impossibility of experience without presuppositions or stand-

14. *Concept of Dread*, trans. Walter Lowrie (Princeton: Princeton University Press, 1944), pp. 32, 83.

points. This invests experience with an irreducible perspectival character. Embodied consciousness always occupies a *standpoint* and apprehends its intended figures in definite perspectives. It stands not only at the center of its territorial space, but is always already positioned in the midst of social and historical situations. Finite consciousness intends its world from *somewhere*. It would be the unique privilege of an infinite consciousness to view the world detachedly from *nowhere*. The embarrassment for the Hegelian is occasioned by the question "Where does he stand when he apprehends himself under the guise of the Absolute Spirit?" Infinite consciousness has neither standpoint nor perspective. Embodied and finite consciousness shows itself in the situationality or contextualism of standpoint and perspective, and it is this which defines its finiteness.

Yet this finitude which shows itself concretely in perception and in man's historical existence is an *open* finitude, a finitude empowered with transcendence. This movement of transcendence is at work in the project of bodily comprehension. The embodied experiencer, although he speaks from particular standpoints and lives in particular perspectives, is not riveted to his situation in the manner of objectified nature. By virtue of the intentional structure of the world which he inhabits he is able to anticipate and appreciate perspectives other than those that he deploys. He is able to perceive objects from a certain point of view and extend the intentional beam of consciousness so as to render copresent perspectives coupled with different positionings of the body. He is able to conceive, by virtue of the operation of representational thought, systems of postulates and theoretical frames of reference which go beyond the given. He is able to understand and appreciate value perspectives other than those he shares. Herein resides the profound freedom and transcendence of finite consciousness, a freedom which is threatened by alien forces, but which consciousness in its struggle for world comprehension seeks to safeguard at all costs. This is why Heidegger is correct in linking transcendence and world.[15] The experience of world is made possible through the projective transcendence of finite consciousness.

15. See particularly his essay, *Vom Wesen des Grundes* (Frankfurt: Vittorio Klostermann, 1955); English translation, *The Essence of Reasons*, by Terrence Malick (Evanston: Northwestern University Press, 1969).

Finitude and transcendence conspire to generate a dialectical tension in the movement of existence. Consciousness, transcending and yet finite, moves within the world while pushing toward the limit of world experience so as to become open to the ontological mystery of the Unconditioned. Transcendence is both a horizontal and vertical movement. Consciousness has the power to open itself to perspectives within the world as well as the power to quest for the unconditional source of world-oriented experience. We agree with Merleau-Ponty when he says that "at the level of being it will never be intelligible that the subject should be both *naturans* and *naturatus*, infinite and finite," but we contest his conclusion from this that beyond time, the body, world, the thing, and other people, "there is nothing to understand." [16] To speak of consciousness as a synthesis of the finite and infinite is an unfortunate rendition of the dialectic of finitude and transcendence. Embodied consciousness remains irremediably finite. By virtue of its power of transcendence, finite consciousness can become open to the infinite, understood as the mystery of the Unconditioned, but the infinite does not become constitutive of finite consciousness itself. Only if the infinity of consciousness is understood to mean becoming open to the Unconditioned can its use be at all justified. Merleau-Ponty is aware of the problematic character of the finite-infinite synthesis, but he unwarrantedly restricts the reach and range of finite world experience in his facile rejection of the possibility of encounter with the Unconditioned. Admittedly, the Unconditioned remains a limit-category for ontological reflection. Its existential resonance shows itself in the concrete and prereflective intentionality of religious experience, and requires for its elucidation a careful and patient phenomenological analysis of the experience of the Holy.[17] At this juncture it is sufficient to point out that a phenomenology of world experience cannot prejudice the case against the testimony of the phenomena of religious experience without undercutting its methodological attitude.

16. *Phenomenology of Perception,* p. 365.
17. Such studies have been carried through with remarkable descriptive insight by Rudolph Otto in *The Idea of the Holy* (London: Oxford University Press, 1924); by Paul Tillich in *The Courage to Be* (New Haven: Yale University Press, 1952); and by William James in *The Varieties of Religious Experience* (New York: Longmans, Green, 1929).

The primal features of embodied consciousness, we have seen, are alienation, finitude, and transcendence. There is another feature of embodied consciousness which requires elucidation—its historical sense. It is sometimes said that Hegel inaugurated historical consciousness. Certainly, in his *Youthful Writings* and in his *Phenomenology of Spirit*, consciousness is infected with a historical destiny. Indeed, its alienation and reconciliation are comprehended only within the context of their historical development. But the notion of history that informed the historicality of Hegel's *spirit* was a notion generated by a representational, subject-object habit of thought. History becomes the property of a historical subject. To be sure, Hegel's titanic efforts to synthesize the objective-historical with the subjective-historical are well known, but as the historicist school, represented chiefly by Dilthey, clearly saw, Hegel's bold speculative project fell short of the mark. As a result the historical subject was summoned to fend for himself in his monadic isolation. The enduring insight contributed by the historicist school was that history has no existence of its own because man himself is history. History, both personal and social, shapes itself through man's decisions and self-affirmative struggles. Consciousness, in such a perspective, never appears as a mute reality in the presence of history; consciousness speaks through history. What the historicist school failed to grasp, however, was the relevance of the experienced world as the proper context for the development of historical consciousness. Dilthey's interest was to return to the historical subject, and his projected "critique of historical reason" had for its theme the elaboration of the interpretive categories which the subject might supply for an understanding of history. It is this historical monadology which a phenomenology of historical consciousness seeks to surmount. A monadic, encapsulated historical subject is as problematic as an epistomological one. A return needs to be staged—however, not a return to the historical monadic subject, but a return to the historical life-world.

Historical consciousness is installed in the concrete life-world in advance of any search for objective facts as well as any isolation of subjective conditions. The twists and turns of history as they are lived through by the historical experiencer are already pregnant with meaning by virtue of the participation and involvement of embodied consciousness. The interpretive frame, disclosed by hermeneutical thinking, in which historical consciousness develops is the frame of beginning and end, origin and goal, source and purpose. The historical drama, in both its personal and social expression, is staged within this world frame. The lived-through decisions and events which constitute the stuff of history require for their elucidation an interpretation of their sense or meaning within the context of movement from beginning to end, origin to goal. Historical consciousness is a drive to the comprehension of personal and social existence in light of the "end of history," which at the same time illuminates the origin of history and the meaning of historical presence. The specific interpretations of the meaning of history (e.g., the Judaic, Christian, Marxist, and Progressivistic) all presuppose this operation of historical consciousness, whereby the end of history—be it expressed through the use of the myth of the New Jerusalem, the Kingdom of God, the classless society, or human perfectibility—illuminates the present and provides directives for historical action. Historical consciousness grasps the meaning of time and space within an eschatological frame of reference. The interpretive meanings of world experience are related, implicitly or explicitly, to this frame. Historical interpretation is already at work when questions about existence and world phenomena are asked. It is for this reason that phenomenology, when it becomes existential phenomenology, cannot avoid at the same time becoming hermeneutical phenomenology.

[4] BODY-AS-MYSELF

THE INTENTIONAL STRUCTURE of experience implicates the experiencer contemporaneously with the intended figures of experience. A reflex of self-imputation is at work in every continuous and undivided portion of experience in which feeling, willing, and thinking occur. At the center of the intentional vectors resides the imputed "*I who* . . . feels, decides, imagines, remembers, anticipates, and thinks." It is this implicated phenomenon of "I who . . ." which becomes the topic of investigation in this section on the body-as-myself. We will attempt to describe and interpret this phenomenon in such a manner that the lived body, as discussed in the preceding sections of this chapter, will answer to the query concerning the "who" of world experience; and we will discuss certain ramifications of the description and interpretation which may lead to a fresh approach to the traditional problems of individuation and self-identity.

We have made use of the grammatical construction "body-as-myself" rather than the construction more commonly employed in existential and phenomenological literature, "body-as-mine." This shift in grammatical construction occurs by design rather than fortuitously, and it is implemented in the hope of achieving more proximate access to the phenomenon in question. The history of Gabriel Marcel's reflections on embodiment is pertinent to the issue at hand. Marcel began with a description of embodiment vis-à-vis the presentment of body-qua-mine, and he carried through an elucidation of the various senses in which the body might be apprehended as a possession and the various senses in which the body is *not* a possession. The relation of *having* thus achieves at best a limited applicability in an elucidation of embodiment. One simply does not own or have his body in the sense that one exercises dominion over one's property. Land, wealth, machines, and tools may be mine, subject to my use and disposal, but my body is not usable and disposable in this manner. There would thus seem to be something semantically misleading in the expression, "the body-as-mine," placing the body into the context of relations of having. Marcel's reflections led him to a substitution of the language of "modes of bodily being" for the language of "relations of having." More precisely, according to Marcel, the peculiar manner in which the self has a body is itself defined in terms of the bodily bearing of incarnated being. "My body is *my* body just in so far as I do *not* consider it in this detached fashion, do not put a gap between myself and it. To put this point in another way, my body is mine in so far as for me my body is not an object but, rather, I *am* my body." [18] The having which is at issue in the phenomenon of embodiment is thus explicated in terms of being. The "body-as-mine" turns out to be the "body-as-myself." It is for this reason that we have chosen to speak of the "body-as-myself." Through this usage we will be able to avoid the concealing connotations of

18. *The Mystery of Being*, trans. René Hague (Chicago: Henry Regnery, 1960), I, 123.

ownership and instrumentality in the locutions involving "having" and "mine," and penetrate more directly to the imputed bodily "who."

The body is not a sign of selfhood, not an indicator of an "I" residing within it. This would place an interval between my body and myself, externalize it, and divest it precisely of that which gives it life and history. To view the body in this manner would, in short, conceal the phenomenon of *embodiment* and reduce the body to a simple corporeal object among other corporeal objects with a special signification. The body as a *way of being embodied*, menaced by threats of alienation and struggling for transcendence as incarnated consciousness, is not a sign of who I am but veritably *is who I am*. I am my body. I exist as embodied. In the very asking of the question "Who am I?" the lived body of the questioner is already implicated by virtue of the intentional structure of experience, and particularly by sentient intentionality. The intentionality of feeling discloses the body-as-myself in the mode of sentience. "I am my body only in so far as I am a being that has feelings," says Marcel.[19] My embodiment initially surges up as a felt phenomenon. Prereflective experience already yields knowledge of myself as body. To say that my body is tired is to say that I am tired. To say that my body experiences pleasure is to say that I experience pleasure. To say that my nerves are taut is to say that I am nervous. The body-as-myself is the "who" of world experience situated as sentient being.

It will be noticed that the question of the "who" or "I" as concerns the contextualized experiencer is raised late in our discussion of embodiment. This has been done in an effort to have the logic of discourse coincide with existential reality. It is not accidental that Heidegger's discussion of the "who" of *Dasein* (*Wer des Daseins*) in *Being and Time* follows rather than precedes his elucidation of world. The phenomenon of *Dasein*'s self-experience is thus placed in its proper perspective as a world-derivative phenomenon. The very question about the self is understood as an existential question, first occasioned through an explication of world involvement. Correspondingly, it is the case that our question concerning the body-as-myself is first

19. *Ibid.*, p. 125.

made possible on the basis of an interrogation of the intentional structure of world experience and the phenomenon of bodily comprehension.

It is within this context that the traditional metaphysical problems of individuation and self-identity can be addressed and reformulated. One could say that the tradition was on the right path in selecting the body as a principle of individuation, but it got off the path when it objectivized the body and postulated an abstract *materia signata quantitate* as the individuating factor. The difficulty in this endeavor was that it circumvented the concrete and personal "I," with the result that the proposed principle of individuation could not individuate on the existential level. The individuating matter with its occult propensity to take on form remained incurably poverty-stricken in accounting for the idiosyncrasy of my body as I live it. It produced the dilemma of vacillating between formal and material determinations of selfhood without touching the concrete I-am experience. The experience of the body-as-myself falls outside of and occurs independently of the metaphysical schema of matter and form. In the last analysis the problem of individuation, as formulated in traditional metaphysics, is removed as a problem through phenomenological analysis. That which occasioned the problem in traditional thought was the need to account for real individuals, given an uncontested doctrine of universal essences or natures. The inquiry-standpoint in a phenomenology of embodiment is significantly different. Here, considerations as to form and matter, the universal and individual, are suspended, not because they are intrinsically wrongheaded—they retain their circumscribed justification when dealing with cosmological issues—but because attention is focused on the appearing of a concrete *existential* individuality with an effort to describe it in its mode of appearing. Individuality then becomes not the material instantiation of a nature, but rather the singularity of a unique, personal, unrepeatable, historical existence. This singularity or existential individuality shows itself in the concerns and involvements of the contextualized experiencer, in the shouldering of his personal guilt, in the summons to resolute action, in the anticipation of a death that implicates him directly. The concerned and engaged embodied consciousness is individuated by his projects which bear the stamp of what Heidegger has suggestively called "personalness" (*Jemeinigkeit*). It is particularly in the confrontation of death as the loss of the possibility of being-in-the-world that Heidegger sees an intensification of the personalness of *Dasein*. Death confronts *Dasein* with a task that is uniquely his own. No substitution of roles is possible; no one can take over my dying. Guilt, despair, resolve, and hope in a similar way determine the personalness of incarnated consciousness. The contextualized experiencer is individualized through his world-engagements and concerns with his body as the center of interest and action.

The problem of self-identity has traditionally been closely allied with the problem of individuation. In providing a fresh approach to the latter, existential phenomenology also repositions the inquiry-standpoint which produced the former. The contextualized experiencer, centered in the flowing stream of experience, is able to apprehend himself as the "same" experiencer as he moves from one context of experience to another. He is the same experiencer who views the steeple from one perspective and then from another, who yesterday decided to become a surgeon and who today either changes his project or resolutely plans for its future actualization. This experience of sameness provides the existential background for the classical doctrine of self-identity. The problem itself arises as a manifestation of existential concern. In this phenomenon of sameness the contributions of time and space, intentionality, and embodiment are already discernible. The task is to explicate their relevance in the restructuring of the traditional inquiry standpoint.

The doctrine of self-identity, in its deliverance through medieval and modern philosophy, accounted for the experience of sameness through a substance-attribute and subject-object categorial scheme. The attempt was made to discover an objective self-identity, securely insulated from the ravages of time. Sameness thus became understood as a *monadic* sameness, unperturbedly resting within itself, without intentionality and without history. The experiencer assumed the status of an enduring substance or an unbroken subjective continuity. The difficulties in this traditional doctrine are two-fold: (1) its justification even within an objectivist scheme of analysis remains problematic, as both Hume and Kant demonstrated; and (2) it conceals the concrete existential character of the phenomenon. The existential phenomenon of sameness is not the monadic sameness of an entity somehow propelling itself through objective time and space. A confusion of categories results when the categories of the representational scheme are applied in the interpretive understanding of concrete historical existence. The traditional view of the self, in which identity is anchored in an underlying substratum or subject somehow riding roughshod over the changing successive instants but itself immune to change, answers the problem of self-identity only at the expense of reducing the self to an object and falsifying its unique temporality and spatiality. The time and space of world experience, as we have already seen, are not objective frames into which a self-identical subject is placed. They are horizon-forms whose ecstasies and boundaries interpenetrate and are marked out by the projects of the experiencer. They indicate the here and now, where and when, not as abstracted and atomistic space-time points and instants but as opportune moments and appropriate places for the deployment of concerned behavior. The nows of experienced time are opportune moments with fringes of past and future. Hence, the experience of "sameness through time" is not the experience of retaining one's monadic identity as one moves from one isolated and discrete now to another. It is the experience of always already existing with time in a certain manner. It is the experience of being embodied with time on one's hand; it is the experience of *my* past and *my* future which is never separable from the time of *my* present.

As the phenomenon of embodiment plays a decisive role in the experience of sameness within an ecstatic temporality, so also it figures in the experience of sameness within oriented space. The body does not function as a self-identical entity exhibited as a composite of material parts. The body as consciousness incarnate is the manner of deployment of territorial space as an abiding *condition* or *situation* that remains throughout the history of consciousness. Admittedly the values and attitudes through which this territorial space is incorporated vary with existence itself, and it is this which accounts for the perspectival character of the self image. The self assumes different postures as it answers to the responses and solicitations of the other. Responding to developing situations the experiencer assumes commensurate roles. The experiencer plays the role of son or daughter, brother or sister, father or mother, teacher or student, employer or employee, citizen or alien, . . . and many more. The self image has multiple expressions, but in each of these expressions and roles the experiencer is already *situated*. There is a fundamental situationality which precedes the posturing of self images. This is the situation of being embodied, of existing in such a manner that one guards, expands, and enriches one's own space through the taking over of various roles and attitudes. My projects vary but my territorial space which marks out my regions of involvement remains my own. It determines my embodiment and accounts for the experience of the body-as-myself.

5 / The Speaking Experiencer

Speaking *designates human reality as it comes to the fore in expression. It is an affirmation of the person in the moral and metaphysical order and not simply a psychological function or a social reality.*
— Georges Gusdorf, *La Parole*

[1] SPEECH AS AN EXISTENTIAL PROJECT

OUR PROGRAM OF STAGING A RETURN to the contextualized experiencer has required, in the preceding chapter, an elucidation of the phenomenon of embodiment. The experiencer exists as embodied, as incarnated consciousness. The act of speaking is inseparable from this concrete life of the experiencer as incarnated consciousness. Human behavior is structured by speech as well as by embodiment. The experiencer, in his prereflective and reflective world-engagement, is installed in the world as a *homo loquens,* a being distinguished by the unique ability to speak. It is thus that speech and language become topics of extraordinary importance in an elucidation of world experience. An analytic of experience must at some juncture give studied attention to the phenomenon of speech as an existential project. This elucidation of the phenomenon of speech needs to proceed hand in glove with an elucidation of man as the being who

[158]

speaks. The problems of speech and language are, on the most fundamental level of analysis, inextricably intertwined with the wider problem of human existence. Speaking is an existential project through which human existence in its manifold concreteness comes to expression.

The phenomenon of speech as an existential project first needs to be understood in the context of its world-oriented development. An investigation of this context will make explicit the background of the world as a field of concerns, against which the peculiar relief and development of speech is discernible. Speech, from bottom up, is a mode of existing-in-the-world. However, it is a mode of existence which enjoys a peculiar privilege. It is operative as a world-disclosing event in a distinctive and decisive way. Speech as an existential project *expresses* and *articulates* the manner in which man exists in the world, his engagement with the world in the perception of objects and the use of tools, his sharing of experiences with friends and colleagues, his working and his playing. Embodied in a gesturing organism, speech discloses and conveys the concerns and preoccupations of everyday life and articulates the sense of the situations through which man lives. Heidegger in his book on language finds the "essence of language" (*Wesen der Sprache*) resident in a "saying" (*Sagens*), understood as a kind of *illuminative pointing* that permits the world to show itself in the ambiguity of its revealedness and hiddenness.[1] Merleau-Ponty brings to bear the world-background in his discussion of speech and attempts to show how the world is the *meaning* of speech.[2] Both Heidegger and Merleau-Ponty clearly recognize that speech is not simply an isolable contingent entity, abstractable from world-engaged speaking. The world is intercalated in the various levels and types of speaking. Through speech the world as the final, although indeterminate, background of lived experience achieves its constitution as a field of meanings. Speech is a manifestation of man's

1. *Unterwegs zur Sprache* (Pfullingen: Günther Neske, 1965), p. 200.
2. *Phenomenology of Perception,* trans. Colin Smith (New York: Humanities Press, 1962), p. 184. Remy Kwant in his phenomenological study of language, which is similar in design to the approach of Merleau-Ponty, has characterized speech as "a living symbiosis of man and the world," (*Phenomenology of Language* [Pittsburgh: Duquesne University Press, 1965], p. 229).

fundamental and vital relation to his perceived and valued world.

Speech, understood as a mode of behavior or an existential project, thus requires for its elucidation attentiveness to the background of world-meanings which insinuate themselves into the manifold modalities of speaking. Admittedly the act of speaking can be isolated and viewed as a physiological function, a psychological event, or a social instrument; but prior to its isolation and abstraction from its living context the act of speaking bespeaks one's installation in a concrete life-world. It is in its living context that the *world-basis* of speaking as an existential project becomes apparent. To make explicit this symbiotic relation of speech and world one may do well to introduce the notion of "en-worlded speech." As the ancients spoke of "en-souled bodies" in an effort to articulate the peculiar and intimate connection between body and soul, so the notion of "en-worlded speech" might aid one in remaining attentive to the phenomenon-background complex that structures the existential project of speaking.

Approached in the above manner, speech understood as the act of speaking is not simply a fact among other facts. It is a distinctive kind of *world-fact*. It is always present *with* the world and never simply *in* the world as an isolable, objective fact. Speaking is present not at all in the manner in which objective facts and the effects of these facts are present. Speech is a primordial world-fact which is presupposed in any objectification of reality. It is that world-fact through which objective facts can be rendered definite and calculable, but it cannot itself be thematized as an object without concealing the phenomenon which it is. Access to the phenomenon of speech needs to be achieved in another manner—through the elucidation and description of the achievement of speaking in its contextual configurations. This demands paying attention to the gestural aspects of speech; to the bodily bearing that accompanies it; to its alliance with thought; to its variegated undertones and overtones; to the dialogic situation of speaker and listener; and to the contribution of silence as a distinctive mode of speech. Speech within this range of attentiveness is not approached as an object or as an essence, which would then require an explanation of *what* it is. The task is to describe *how* speech discloses the world and articulates one's behavioral designs in it. What is required is a Kierkegaardian turn to the concrete speaker (whom we will find to be inseparable from the concrete thinker) so as to accomplish a recovery of speech through an elucidation of the existential project of speaking.

The en-worlded speech of the concretely existing speaker appears within two dialectically related perspectives. These two perspectives constitute the developmental cross-section, as it were, of the existential act of speaking. Speech appears in the one perspective as the rendition of words, phrases, sentences, and meanings which have already been uttered and which have found a place in the cultural history of man. We will refer to this perspective of the phenomenon as the "word-already-spoken," or more simply, "the spoken word." Speech appears in the other perspective as the *creative presence* of speaking. This is the perspective of the "word-as-being-spoken," or more simply, "the word as spoken." Designated by this formulation is the creative and originative aspect of speech, which displays a drive toward new meanings. The spoken word and the word as spoken constitute the internal structure of speech. It is important to keep in mind however that these two perspectives are "copresent" in the act of speaking. Although distinguishable, they are interwoven. Whenever I am engaged in speaking I make use of words which have already undergone institutionalization, either explicitly or implicitly. The spoken word is present in the word as spoken. It is present as a collocation of generally accepted ways of speaking. The spoken word is the repetition of something already said, either by the original speaker or by someone else. The spoken word puts an accepted grammar and extant meanings into play. These extant meanings not only determine the semantical referents of speech but they exert a power over one's style of existence. The spoken word has the power to define one's mode of life. Jean Genet, for example, accepted the word "thief" and defined his life in terms of its collocated meanings, thus providing an illustration of the ontological dimension of speech.[3] A relatively clear example of what we mean by the spoken word is the repetition of proverbs. A proverb has already been spoken and can be repeated. However, when we reflect on the *genesis* of the proverb we realize that there was a time when it was first

3. See Jean-Paul Sartre, *Saint Genet: Actor and Martyr,* trans. Bernard Frechtman (New York: George Braziller, 1963).

spoken. This *having been spoken for the first time* points to the other perspective in the phenomenon of speech—the word as spoken. The word as spoken is an originative act of speaking. The spoken word is subject to the self-limitation of already delivered meanings. The word as spoken gives rise to new points of view and creates meaning through a transfiguration of the spoken word.

We have characterized the word as spoken as an originative act in which something is uttered for the first time. But there are many senses of "first." A proverb is spoken or written for a first time. No sentence has ever been formulated in such a manner with such a meaning. Yet the proverb makes use of particular words that have already been spoken and suggest familiar meanings. If this were not the case no understanding of the proverb could occur. Hence, although it would seem clear that there is a sense in which a proverb when originally formulated is uttered for the first time, the firstness at issue is not that of creation *ex nihilo*. There is also the first speech of a child. Here first has a different sense. The child, unlike the producer of proverbs, has never spoken before. In a quite literal sense the child speaks the first word. But that which he speaks in his first act of speaking is something already spoken before. The child repeats that which he has learned from his parent or guardian. So the firstness of the newly spoken word of the child, like the firstness of a new proverb, needs to be qualified. Yet one can discern in both cases legitimate senses of being first. The creation of new words and phrases by the original thinker and the poet may afford a more precise illustration of the word as spoken. The original thinker and the poet often create new words and new sentences which depart from standardized grammar and lexicology. With these new words and sentences meanings hitherto unexpressed are put into play. The thinker and the poet exhibit a relative freedom from the spoken word and introduce something that has remained unsaid. Although even here the creation of meaning is not *ex nihilo* in a strict sense the firstness of the word as spoken becomes more explicit. There is also the speech of the first man which provides yet another sense of firstness. The first man spoke that which had never been spoken before. He veritably *introduced* speech. He spoke for the first time, unfettered by the sedimentation of collocated grammar and usage. Grammar and usage came into being with the utterances of the first man, and hence it could be said that the spoken word was introduced through the word as spoken. There is in this example a more radical sense of first which helps to throw into relief the primordiality and originative character of the word as spoken.

The above delineated senses of first are not offered as an exhaustive listing, but they will serve to provide indicators of the criterion of firstness in its applicability to the word as spoken. There is, however, another distinguishing feature of the word as spoken. This is its *concreteness*. The word as spoken is an act of concretion. Here one does well to heed the contribution of etymology in elucidating the term: the English term "concrete" comes from the Latin *concrescere,* which means "to grow together." The insight that is generated in such an explication is that the model governing the word as spoken is *organismic-developmental* rather than *mechanistic-inventive* in character. Originative speaking is more like the growth and development of an organism than like the mechanical arrangement of parts given in advance. Even in making use of institutionalized grammars and vocabularies speech does not shed its originative character. The collocated usages and meanings of the spoken word are appropriated in the concrescence of speaking and put into operation as the connective tissues of an on-going and developing organism. The word as spoken and the spoken word interpenetrate. The act of speaking organismically knits together that which has already been said with that which is yet to be said. Extant meanings and usages infect the creativity of the word as spoken. But this does not deprive the word as spoken of its creative possibilities. The word as spoken, even if it is the very same word that has already been uttered in the past, is in some sense novel in each of its situational utterances. To this extent Delacroix was right when he said that "the word is created each time that it is uttered." In the act of speaking the spoken word is kept alive, charged with fecundity, and vitalized through new contextual meanings. The meanings that arise and are disclosed through the existential project of speech are never final and exhausted. It is precisely the living character of speech that keeps words from becoming sedimented into atomistically discrete entities that can be catalogued and filed away. Living speech is a creative project in which the spoken word and the word as spoken nourish each other in a consummate reciprocity.

These two perspectives of speaking as an existential project provide the basis for the commonly accepted distinction between language and speech. Language is an investigatible object, transparent to theoretical analysis and amenable to practical manipulation. Speech is a developing and organismic event, so inextricably bound to the speaker, his bodily bearing, and his wider situation that it escapes any exhaustive objective determination. Speech, as an organismic and developmental phenomenon, is never able to come to rest and posit itself as a given datum. It has the peculiar destiny of being always on the way, moving beyond that which has already been said in a continuing drive for further explication and articulation. It ever eludes us as a calculable and controllable object because of its transitory and developing character. Language, on the other hand, can be objectified and controlled. It is precisely at this juncture that the distinction between language and speech achieves its full force. Language is objectified, abstracted, and disembodied speech; and the proper approach to it is through linguistics as the science of language. Different objectifiable aspects of language are investigated in each of the areas of linguistics. Phonetics, phonology, grammar (syntax and morphology), semantics, pragmatics, etymology, and lexicology are able to explore language as an objective and already given datum. Through carefully formulated methodological procedures, these subdisciplines are able to isolate words as optical and acoustical data from the streaming and transitory presence of their occurrence. The streaming presence of the word as spoken is brought to a standstill, and its abstracted components are objectively analyzed. Thus the science of language cannot avoid the reduction of speech to classified sounds, parts of speech, rules of formation, social instruments, and standardized usages. Through this reduction speech becomes objectified and institutionalized. Language, in short, is objectified and institutionalized speech. Speech, from which language is an abstraction, is if not a quite different phenomenon at least a quite different manifestation of the same phenomenon. This qualification is required because speech and language remain interlaced on at least one level by virtue of the inseparability of the word as spoken and the spoken word in the existential project of speaking. Speech provides the living context out of which linguistic abstractions and objectifications arise. It is a dynamic and developmental process through which the manifold and pervasive intentionalities of world experience come to expression.

Speech and language are thus distinguishable in the above manner. The recognition of this distinction provides the possibilities for the formulation of a phenomenology of speaking on the one hand and a logic of language on the other. The question as to the relation of these two disciplines remains one of the more thorny problems for any comprehensive critique of language. Some of the basic issues involved might be clarified through an examination of the discussions of language and speech in the philosophies of Edmund Husserl and Ludwig Wittgenstein. It is well known that there are two phases in Husserl's philosophy of language. There is the *eidetic* phase in which Husserl addresses himself to questions about an ideal language and a pure grammar. Then there is the *Lebenswelt* phase which involves a return to the concrete speaking experience with language. Correspondingly similar phases become apparent in the philosophy of Wittgenstein. In the *Tractatus Logico-Philosophicus*, Wittgenstein develops a truth-functional view of language. In his later works one finds a preoccupation with *ordinary* language, which boils down to speech viewed as a form of life (*Lebensform*).[4] We are not able at this juncture to move to a consideration of the central

4. For an illuminating discussion of the relation of Husserl and Wittgenstein on the problem of language the reader is referred to J. N. Mohanty, *Edmund Husserl's Theory of Meaning* (The Hague: Martinus Nijhoff, 1964), pp. 54–76. Also of interest would be C. A. van Peursen, "Edmund Husserl and Ludwig Wittgenstein," *Philosophy and Phenomenological Research*, XX (1959), pp. 181–97. There is yet another aspect of Wittgenstein's relation to the phenomenology of language, discussed neither by Mohanty nor by van Peursen, which has opened up as a result of the publication of *Philosophische Bemerkungen*, ed. Rush Rhees (Oxford: Basil Blackwell, 1964). This work comprises selections from the *Nachlass* of Wittgenstein. In it numerous references to phenomenology and phenomenological language are made, which at the same time indicates a broadening of philosophical interests on the part of Wittgenstein and a developing of the *rapprochement* between linguistic and phenomenological analysis. (See particularly #1, p. 51; #57, p. 88; and #213, p. 267). For a discussion of these issues opened up principally through the publication of Wittgenstein's *Nachlass* the reader is referred to Herbert Spiegelberg's article, "The Puzzle of Ludwig Wittgenstein's *Phänomenologie* (1929–?)," *American Philosophical Quarterly*, V (1968), 244–56.

issues in such a comprehensive critique of language and speech. Our interest in bringing into thematic focus the phenomenon of the contextualized, speaking experiencer requires that we bracket the purely linguistic and logical approaches to language. But to bracket them is not to displace them. Language and speech alike are rooted in the existential project of speaking—in the perspectival expressions of the spoken word and the word as spoken. Language and speech are prethematically present in the contextualized dialectical interplay of the spoken word with the word as spoken, and both the phenomenology of speech and the logic of language proceed at peril if this interplay remains unrecognized.

[2] GESTURAL SPEECH

IN THE PRECEDING SECTION we sought to elucidate the world-orientation of speech as an existential project and explicate its dialectically interpenetrating constitutive elements. We saw that, in his speaking, man is oriented toward the world, condemned to an unimpeachable alliance with it. Speech, considered in its ontological dimension, is an expression of the symbiotic liaison of man with world. Speech is a modality of existence itself, expressing a certain lodgment of man in the world. Thus we find that the question about the phenomenon of speaking is at bottom a question about the being who speaks. The elucidation of en-worlded speech leads to an elucidation of man as contextualized experiencer. The experiencer, as we learned in the foregoing chapter, exists within the context of his embodiment. It is now our task to discern how the contextualism of his embodiment bears upon the contextualism of his speech. We need to show how the phenomenology of speech is linked with the phenomenology of the lived body.

The lived body, we have seen, achieves a privileged status in the elucidation of the experiencer. His various projects and concerns find in the lived body an anchorage and a unitary base. Perceptions and movements radiate from it, and distances are measured by it. The body is that by which I am in contact with the world, that which makes the world accessible to me. It is by virtue of my embodiment that I am able to lay hold of the world and deploy purposive movements in it. My embodiment marks out regions and directions and locates perceptible objects within these regions and directions. The lived body is the occasion for existential spatiality and provides the vantage point of perceptual perspectives. My body is wherever there is something to be seen, done, and valued. In short, the lived body is the center of the world as experienced and functions as its base of operation.

What are the implications of this status and role of the lived body for a comprehension of the phenomenon of speech? Speech, along with perception, is as an existential act anchored in the lived body. En-worlded speech is at the same time embodied speech. Wherever speech is there is body also. In the act of verbal speaking bodily movements and posturing already contribute a spectrum of nuances that speak between the lines of verbal utterances. But body and speech are yet more intimately connected. The body itself is a project of speech in the mode of gesture. Embodiment provides the occasion for gestural speech. The speaker is inserted into the world as embodied speaker, and as embodied he is able to speak through gestures. Gestures, properly understood, constitute a mode of speech. Through gestures a situation can be articulated and the sense of it made manifest. Gestures exhibit a power of expression and communication, through which the world and the engaged experiencer are co-revealed.

It is now our task to elucidate with some care how the lived body speaks. How do the gestural movements and configurations of embodied existence disclose dimensions of the world and communicate the sense of the situations through which man lives? The thesis that we wish to maintain is that gestures secrete their own expressive and communicative meanings. They display an intrinsic power of sense-giving. Indeed meaning is so closely linked with the deployment of gesticulation that one would remain more proximate to the phenomenon by saying that a gesture *is* meaning rather than that a gesture *indicates* meaning. The mode of manifestation of gestural meaning is such that gesture and meaning conspire and develop as a phenomenal unity. Gesture and meaning are intimately associated.

We will seek to clarify our thesis about gestural speech first of all through a delineation of some common interpretations of the status and role of gestures rejected by our position. Specifically, our thesis entails a rejection of three views that have recurred throughout the history of philosophy: (1) the view that gestures are lower-order modes of expression, at best a kind of material basis for the spoken word, requiring for their purification a translation into audible speech; (2) the view that gestures express and communicate private and internal psychic states or events; and (3) the view that gestures are external *signs* functioning as indicators of some hidden meaning. Sometimes the three views about the phenomenon of gestures have been combined. This is particularly the case with (2) and (3), resulting in the theory that gestures are signs pointing to inner or private states.

The first of these interpretations might be called the Platonic prejudice, for it involves the Platonic metaphysical presupposition of a dichotomy of matter and spirit. A modern version of this Platonic prejudice is discernible in the philosophy of language of Max Picard. It is the view of Picard that "gesture belongs to a totally different category than language." He views gestures as lower-order significations, enmeshed in matter, tainted with desire, standing in need of redemption by spirit.

> Gesture is unfree, unredeemed, still completely mixed with the material it uses in its attempts at self-representation. It is still inside the material and bound up with it, not approaching the material freely from the outside as the spirit approaches the world.[5]

It is precisely this implied essentialism and Platonism of Picard's approach that our phenomenological analysis of gesture and speech seeks to overcome. The traditional metaphysics of a matter-spirit dualism, and the accessory scaling of being, needs to be suspended so as to permit the phenomenon of gestural speech to show itself and speak for itself.

The other two interpretations would seem to be the peculiar legacy of modern rationalism and empiricism, although suggestions of a sign theory of gestures already occur in ancient and medieval philosophy. In modern rationalism and empiricism, the theory of gestures is developed in much closer concordance with the design for formulating a defensible theory of knowledge. Epistemological interests come to the forefront and the theory of gestures is subordinated to it. Although rationalism and empiricism each seek to solve the problem of the relation of

5. *Man and Language,* trans. Stanley Goodman (Chicago: Henry Regnery, 1963), p. 22.

gestures to speech in its own way, they share the prejudice that, at bottom, gestures are signs. For the rationalist, they are signs of some recessed process of ideation or categorial operation; for the traditional empiricist, they are signs of private impressions and inferred meanings. It is precisely the prejudgment of gestures as signs, shared by both traditions, that needs to be called into question and reassessed.

What is lacking in all three of the above interpretations under indictment here is the recognition that gestures are projections of existential behavior. The phenomenon of gesturing needs to be given the freedom to show itself in its varied world-oriented deployment. The essentialist's criterion, whereby gestures become the fettered and tainted movement of matter, as well as the sign theory of gestures, needs to be held in suspension so as to permit the phenomenon in question to show itself without reduction. A more adequate method of "seeing the phenomenon" might well be an unmediated inspection of the bodily behavior of the world-engaged experiencer. What becomes evident through such an inspection is that gestures are modes of comportment, projections of the behavior of an embodied experiencer, which secrete meanings in the act of gesticulation. Gestures carry their own meaning and display an intrinsic power for illuminating the sense of the situation. To express meaning they need not wait for a transposition into verbal utterance, nor for a category or an idea to swoop down from on high to liberate them from their bondage to matter. There are the common gestures of love, grief, and anger. In the deployment of each the situationality of the one in love, the one in grief, or the one in anger, is expressed without mediation. The caress by the lover's fingers, the anguished wringing of hands by the bereaved at a death-bed, the clenched fist of the angry business associate who has been betrayed, all secrete meanings which reside in the gestural acts themselves. Love, grief, and anger are not hidden behind the gestures. They are not private states within an encapsulated psyche which first become externalized through the proper gesticulation. Love resides in the caress, the kiss, and the embrace; grief is on the anguished face and the depressed posture of the bereaved; anger is in the shaking of the fist and the stamping of the foot. The meanings of love, grief, and anger are written across their gestural configurations. Here there is no distinction between the meaning and its manner of manifestation. If one speaks of gestures manifesting meaning one must speak of self-manifestation. Gestures manifest meanings which are embedded in the act of gesturing. Such a view of gestures, whereby gestures are understood as displaying an intrinsic power of sense-giving, provides a place for gestures in the wider intentional structure of world experience. Gestures are movements of intentional experience in its expressive and communicative projection. It is not that gestures simply indicate or point to the intended contents of feeling, willing, and thinking; they are the concrete embodiment of these intentionalities.

In the preceding chapter we explored the connection of embodiment and spatiality and found that the lived body is open and exposed to the world through its territorial and lived space. The space disclosed through embodiment is, we have seen, the spatiality of situation rather than the space of geometry and metric coordinates. Now, with the intimate connection of speech and embodiment in the mode of gestural behavior made explicit, we are able to grasp the spatial scope of speech. The spatial scope of speech reaches into the regions and directions mapped out by the intentionality of bodily projection. The situation of my embodiment is such that all of its projects move out from a natural center, a "here," or a position from which objects are perceived, tools manipulated, and other selves encountered. The directions of right and left, above and below, proceed from this natural center and mark out the "there" and the "toward which . . ." of the body's intentional operations. The spatiality of the lived body is thus a region of possible places and movements determined by value-laden references to a here and a there, a circumscription of territories and vicinities inhabited by a concernful existence. The proper and improper places of utensils, objects, and persons are defined within the context of these regions and territories. Gestural speech provides a privileged expression and disclosure of these regions and territories. Through gestures, and principally through the gestural use of the hands, I define for myself and for others the territorial space of my lived body. Gestures order this space in a certain manner. Through gesturing I make it known that I am ready to defend my space, to expand it, or to make it open to the other so that certain shared experiences might occur. In the gesture of the handshake I invite the other to participate in my territorial space. The gesture of pointing expresses an intentional expansion of my lived space. In the indignant shaking of the finger, in the clenching of the fist, in the outstretched arms, and in the posture of prayer, various intentionalities and values of my lived space are expressed and communicated. My gestural embodiment reveals the structure and dynamics of my lived space as infused with meaning and value.

[3] SPEAKING AND THINKING

SPEAKING, AS AN EXISTENTIAL PROJECT, is at the same time a project of thought. Speaking and thinking are both anchored in embodied existence, interlaced in such a manner that speaking can be understood as thought in action or as the presence of thought in the world. The pressing demand thus becomes that of clarifying the manner of connection between speaking and thinking. We have already given some attention to the nature and dynamics of thought in our discussion of noetic meaning in Chapter 3. We found that thinking is a complex phenomenon, displaying a variety of forms. We singled out for discussion two readily distinguishable types—representational thinking and hermeneutical thinking. The former we found to be characterizable as an objectifying thinking whereas the latter deals with nonobjectifiable contents. Our present task is not that of further amplifying this distinction, however desirable such a further amplification might be, but rather that of pursuing a patient inquiry into the peculiar connection of speaking and thinking. This connection, we propose, will obtain both in the operation of representational and hermeneutical thought. In the succeeding section of this chapter we will have the occasion to see how the distinction between the objectifying and the nonobjectifying determines respectively the possibilities of direct and indirect communication. In this section our explicit task is that of investigating certain features of the connection of the act of thinking with the project of speech.

We begin by seeking an inquiry-standpoint in which the problem of the relation of thinking and speaking can be approached without the honoring of certain *a priori* metaphysical and epistemological claims. Of these claims, the ones that have most effectively concealed the phenomenal complex in question are that thought is in some sense a copy of reality and that speech is a sign of thought. These may well constitute the dominant prejudices of traditional metaphysics and epistemology concerning the relation of speaking and thinking. In such a scheme thought is placed at a second remove from reality and speech is accorded a still lower status, somehow functioning as a sign or instrument of thought. Speech and language become vehicles which carry and convey thoughts, signs which point to some categorial operation prior to the act of speaking. In this view, speaking is destined to remain exterior to the thought process itself.

It is this exteriority of speech in relation to thought that we wish to call into question. The unnamed presupposition, which masquerades as self-evident, in this traditional view is that speech and thought have some kind of entitative status. They are *things* of some sort or another. Admittedly, they are not viewed as things in the sense that ashtrays and turnips are things, but nonetheless they are defined within a general ontology of thinghood as pieces of the world that can be analyzed as determinable entities. They are, in the language of Heidegger, viewed under the rubric of on-handness (*Vorhandensein*), placed over against a detached observer who can fit them neatly into the categorial scheme of substance and attribute, essence and accident. Given such an ontology, the relations of external or exterior *vs.* internal or interior cannot be suppressed, and when speech is fitted into this pre-delineated scheme it comes off rather badly. At best it becomes an attribute of rational man through which the exteriorization of thought occurs. Exteriority and interiority are both relations determined by an ontology of thinghood. This ontology will need to be overcome if the phenomena of thought and speech are to be elucidated as they show themselves in human experience. If there is to be any talk of ontology at all, it will need to be an ontology of world experience, an ontology of embodied behavior and life styles in which thinking and speaking are not juxtaposed and externally related entities but reciprocating ways of existing in the world. The view which we are suggesting comes down to the proposal that dialogue provides the experiential basis for speaking and thinking alike. Thought, although it may be tested in the monologue of solitude, does not find its genesis in a colloquy with oneself. Indeed, such a silent colloquy already implicates another self as the second term of a dialogic relation, either remembered or anticipated. The reciprocity of thinking and speaking is thus most readily discernible in the interpenetration of the dialectical feature of thought with the dialogic character of speech. This would seem to be the insight expressed by Feuerbach when he wrote: "The true dialectic is not a monologue of a solitary thinker with himself; it is a dialogue between I and thou." [6]

Only by keeping our attention fixed on the primordial phenomenon itself—speaking as an existential project—will it be possible to discern the intimate connection of speech and thought. Thought is copresent with speech. It is in the act of speaking that thought is accomplished and approximates its completion. The word as spoken is not a sign of an internal recognition of a concept made possible through some species of categorial operation. Conceptualization does not hide behind its expression in a secure and hermetically sealed region of mind. Conceptualization first achieves form and constitutes its intentional objects through its incarnation in the word. To say that words are external to thought, functioning as signs of an internal recognition, belies a prejudicial assessment of both speaking and thinking. The word as spoken is shorn of its immediate and manifest meaning, and thought is construed as a finished product. A more primordial grasp of the phenomena is required for an elucidation of the interlacing of speaking and thinking. In the existential act of speaking, thought is being accomplished without ever attaining completion. In speaking the embodied experiencer *thinks something through.* But that which is thought through is not an object with a definite beginning and a definite end. A thought is never self-enclosed, final, and complete. It remains exposed to the world and retains an open-ended character. Thought is vectorially directed toward the world, disclosing figure and background in a synoptic totality. This is to say that thought is accomplished within the manifold of intentionalities of world experience. A worldless thought is a fictive abstraction. Thought never appears in the world, understood as a field of concerns, as a thing or an investigable object. Thought is a project of world-engagement which first provides the condition for the objectification and classification of things.

As the nature of thought is falsified if it is construed as an

6. *Principles of the Philosophy of the Future,* trans. Manfred H. Vogel (Bobbs-Merrill, 1966), p. 72.

object, surreptitiously determined by an ontology of thinghood, so likewise speech as an existential act is concealed so long as it is defined as a juxtaposition of objectifiable acoustical signs. Speech is not a sign which points to thought, nor is it an instrument of translation whereby thought is rendered into verbal or gestural expression. Speech *is thought expressed,* and there is no phenomenological justification for the postulation of an "in-itself" of thought which stands behind the expression. The problematic relation of sign and object signified becomes an issue only if speech and thought are viewed as separately given entities. Words are the presence of thought in the world, not arbitrary instruments or interchangeable garments which can be substituted at will without altering the intended meaning. It is interesting to note that two contemporary philosophers, commonly alleged to be of quite different persuasions, are in solid agreement in their rejection of the traditional separation of thinking and speaking. "Thinking," says Wittgenstein, "is not an incorporeal process which lends life and sense to speaking, and which it would be possible to detach from speaking." [7] Heidegger, although his ontological concerns are more pronounced than those of Wittgenstein, makes a similar point when he writes:

> Words and language are not wrappings in which things are packed for the commerce of those who write and speak. It is in words and language that things first come into being and are. For this reason the misuse of language in idle talk, in slogans and phrases, destroys our authentic relation to things. [8]

Speaking and thinking conspire to produce meaning. Speaking as a mode of behavior carries meaning within itself. The meaning that emerges through the interplay of word as spoken and spoken word is not a borrowed meaning, a mere translation from the domain of thought. The peculiar irony in the sign theory of language is that there is no account of the meaning of discourse itself. According to the sign theory, words themselves do not have meaning but in some quasi-mystical manner point to a categorial operation behind the words which first gives rise to

7. *Philosophical Investigations,* trans. G. E. M. Anscombe (New York: Macmillan, 1953), no. 339, p. 109.
8. *An Introduction to Metaphysics,* trans. Ralph Manheim (New York: Doubleday, 1959), p. 11.

meaning. But meaning infects the total field of world experience. It is not encased in a private thinking subject, whose existence at least on one level is itself problematic. Meaning, particularly in the workaday world of the engaged experiencer, has to do with the sense of his situation in its colorful variety. This situation is deployed through the comportment of the lived body, which occasions a gestural and verbal behavior that is already sense-expressive. Speech, which must always be understood to include its gestural mode, would thus seem to have a privileged role in the expression of meaning. Far from being devoid of meaning, it is the upsurge of meaning in the world. Speaking and the sense of the situation are inseparable. Sense or meaning is simultaneously constituted as word and thought.

Yet it may be objected that some experiences of everyday life stand to confute our claim that thinking and speaking are inseparable. This would, indeed, prove to be quite embarrassing for a phenomenology of speech which purports to take seriously the testimony of everyday experiences! Does one not, it might be asked, often realize that he has spoken without thinking, and then thoughtfully corrected that which he had misspoken? Is it not possible to have thoughtless speech? Does not the prevalence of the common adage "Think before you speak" indicate that much of what is said in everyday life is said without thought? Even a cursory acquaintance with the chatter, gossip, and superficial talk that plays such a leveling role in our social existence would seem to testify that thought may indeed be far removed from speech. This possible objection to our thesis is more than of superficial significance. It calls for a more concrete justification of our claim that speaking and thinking are inseparable.

What, precisely, is at issue in the statement that someone has spoken before he has thought, or that he has spoken thoughtlessly? Is it possible to clarify the sense of this without recourse to a separation of thinking and speaking? Can one interpret this by avoiding the traditional prejudice that speech and thought are two entities which can appear either conjointly or in separation? A patient examination of the phenomena might preclude an invoking of the traditional mode of analysis with its bifurcation of thought and speech. Is it indeed the case that thinking is somehow totally absent when one "speaks before one thinks"? Or is it not, rather, that thinking is already present, although in an imprecise or equivocal manner? The everyday locution, "He spoke without thinking," would seem to mean that he spoke imprecisely, unclearly, confusedly, cumbersomely, or equivocally; but this does not imply that thought was absent in his speaking so much as it implies that his thinking in his speaking was also imprecise, unclear, confused, cumbersome, or equivocal. When something is rephrased or restated, it is also reconsidered and rethought. When something is poorly said, it is poorly thought. When something is well said, it is well thought. Thinking, in some manner or form, would thus seem to be already present in speaking. If thinking were not present it would be difficult to account for the utterance of a particular word or phrase rather than some other, or even for the utterance of any words at all.

It would thus seem to be the case that there is no speaking without thinking, but is the converse also true? Cannot one think without speaking? Is there not a solitary thinking, a thinking without gestures and without words? The deaf-mute does not speak a verbal language, but are we led to conclude from this that the deaf-mute does not think? The aphasiac has lost his power of speech; does this mean that he has also lost his power of thought? Clearly, the situations of the solitary thinker, the deaf-mute, and the aphasiac are different in detail, but they all force us to delineate more precisely the connection between speaking and thinking. First, it should be made clear that what we are seeking to elucidate is the *inseparability* of speaking and thinking. Nowhere have we argued for their *identity*. Thus we can allow for an asymmetry in the connection between speech and thought without dissociating them. Thinking is present in speaking in a way different from the presence of speaking in thinking. The issue ultimately revolves around the difference with respect to the use and meaning of the preposition *in*. Thinking is present *in* speaking in the sense that speech is an accomplishment of the intentionality of thought. One is already thinking in one's speaking, although on different levels of clarity and disclosure. But speaking is present *in* thinking in a different manner. Assuredly I am able to think in solitude without engaging in an overt act of speaking. Yet my thinking even in solitude does not occur in a vacuum. I think *with* words that I have spoken at some previous time or that I have heard spoken by someone else. Sometimes I even express these words audibly to myself, in the hope of achieving greater clarity thereby. So even in my solitude I seem to be condemned to think with words. My thought is borne by the remembered word as spoken. The situation of the deaf-mute and the aphasiac, however is different. The deaf-mute lacks the ability for verbal speech; the aphasiac has suffered an impairment of this ability. Yet, with our broadening of the existential project of speaking to include gestural expression and communication it cannot be said that either the deaf-mute or the aphasiac are totally bereft of the power of speech. By virtue of their bodily comportment they are able to relate themselves meaningfully to the natural and social world and speak through the intentionality of gestures. Even the deaf-mute remains within the scope of speech. His bodily bearing and his gestures are his means of expression and communication and it is in them that his thinking is displayed.

[4] Speech as Communication

AT VARIOUS POINTS throughout our preceding discussion we have referred obliquely to the speaker-hearer context as a structural element in the existential project of speaking. A thematic focus on this speaker-hearer context will throw into relief the communicative aspect of speech. Speaking is an act of communication. In virtually every treatment of the subject of communication a distinction between the expressive and communicative function of speech is made. That a distinction can be maintained is not at issue here, but very often the distinctions that are made involve a cluster of questionable assumptions. It will hardly do to say that expression is a private affair and communication a public affair. The distinction between private and public does not arise on this level. The expression which occurs in speaking as an existential act is already exposed to the world of the other. Expression can never be wholly private because the existence of the experiencer is never wholly private. The experiencer is always already installed in a public world. Likewise, it will not do to say that the expressive function of speech is emotive whereas the communicative function is intellectual. Thought can be expressed as well as anger, and feeling can be communicated as well as ideas. However, the expression of the sense of a situation does not as such insure the communication of that sense. Although interwoven with communication when it is achieved, expression does not by necessity result in communication. Communication can break down through the introduction of existential negativities. The peculiar relation between expression and communication would thus seem to be that communication is the fulfillment of expression.

Karl Jaspers, more than any other contemporary philosopher, has made the theme of communication central to his philosophy. The basic task of the philosopher, for Jaspers, is understood in light of the will to communicate. According to Jaspers, knowledge is the result of mutual discovery, and truth is communicability. Amidst the various threats to communication which contribute to its breakdown the philosopher engages in a loving struggle to engender understanding and trust in spite of diverging points of view. Indebted to Kierkegaard for his insights into the nature and role of indirect communication, Jaspers has attempted to formulate a philosophy of communication which provides a fresh approach to the nature of philosophical inquiry. Our present elucidation of speech as communication will proceed along the paths already opened up by the reflections and investigations of Kierkegaard and Jaspers.

That communication occurs on various levels is a phenomenological fact of the concrete life-world, and, like other facts of the life-world, it provides an occasion for wonder and reflective inquiry. We have already found it to be the case that world phenomena present themselves in a multiplicity of modes. The phenomenon of communication is no exception. There is communication by verbal speech, communication by gestures, communication by silence, and communication by both visual and nonvisual arts. Within each of these modes one finds a plurality of forms. Communication by silence, for example, varies with the sense of the situation of the communicator. As Gusdorf has pointed out there are silences of poverty as well as pregnant silences.[9] Silence can communicate the impoverishment of knowledge, as when one remains silent because the proper verbal response to the situation eludes one. There is the silence of embarrassment which discloses some personal threat in the relation of self with other self. There are silences of despondency and despair which communicate the quiet desperation of every-

9. *Speaking*, trans. Paul T. Brockelman (Evanston: Northwestern University Press, 1965), p. 90.

day existence. And there is the psychotic silence of the disturbed personality. But there are also pregnant silences, silences which secrete meanings which would be lost through verbalization. These silences express a mastery of the situation and are filled with positive meanings. The silence of one falsely accused, the silence of the lover, and the silence of one struck by the awe-inspiring beauty of nature provide illustrations of silence as pregnant and enriched.[10]

One of the more interesting features of communicative speech is that it falls along a continuum moving from direct to indirect and indirect to direct. It was the genius of Kierkegaard that perceived the need for an elucidation of the ways of indirect communication so as to become clear about the communicability of religious truth. What is required, however, is a broadening of the method and use of indirect communication and a more precise delineation of its distinction from direct communication. Our inquiry-standpoint for the discussion of direct and indirect communication has already been positioned by our phenomenological investigation of the character of thought and the inseparability of thinking and speaking. There is, we have observed, an objectifying form of thinking, which we have called representational thinking. The distinguishing feature of this representational thinking is that it strives for controlling knowledge,

10. Kierkegaard and Jaspers have given particular attention to the communicative importance of silence. Kierkegaard interprets the silence of Jesus before Pilate as subjective existence impregnated with meaning. The silence of Jesus was not simply an objective time-span which might have been filled in with verbal speech; it uttered its own meaning and "spoke" decisively to the situation which Pilate had misconstrued as one requiring objective truth rather than truth as subjectivity. One is here immediately reminded of the Grand Inquisitor section in Dostoevsky's novel, *The Brothers Karamozov*. The Grand Inquisitor is a master of argumentation and verbal persuasion. But all the while Christ remains silent, and in the end the impact of this silence is stronger and more convincing than the compelling logic of the Grand Inquisitor. Jaspers, in his discussion of silence in the section on communication in his three-volume *Philosophie*, provides an interpretive category for the phenomena which Kierkegaard and Dostoevsky elucidate in a more metaphorical manner. This is the interpretive category of "revelatory silence" (*offenbares Schweigen*). As distinct from the impoverished types of silence there is, says Jaspers, a silence that reveals the depth dimension of the human spirit and needs be counted as a mode of authentic speech. ([Heidelberg: Springer, 1948], pp. 358–61).

whereby the object of thought can be isolated and tested so as to yield information about a given state of affairs. Representational thinking takes place within the context of an information-scheme. The communication of the contents of representational thought can thus be properly understood as a transmission of information. The communicative speaking allied with representational thinking is the communication of information about objects and their functions. Hermeneutical thinking, which we have contrasted with representational thinking, does not strive to control its intentional content within a presupposed subject-object frame of analysis, but rather seeks an elucidation of life styles and forms of embodied behavior. Hermeneutical thinking does not control the phenomena through objectification, but rather lets the phenomena be and permits them the freedom to show themselves in their configurative presentment. The communicative speech of hermeneutical thinking thus becomes a struggle to elicit personal and historical meanings rather than a project of transmitting information about objectifiable properties and functions.

It is within the context of this distinction between representational and hermeneutical thinking that the discussion of direct and indirect communication needs to proceed. The speaking allied with representational thinking is designed for direct communication. The communicative speech of hermeneutical thinking makes use of the maieutic of indirection. The point at issue might be expressed as follows: corresponding with the modes of objectifying and nonobjectifying thinking are objectifying and nonobjectifying types of speaking. Direct communication requires a communicable content, a stock of items of information, which are receptive to objective measurement, quantification, and control. Direct communication can thus be properly understood as *denotative* communication. For example, in speaking about the solubility of sugar one communicates something about the denotable properties of sugar. The communication of these denotable properties is direct because what is said stands open to verificational analysis. That which is communicated is allegedly a scientifically verifiable fact subject to control, measurement, and prediction. The meaning of a proposition referring to a verifiable state of affairs can be directly communicated.

Speech and language function in nonverificational as well as strictly verificational contexts. Communication in such contexts becomes more a matter of elucidation and evocation than denotation. It becomes indirect rather than direct, suggesting possible perspectives rather than cataloging denotable properties, delineating styles of existence to be chosen rather than transmitting information. When the poet speaks of jealousy as "the green-eyed monster," when the statesman speaks of "manifest destiny," when the religious mystic speaks of "the dark night of the soul," they are seeking to communicate something about the human situation, something about the self-destructive character of the human emotions, the motives for political involvement, and the character of religious experience. What is at stake for the poet, the statesman, and the mystic are not denotative entities (objects, properties, or relations) but peculiar world-facts arising within certain configurations of experience. Although not under the umbrella of the verificational theory of meaning these world-facts are not bereft of meaning. Their meaning is bound up with the projects and life styles of the poetic, political, and religious modes of existence. These projects and life styles can be communicated only indirectly, requiring some degree of participation in the situation that is being elucidated. There is operative here a different style of speaking and a different use of language.

The different existential stance in speaking and the different use of language that distinguishes direct from indirect communication have a bearing on the type and degree of fulfillment of the communicative act. Direct communication is a communication of general truths, susceptible to clarity and distinctness, and readily accessible by following a prescribed chain of reasoning or controlled process of experimentation. The truths of indirect communication are not generalizable in this sense for the language employed does not carry the same denotative significance. Indirect communication remains a struggle and a risk. The American and the Russian diplomat, the romantic and the transcendental poet, the Buddhist and the Christian, would not be likely to encounter any communication problem in talking about the solubility of sugar or the Pythagorean theorem; but when political ideologies, poetic perspectives, and religious convictions are at issue, communication is not as readily achieved. The beliefs and convictions that capitalism is superior to communism, that the poetic vision lays hold of the transcendent as opposed to the merely human, that Christ is the incarnate Son of

God, are rooted in a personal-historical perspective as contrasted with the more impersonal-scientific perspective of direct communication. Both the attitude and the intended content differ in these two types of communication. Direct communication displays an attitude of detachment; indirect communication issues from an attitude of involvement. The intended content of direct communication is circumscribed by a region of objectifiable and generalizable fact; the intended content of indirect communication is within a region of world-fact whose fabric is an interwoven complex of personal and historical meanings. For the latter communication remains a struggle, a search for common frames of life amidst diversities, an experimentation with locutions and types of language in order to elicit or evoke common attitudes and insights. Ian Ramsey has given some studied attention to what we would call indirect communication, and although Ramsey's philosophical orientation is somewhat different from that of Kierkegaard, on this particular issue the similarities between the two men seem to be more striking than the differences. Ramsey describes the religious situation as one of commitment and discernment, requiring for its communication a language whose use is qualified until the "penny drops," "the ice breaks," "the light dawns." [11] This seems to be highly reminiscent of the indirect method of communication employed by Judge Wilhelm in Kierkegaard's maieutic essay, *Either/Or*. In each case a life style is elucidated and the reader is left to discern and choose for himself.

Thus far in this section, we have centered our discussion of communication around the distinction between direct and indirect communication and have sought to explicate the peculiar character of each. In concluding this section we will focus upon an issue which is central to the inquiry into the conditions which make communication possible. What is it about the character of speech that makes communication, either of a direct or indirect style, possible? Our proposal is that one of the basic conditions that underlies the relative achievements of communicative speech resides in the promise-making character of speech. Speech as communication is a form of promise-making. The recognition of this opens up the ethical perspective of speech. A

11. *Religious Language: An Empirical Placing of Theological Phrases* (New York: Macmillan, 1957). See particularly Chapter I: "What Kind of Situations Are Religious?"

phenomenology of speaking cannot avoid coming to grips with the ethics of speech. Speaking, as it is motivated by the will to communicate, implies an ethical bond between speaker and listener. For communication to occur there must be a relation of mutual trust which binds the speaker and the listener. The speaker, in the words that he speaks and in the manner in which he speaks them, makes a promise—a promise that what he says is trustworthy. In his speech he offers a promise and invites a communicative response from the listener. The listener responds either in word or deed, trusting the speech of the speaker and the speaker himself. It is at this juncture that one is able to discern in particular the inseparability of speech and the speaker. In trusting the veracity of the words that are spoken one trusts the truthfulness of the speaker himself. In ordinary speech we often say "He has given his word." To give one's word is to give oneself. To trust a person's speech is to trust that person. Speaking thus appears to imply a promise—a promise that what is said is said with the will to communicate rather than the will to deceive. The communicative circuit is completed when the listener responds to the promise in an attitude of trust. He enters a bond of loyalty with the speaker, trusts the speaker and his spoken word, and is satisfied that what is spoken can be appropriated as the truth of the speaker. These conditions apply not only to the explicit ethical situations of making particular commitments, pledging loyalties, and giving vows; they apply also in the more objectifying realms of discourse. Even in scientific discourse about verifiable matters of fact, the speaker interested in communication makes an implicit promise that his speaking will not misconstrue the facts as he interprets them. The speaker makes a promise that if such and such verificational operations were to be carried through the truth of what he says would be borne out.

The promise-making character of speech that underlies the achievement of communication provides the clue for the existentialist's distinction between authentic and unauthentic speech. The distinction between the authentic and the unauthentic can be found in virtually all of the existentialist thinkers. Kierkegaard and Heidegger, in particular, have given attention to the issues involved in the distinction. Kierkegaard in numerous writings inveighs against the depersonalization of speech as illustrated in the prevalence of the idle talk of chatter, gossip, and sterile repetition of cliches. In these unauthentic forms of speech, no genuine content is communicated. There is only a display of counterfeit meanings. Idle talk divests communicative speech of its personal quality and renders it into a mere garment that can be interchanged at will. Unauthentic speech proceeds in abstraction from the speaker himself.[12] Heidegger has further clarified the meaning of the unauthentic and the authentic with respect to the project of speech in his distinction between *Rede* and *Gerede*. *Gerede* as idle or mere talk is an unauthentic modification of *Rede* as genuine speech.[13] Admittedly, even idle talk expresses certain features of *Dasein*'s world-involvement, but what comes to expression is the flattened, shallow, and conventionalized mode of the anonymous and impersonal one (*Das Man*). No genuine communication is achieved because the speaker remains accidental to what is said. The originative and creative character of the word as spoken is threatened and speech degenerates into a morass of cliches and superficial observations. What is at issue is no longer the fecund word which is created each time that it is uttered, but rather the sterile locutions of a flattened existence.

The promise-making element in communicative speech is one of the main factors in the distinction between authentic and unauthentic speech. In authentic speech a promise is made by the speaker to the listener. The speaker opens himself to the listener as a man of his word and strives to communicate the various feelings, volitions, and ideas which comprise the intentional structure of his world experience. The authentic speaker makes the promise to communicate himself in his lived concreteness. Unauthentic speech either remains indifferent toward the promise-making element in communication or consciously wills to deceive. Lying, hypocrisy, and perjury are inseparable from speech as an existential project. They indicate certain modes of existence of the embodied speaker, modes which threaten the achievement of communication. It is at this point that a phenomenology of speech moves into an ethics of speech and arrives at the foundation of the unity of language and morality.

12. See particularly *The Present Age*, trans. Alexander Dru and Walter Lowrie (London: Oxford University Press, 1939), p. 59.
13. The most explicit discussion of the distinction between *Rede* and *Gerede* is found in *Being and Time*, trans. J. Macquarrie and E. Robinson (New York: Harper & Row, 1962), pp. 211–14.

6 / The Social Experiencer

*The individual cannot become human by himself.
Self-being is only real in communication with
another self-being. Alone, I sink into gloomy isolation—only in community with others can I be revealed in the act of mutual discovery.*
— Karl Jaspers, *On My Philosophy*

[1] THE PHENOMENON OF SOCIALITY

THE PHENOMENON OF SOCIALITY provides the third
contextual structure in our elucidation of the world-engaged
experiencer. Situated in the territory staked out by his embodiment and expressing meaning in various modes and projects of
speech, the experiencer exists amidst the attitudes and actions of
other selves. Embodiment, speech, and sociality provide the intercalated contexts of the experiencer as intentional consciousness. They comprise three of the more encompassing features of
the engaged experiencer. It is of some importance to note at the
outset that the characterization of the experiencer vis-à-vis his
sociality is not merely an additional item adventitiously attached
to the preceding two characterizations. The phenomenon of sociality is already present in the lived experience of one's embodiment and in the projection of one's existence as speaker and user
of language. My embodiment already discloses the territorial

[185]

space of the other self and the peculiar value significations which reside in it. Speaking, particularly in its communicative aspect, places me in an unmediated confrontation with the other self within a speaker-hearer context. Embodiment and speech are already socialized, and in their deployment the presence of the other is announced.

It is necessary to specify at the outset the peculiar use and range of signification of our characterizing term "sociality." Sociality as a contextual feature of the experiencer is not a designation *per genus* through which one kind of experience would be marked off from another, as for example in the problematic distinction of "social experience" from "religious experience," from "ethical experience," or from "aesthetic experience." Nor is it a classificatory rubric for the social sciences under which particular disciplines and methodological procedures are subsumed—such as sociology, social psychology, social anthropology, psychotherapy, and social work. What is at issue is the use of "sociality" as indicating or pointing to a mode of world-engagement, to an expression of one's installation in the world. Sociality does not function here as a classificatory concept, nor is it the region of the social as a nexus of objectifiable properties and relations. It has to do, initially at least, with the prereflective involvement and functioning intentionality from which all forms of reflection take their rise. There is a *sociality of situation* which precedes objectifying distinctions and which antedates the methodological scaffolding of the social sciences. This sociality of situation is my situation as lived through with the other. It is the situation of awareness and action in which meanings contributed by the other both limit and enrich my own existence as a project of meaning. It is the situation of living through experiences with the other on your hands, at your mercy, in the way, as a source of comfort, as a desirable colleague, as someone to be feared. The manner of this appearance of the other within my situation will need to be explored in some detail—and we will discover that the transaction of dialogue assumes a privileged role in the appearance and disclosure of the other—but at this juncture we are interested in clarifying our usage of a term which has an almost unmanageable range of meaning. Like embodiment and speech, sociality is the discrimination of a manner of existence. It is the characterization of a phenomenon as it appears in its lived concreteness rather than a denotable property attached to a pregiven substance. It is not that the experiencer has the property of sociality along with other properties; the experiencer *is* socialized existence. Man does not first exist and then assume a property of social relatedness in the way that one might add a new set of photographs to one's travel album. Man exists in the first flush of consciousness as a social being.

This proposal, that sociality be understood as an existential structure inseparable from man's being-in-the-world, requires a reexamination of the allegedly privileged standpoint of the ego or the "I" in egological philosophies. Scheler, in developing his perceptual theory of the alter ego, had already succeeded in calling into question the bold claim by the egologists that the first datum given to each of us is his own self. Scheler presented evidence for the priority of the sphere of the "we" over the sphere of the "I." [1] As a result of his trenchant studies on the nature of sympathy, Scheler opened up the path to a phenomenology of the "we-experience." Marcel has moved in a similar direction in his philosophy of intersubjectivity by taking as his starting point not the interiorized "I am" experience of Descartes but the more global "we are" experience. [2] The pressing demand bequeathed to contemporary philosophy of existence by Scheler and Marcel is that of a patient exploration of the structural development of the "we experience" in an effort to overcome the difficulties inherent in an egological inquiry-standpoint—difficulties which Husserl himself confronted, particularly in his *Cartesian Meditations*.

We have already urged that a philosophy which professes to provide an elucidation of experience needs to assume as its fundamental project a return to the concrete life-world, which antedates any constitution of essences grounded in the constituting activity of a transcendental ego. Such an ego is a relatively late arrival, occasioned by the constituting intentionality of representational thinking. Returning to the life-world places in the forefront a prior and foundational investigation which is geared to an elucidation of the world-oriented posturing of experience. The life of the transcendental ego is not the result of its constituting activity but rather the basis for it. Transcendental philoso-

1. See particularly *The Nature of Sympathy*, trans. Peter Heath (London: Routledge and Kegan Paul, 1954), pp. 238 ff.

2. *The Mystery of Being*, trans. René Hague (Chicago: Henry Regnery, 1960), II, 10.

phy is itself rooted in a phenomenology of the dialectic of lived experience. Existential dialectics, as both the early Hegel and Kierkegaard had already known, precedes any regression to an ego-standpoint. The existential dialectic which is at issue in our explication of the phenomenon of sociality, and which requires attention, is the dialectical movement of the "we-experience." Being-with-others as a phenomenon of the life-world makes its appearance as an undivided portion of experience which contains within it the polarity of self and other. The self and the other are ensconced in the we-experience in such a way that they direct the movement of consciousness without becoming thematically explicit. They are incorporated in the prereflective movement of consciousness and solicit corporate meanings. It is this which makes it possible for one to say "we" when one is describing or assessing a project. The "I" is already contained in the "we," whereas in the egological approach the sphere of the "we" is bracketed and the distillation of its referential meaning is deferred until the monadical ego has been constituted. The self and the other are copresent in the we-experience and first become thematically explicit through the operation of reflective consciousness. The historical route of this emergence follows a dynamic, dialectical struggle for self-consciousness and consciousness-of-the-other. We must now clarify this dialectical movement.

In a preceding chapter we explored the phenomenon of self-imputation in the intentionality of feeling, will, and thought. Sentient, volitional, and noetic experiences have the peculiar feature of implicating a self who feels, wills, and thinks, through which a variegated spectrum of self-awareness (for example, self-love, self-hate, self-denial, self-affirmation, self-distrust, self-knowledge, etc.) is postured. We are now able to examine the development of this self-imputation resident within the intentional structure of experience as a socially contextualized self-imputation. The historical route of self-imputation and the resultant self-awareness is not the serene and untroubled unfolding of a solipsistic self-reflexivity, but rather it is a dynamic struggle of self-establishment through a resisting encounter with the other. The movement of self-awareness is not insular or self-contained. It feeds on the resisting tendencies of otherness supplied by a society of selves. The self-reflexivity which is operative in self-hate and self-affirmation requires a *field of operation* supplied by the distance of otherness. I can hate myself only because an image of who I am has already been put into play through the attitudes and responses to my speech and action by the other. I affirm myself in word and deed in response to the word and deed, and consequent meanings, contributed by the other who invades my time and space. The phenomenon of existential resistance is a decisive index of the social dimension of being-in-the-world. Self and other are co-revealed through the immediacy of existential resistance. Through his resistance, the other creates the distance which occasions the eruption of my self-awareness. This makes for a mutual discovery of self and other and gives credence to Jaspers' claim that man cannot become human by himself.

Our introduction of the category of existential resistance and the proposal that it points to a primordial world-fact requires further comment in anticipation of possible misinterpretation. It is important to keep in mind even at this initial stage of our elucidation that the existential resistance that determines the mutual discovery of self and other in the "we-experience" is not by necessity a movement of estrangement or alienation. Estrangement is not ontologically necessitated by the experience of resistance. Resistance has a creative as well as a destructive expression. It is an occasion for value as well as disvalue. It resides on the hither side of good and evil. Good and evil are first posited in the course of its dialectical development. The chief fault of Sartre's otherwise penetrating analysis of the concrete relations with others resides in his neglect of the creative side of resistance. Resistance for Sartre becomes an effort at displacement of one self by another. After the realization that the other self cannot be displaced, that he is part of the facticity of my situation, then he is reduced to the material for my freedom, eternally alienated by my gaze and depersonalized by my project of self-affirmation. What is not accounted for by Sartre's view of the self-other relation is that existential resistance can spur a dialogue to mutual self-discovery and the clarification of concepts and projects (as was the case in the dialogic activity of Socrates). Resistance can drive the self and the other to transcending perspectives and a mutual expansion of meaning. Existential resistance, in disclosing the irremovable finitude of self

and other, can initiate what Jaspers has called a "loving struggle" for communication in which there is a mutual acceptance in
spite of differing points of view. Hence it is the source for love,
sympathy, and forgiveness as well as hate, conflict, and rejection. This double aspect of the phenomenon of existential resistance will become the subject of inquiry and elaboration in our
later discussion on conformity and community.

Attentiveness to the dialectical interplay and mutual discovery of self and other through the developing struggle of existential resistance leads to a questioning of the egologist's claim that
the self is somehow given to itself by itself. Monadological subjectivity, in selecting an egological inquiry-standpoint, conceals
a primordial region of world-facts—facts attested to by the revealing power of the "we-experience." We have already suggested
that embodiment and speech are basic situational determinants
in the dialectical disclosure of self and other. The fact of dialogue, in its concrete embodiment, plays a particularly crucial
role in the mutual discovery of self and other. The dialectic of
existential resistance finds its peculiarly appropriate concrete
illustration in the dialogic transaction between speaker and
hearer. It is to a discussion of this that we must now turn.

[2] THE DIALOGIC TRANSACTION

THE DIALECTIC OF MUTUAL SELF-DISCOVERY in the
emergence of the we-experience achieves its most forceful expression in the dialogic encounter. Speech plays a privileged role
in the perception of the other. The we-experience is constituted
principally through the experience of dialogue. This experience
of dialogue has a transactive structure in that it involves action
moving from speaker to hearer, and, through an interchange of
roles, from hearer to speaker. The dialectical feature of this
transactive experience consists in the reciprocity of roles in the
speaker-hearer relation. In the unfolding of a dialogue, the
speaker becomes hearer and the hearer becomes speaker—not
simply through a mechanical reversal of roles but rather through
an organic development in which resistance and appropriation
are at work. The hearer listens to the speaker, responds by
affirming or denying (or partially affirming and partially deny-

ing) what has been said, and thus takes over the role of speaker. But in thus taking over the role of speaker the utterances and meanings which are achieved are in some sense shaped by that which is proposed, questioned, or denied by the previous speaker. The assumption of the role of speaker in the dialogic transaction involves a response to prior speech in such a manner that this prior speech is taken into account. A breakdown of dialogue occurs when this dialectically transactive interplay between speaker and hearer is disrupted, and there remains nothing more to be proposed, contested, denied, or agreed upon. Our specific task in this section is that of elucidating the dialogue situation as speech-in-action in an effort to show in what manner the presence of the other is displayed and known.

In the experience of dialogue the other is present in such a manner that he is already constitutive of the situation. Encountering the other through dialogue is not a matter of integrating an additional item existing alongside other items into my experiential field. The other, through his interchanging of roles as speaker and hearer, is already lodged in the situation as a coexisting center of projective speech and action. This is what is meant by the "we-experience" in the dialogic transaction. It is the experience of a common background in which the composition of the thought, speech, and action of the other is interwoven with the composition of my thought, speech, and action. The other is revealed in the dialogue situation not as an external entity somehow added to my world, but as a coemergent in a world shared by both of us. It is this that determines the dialogue as a *shared* experience in which the contribution of the other and the contribution of myself coalesce to produce a joint project. The dialogue situation is neither created singularly by the other nor singularly by myself. Admittedly, the other's thought, speech, and action can be said to be his. They occur over there, not here. They fill his lived space, not mine. But there is no phenomenological evidence for the claim that this composite of thought, speech, and action is interiorized in an encapsulated and hermetically sealed subject. The composite is present in the *transaction* of speaking and listening and listening and speaking. His thoughts are embedded in his speaking, which is interwoven with my speaking in a consummate reciprocity. He speaks as he speaks and thinks as he thinks in a particular dialogue situation by virtue of an appropriation of certain leads and suggestions in my speaking and thinking. His speaking and thinking is nurtured by mine, and my speaking and thinking is nurtured by his. That which emerges in the dialogue situation is thus a collaboration of thought and speech which conspires to create meanings in a project of shared experience. The other is perceived within this collaborative activity. His resistance through counterproposals, critical comments, and demands for clarification is concretely experienced in the deployment of our mutual project.

The mutual discovery of self and other in the experience of dialogue proceeds in close association with our previously delineated determinants of embodiment. Our discussion of the embodied experiencer already pointed the way to the phenomenon of social existence. The lived body opens the world not only as a world of objects and utensils but as a social world as well. The lived body deploys a field of action in which the presence of the other is discernible. The territorial space which surrounds my body is bordered and limited by the space of the other. The other contributes to the definition of my space; at times he threatens it and at times he aids me in filling it with meaning. The presence of the other is felt on the fringes of my lived space. His "there" is acknowledged as being contributive to the sense of my "here." The other announces his presence and reveals me to myself through the spatiality of his embodiment.

The spatiality of one's embodiment thus already displays social meanings connected with the presence of the other. Embodiment is indelibly and irrevocably *social* embodiment. One needs therefore to speak of *intercorporeality* or corporeal coexistence. The space of the other coexists with my own, and in this space of the other a certain style of life and assignment of significations to objects and tools become manifest. I find that the figures which my lived body intends are taken over by another embodied center of world experience. Meanings, not the result of my own doing, are attached to these figures. The tools which are at hand for my use are used by another as well, and the space which is oriented through a manipulation of these tools finds its center in another world locus. I may engage in efforts to reconstitute the meanings which emerge through the manipulative and perceptual activity of the other, but I can never displace the other and his oriented space. The other is irreducibly given in his embodied existence, and ultimately I am forced to acknowledge the other as a coexisting center of world experience who is able to project a world remarkably similar to my own. Merleau-Ponty's seminal investigations on the topic of intercorporeality are particularly illuminating on this point. In an insightful passagē he puts us on the path to seeing the phenomenon in question:

> No sooner has my gaze fallen upon a living body in process of acting than the objects surrounding it immediately take on a fresh layer of significance: they are no longer simply what I myself could make of them, they are what this other pattern of behaviour is about to make of them. Round about the perceived body a vortex forms, towards which my world is drawn and, so to speak, sucked in: to this extent, it is no longer merely mine, and no longer merely present, it is present to x, to that other manifestation of behaviour which begins to take shape in it.[3]

The phenomenon of the we-experience, manifest in the dialogic transaction, provides the anchor for the more indirect disclosure of the other by way of cultural objects. Husserl had already spoken of "spiritual predicates" which attach to cultural objects and reveal a cultural community to which they belong.[4] Books, paintings, buildings, roads, historical markers, and battlegrounds are accompanied by social meanings which point to human actions and purposes already projected and carried through. Someone has written the book which I read; someone travels the highway through the mountains; someone frequents the church on the town square; someone is commemorated by the historical marker. It is principally by virtue of these cultural objects that the wider dimensions of the social world are disclosed. They intend both a world of contemporaries, whom I do not meet in the face-to-face situations of the dialogic transaction, and a world of predecessors, whom I cannot meet in face-to-face situations. Museums, antiques, and historical markers point to a world of social meanings no longer extant, but a world which nonetheless solicits clues for its understanding and inter-

---

3. *The Phenomenology of Perception,* trans. Colin Smith (New York: Humanities Press, 1962), p. 353.
4. *Cartesian Meditations,* trans. Dorion Cairns (The Hague: Martinus Nijhoff, 1960), p. 92.

pretation. Even the social world of the past can be reentered and reconstructed through a hermeneutical understanding.[5]

It is also against the background of the direct, face-to-face dialogic encounter that the so called "problem of the existence of other minds" is to be assessed to see if a phenomenological reformulation of the issue might provide a fresh approach. It would indeed seem that if we have as much as approached the phenomenon of sociality through our description of the dialectic of the we-experience (to which the dialogic transaction and the intentionality of the lived body provided a privileged access) the much discussed problem of other minds would emerge as a problem only in retrospect. The inquiry-standpoint from which the traditional problem is raised directs the investigation toward a search for confirming or confuting evidence for the existence of a private episodical history or private consciousness owned by the other. But this is to give a priority to private consciousness, both with respect to myself and the other, which our phenomenological analysis has found to be untenable. The sphere of the "we" takes priority over the sphere of the "I" in the concrete dialogue experience. Only after one has distanced himself from the dialogue situation can one record the results of the dialogue and separate that which belongs to my private history and consciousness from that which belongs to the other. When one does this, however, one is no longer engaging in a dialogic transaction; one is performing a post-mortem on the dialogue. One is dissecting that which originated as an organismically function-

5. The studies of Dilthey become particularly relevant at this point. It was Dilthey who introduced the "category" of *Verstehen* to indicate a method of social interpretation, later taken over by thinkers like Max Weber and Karl Manheim in the formative development of the school of *Verstehendes* sociology. *Verstehen* is for Dilthey a kind of historical imagination through which one is able to project himself into the past and enter the mind of a philosopher or the ethos of a culture. But Dilthey never succeeded in freeing his theory of hermeneutics from an underlying Kantian constructionist epistemology, and hence the phenomena of historical existence are never quite permitted to speak for themselves. According to Dilthey, the historical interpreter carries with him on his projective journey into the past a categorial scheme of values which he himself has supplied. There is no clear recognition of the solicitation of meaning by the phenomena themselves as they are presented to the interpreter in his historical existence. Heidegger is more clearly aware of the phenomenological dimension of hermeneutical interpretation.

ing totality. As a result of this post-mortem, the distinction between private and public is born. The distinction is a late arrival, a product of the afterthought of retrospection. It is an abstraction from the primordial phenomenon of shared experience in the *lived through* transaction of dialogue. The secrets of coexistence are unlocked through attentiveness to this primordial phenomenon.

The time-honored theories of explanation which have been recurringly invoked to provide confirmation for the existence of other minds and the occurrence of a private episodical history (such as the theory of inductive inference, the theory of projective analogy, and the theory of empathic identification) seem to share an egological inquiry-standpoint in one form or another, principally of either a transcendental or empirical-behavioristic variety. As already indicated the accepted axiom of the egologist is that the datum of one's own self or consciousness is given as a privileged datum. I first know myself—allegedly through some species of internal reflection. A related axiom for those making use of inferential and analogical arguments for the existence of other minds is that the first perceptual evidence for the reality of another human being resides in the observation of objectifiable bodily movements and physiological processes. Both of these axioms need to be subjected to careful scrutiny, for as we have seen there is phenomenological evidence which counts against both. It is not at all evident that knowledge of myself is given prior to an encounter with other selves. Both phenomenological description and psychological studies in child development would indicate that the we-experience precedes the I-experience.[6] Regarding the problematic character of the second axiom, we need only remind the reader about our analysis of concrete embodiment, which undercuts the objectification of the body as a physiological entity and proposes a much closer connection

6. Jean Piaget, in his psychological explorations of the life-world of the child, has contributed evidence and insights which support the claim that in the genetic development of the child consciousness of the other precedes consciousness of self. See particularly *The Child's Conception of the World,* trans. Joan and Andrew Tomlinson (New York: Humanities Press, 1951); and *The Construction of Reality in the Child,* trans. Margaret Cook (New York: Basic Books, 1954). See also Merleau-Ponty's essay, "The Child's Relations with Others," in *The Primacy of Perception,* ed. James M. Edie (Evanston: Northwestern University Press, 1964).

between body and consciousness than is admitted by traditional theories of mind. Consciousness, we have seen, surges up in the world only as it is embodied. Thought is interlaced with one's bodily bearing. It is not a hermetically sealed entity to be inferred from external, material properties and movements. Alfred Schütz, in his exploration of the social world, has contributed an observation and suggestion that would seem to come close to the heart of the matter. The traditional theories of mind which make use of inferential and analogical argumentation, as well as the theory of empathy, he says, underestimate the difficulties of self-perception while overestimating the difficulties of perceiving the thoughts of others.[7]

Only if we hold our attention to the phenomena themselves —the living experience of dialogue and the fact of intercorporeality—will the preinferential character of our knowledge of other selves be established. Perceptual experience, in the broadened form which we have suggested, will provide its own evidence. We perceive the other's mind at work as it is interwoven with our own in the dialectical interchange of dialogue. We perceive the intentional feelings and volitions in the other's bodily comportment and gestural complex. His presence is announced in the anger of his shaking fist, in the disapproval of his frown, in the happiness of his smile, and in the sorrow of his tears. These features of his consciousness are directly discernible in the immediacy of the situation and need not wait for the corroboration of an inferential argument or an empathic projection. Admittedly, one can mistrust one's perceptions and doubt the veracity of a particular gesticulation. His smile may hide his sorrow, but "smiling to hide one's sorrow" is also a phenomenon which can show itself, but whose perception requires taking into account a wider framework of his bodily bearing and his personal history. The perception of the other, it need be added, is never a finished fact. It proceeds and grows with the historical development of dialogue and intercorporeality. Although known through the situation of encounter, the other is never completely and exhaustively known. As I never become fully transparent to myself, so the other never becomes fully transparent to me. Knowledge of the other is historical knowledge subject to the contingencies of historical becoming.

7. *Collected Papers, Vol. 1: The Problem of Social Reality,* ed. Maurice Natanson (The Hague: Martinus Nijhoff, 1962), p. 161.

[3] COMMUNITY AND CONFORMITY

OUR RETURN to the contextualized experiencer, which has followed the leads afforded by the self-imputation within the intentional structure of experience, has taken a different path than that of a search for a quietly reposing transcendental ego. The transcendental ego, as we have seen, is a construction arising from the intentionality of representational thinking, and it does not carry the status of privilege which so often has been assigned to it. Our uneasiness about Husserl's *Cartesian Meditations* concerns this point in particular. The transcendental ego of Husserl's phenomenological idealism remains lifeless and untroubled, insulated from the negativities that infect the life-world. Correspondingly, his theory of the alter ego, in his doctrine of intersubjectivity, does not sufficiently account for the movement of estrangement within the we-experience. In his later writings Husserl seems to recognize the phenomenon clearly enough, but the fact remains that, given his program of transcendental-phenomenological idealism, it is difficult to see what role estrangement would play in the streaming concreteness of consciousness. It was assuredly sensitivity to this issue on the part of phenomenologists like Sartre and Merleau-Ponty which drove them in the direction of existential phenomenology, through which alone an account could be rendered of the negativities that pervade man's social existence. Sartre and Merleau-Ponty also realized, as many other existentialists and phenomenologists did not, that such an account could not be given without again taking up the study of Hegel. It was Hegel who coined the categories of "estrangement" and "unhappy consciousness" and made them philosophical tender. But the basic error of Hegel followed closely on the heels of his profound discovery. He prevented estrangement from becoming a *decisive* fault by subordinating it to the essentialist structure of pure thought. Estrangement is overcome, believed Hegel, through the metaphysical optimism of an essentialist theory of history. It was left to the anti-Hegelians, particularly Kierkegaard and Marx, to show that reconciliation is a matter of anticipation and that estrangement still remains in force, both in one's personal and in one's social existence. Sartre and Merleau-Ponty reopen this dialogue between Hegel and the anti-Hegelians, perceptively aware of the need for a dialectical approach to supplement that of phenomenological description in order to deal with the issue at hand. Contemporary reflection on the positivities and negativities of social existence seems to stand at the crossroads of this dialogue and debate, and it beckons one to rethink the philosophical past to become clear about the present.

Hegel's phenomenology of the alienated consciousness, which is at the same time an exercise in the highest abstraction and a project of concrete description, may indeed have been his unique contribution. According to Hegel, consciousness in its drive for purification seeks to become master of itself. Through the hard struggle for self-mastery, consciousness evolves as a striving for sublimation, self-knowledge, and self-affirmation. In this struggle for self-mastery, the presence of the other is disclosed, not as a simple objective entity but rather as a fact of social resistance. Self-mastery is achieved within this dialectic of self and other, which in its initial stage of development is structured as a dialectic of master and servant. Consciousness affirms itself by making use of the labor, desires, and thoughts of the other. Consciousness satisfies its needs and achieves self-fulfillment by enjoying the services performed by another—the encountered self in the role of servant. The master enjoys that which the servant delivers and makes accessible to him. Thus is constituted the basic situation of self as master and other as servant. But the dialectic of sociality drives beyond this initial posturing of the relation between self and other. The servant as another consciousness, and not simply a manipulable object, is himself capable of self-reflection, and in the movement of this self-reflection becomes aware that the master is dependent upon him for the services which he renders. Only through the work of the servant does the master achieve satisfaction. The master thus becomes dependent upon the servant in the realization that only through the servant does he have that which he now enjoys. The master, rather than an independent "being-for-himself," recognizes his dependence upon another being who labors for him. The pure freedom of independence is transformed into the mixed freedom of *inter*-dependence, and a mutuality of egos is established.

Sartre, in his phenomenology of concrete relations with others, transposes Hegel's dialectic of master and servant into an

existentialist key. The *pour-soi* strives for self-mastery by transforming the encountered other into the servile role of being-for-
him. Sartre makes use of the phenomenon of the look (*le regard*) to illustrate the dialectical movement of mastery and
servitude. Through the look I am able to reduce the other to an
object-for-me, an entity whose significance is defined in terms of
my region of concerns. The other becomes an item in my world,
stripped of his subjectivity, deprived of his freedom. The meaning of his existence is that which I confer upon it. Through my
look I occasion his fall into objectivity by shattering his subjective world. But the other is not defenseless as he stands in the
beam of my regarding consciousness. He can look back in an
effort to beat me at my own game and put my world out of play.
The other as an irreducible fact cannot be removed. He stands in
his lived space and threatens to encroach on mine. My only
recourse, according to Sartre, remains that of redeploying my
self-affirmative forces in an existential counterattack. For Sartre
apparently there is no end to this sort of thing. The alienating
movement within sociality goes on and on. The breakdown of
genuine communication is final—indeed communication is
never achieved—and the mutuality of egos which Hegel envi-
sioned remains a vain expectation.

Hegel and Sartre, in spite of the rather sharp differences in
their phenomenologies of consciousness, have been contributing
factors in the development of existential phenomenology. One of
the main features that differentiates existential phenomenology
from phenomenology as transcendental idealism is the recognition of the negativities that threaten consciousness in its drive to
actualization and self-affirmation. Hegel and Sartre recognized
these negativities clearly enough. The philosophical use which
they made of them is, of course, quite a different matter. Hegel
had a metaphysical system within reach, through which the
whole of reality could be comprehended in the fashion of a
God-like survey. Estrangement, in this system, is but a moment
in the history of consciousness destined to be "taken up" and
transformed by the reconciling work of the Absolute Spirit incarnate. The philosophical use which Sartre made of estrangement
is of a quite different genre. Sartre has no metaphysical idealism
into which his illustrations of estrangement might be fitted. He
proceeds more descriptively and less speculatively. Yet his descriptions of consciousness, illuminating though they are, are

peculiarly impoverished with respect to their encompassing range. From a number of engaging illustrations of alienated consciousness there emerges a rather bold generalization that such is the only mode or manner in which consciousness exists, and thereafter his examples are carefully selected so as to fit his generalization. Phenomena which bespeak the creative expression of the we-experience (such as love, sympathy, trust, loyalty, and communal hope) are either neglected or made to fit the generalization that estrangement and self-destruction play the trump card.

We use Sartre against Hegel in rejecting idealistic metaphysics and the God-like survey. But in turn we indict Sartre for his unwarranted generalizations from carefully selected illustrations of the alienated we-experience. Phenomena should be given more freedom to speak for themselves. Generalizations, both of a metaphysical and phenomenological variety, remain forever a matter of risk and one needs to be reminded of their tentative character time and again. We will suggest a descriptive scheme of analysis which hopefully will allow for greater modulations in the phenomenon of sociality than appear in Sartre's analysis.

Our exploration of the we-experience has uncovered the dialectical interplay of self and other as its constitutive structure. This dialectical interplay is concretized in the experience of dialogue and the experience of intercorporeality. It is now our task to elucidate this dialectical interplay from the perspectives of the modulations of being-alone and being-with. Being-alone is the existential intensification of the self-experience. The self that is imputed in the intentional structure of world experience is not, in the first upsurge of selfness, a transcendental ego; rather, it is a self that can be alone. Aloneness is the existential expression of selfhood. But aloneness remains determined by the we-experience, which retains its priority. I can only be alone because the other is absent. In the experience of being-alone the world of the other remains on the fringe of consciousness and determines my separation from the other. But separation from the other is not necessarily estrangement from the other. Estrangement is not a necessary implication of existential separation. It is this that allows for an authentic or creative being-alone, the being-alone of self-mastery and personal creativity. Solitude, we submit, is a creative way of being-alone. Loneliness is a self-destructive way of being-alone. Loneliness is aloneness under the conditions of estrangement.

The phenomenon of loneliness has received a great deal of attention in the existentialist literature, particularly by writers of the literary wing. Kafka, Dostoevsky, Camus, Malraux, Rilke, Auden, and others whose writings illustrate existentialism as the exemplification of a mood or an attitude, have provided penetrating depictions of various expressions of loneliness.[8] The media of the novel, short story, drama, and poem are peculiarly adapted to the elucidation of the phenomenon of loneliness in its concreteness, and it is for this reason that existential phenomenology has much to learn from existential literature. In existential phenomenology, the loneliness—exemplified poetically in literature—is explicated with respect to its structural configuration as a possibility of world experience. The experience of loneliness can be characterized phenomenologically as a discontinuity of lived space and lived time, and as a peculiar fracture in the intentional structure of world experience. The lonely self is spatially isolated. The vicinity of his lived space is walled off from the other. However the presence of the other is still felt, and often with an accentuated poignancy. It is precisely the possibility of a creative being-with-others that produces the anguish in

8. Franz Kafka's novel, *The Castle,* is a particularly poignant exemplification of the negative side of being alone. The central character's passionate efforts to enter the society of the Castle prove to be abortive; at every turn there is a breakdown of communication and the isolated "hero" is subjected to the destructibility of loneliness. In Malraux's novel, *Man's Fate,* the revolutionary hero seeks to escape the anguish of his isolation through a participation in the Chinese Communist revolt, but even in the physical togetherness of executing a siege against the enemy he cannot forget his tragic loneliness. Roquentin in Sartre's novel, *Nausea,* is repeatedly threatened with isolation from creative communal existence. The inhabitants of the plague ridden city in Camus' *The Plague* experience the pangs of loneliness. Gogo and Didi in Beckett's shocking drama *Waiting for Godot* exemplify the disturbing experience of a complete breakdown of communication. W. H. Auden in his celebrated baroque ecologue "The Age of Anxiety," expresses the tragic situation in which man's personality is threatened by absorption into cosy crowds and by the tyranny of statistical averages. In all of these writers there is a profound depiction of loneliness as a determination of mood in human existence.

loneliness. Loneliness is not a solipsistic phenomenon. One of the more disquieting experiences is that of being lonely in the midst of a crowd, where the other is present, but as a nameless and faceless self whose lived spaced remains sealed off from mine. There is no sharing of lived space, no assessment of it in terms of common directions and places for the joint actualization of projects. Correspondingly, the horizon-form of lived time is restricted and flattened. The lonely self has no anticipation of creative associations, and the past which he remembers is cut off from the present. The past is objectified as a serial succession of experiences which have gone by, no longer nourishing and enriching the present. This discontinuity within the experience of space and time produces a disturbance in the intentional structure of experience. This accounts for the threat of meaning that accompanies loneliness, and makes possible the understanding of loneliness as a form of existential meaninglessness. The lonely self is cut off from the meanings of his sentient, volitional, and reflective existence. He is unable to affirm the creative contents of his cultural heritage. He no longer derives meaning through an active participation in the political, religious, and aesthetic life of the community. The region of the social world no longer affords opportunities for satisfying dialogue and involvement reaching into the total sentient, volitional, and intellectual life of man. Felt, willed, and noetic meanings are all infected with doubt and the whole intentional structure of world experience is threatened.

Solitude is a creative rather than a self-destructive way of being-alone. Solitude is separation without alienation. One can experience solitude without becoming an alien or a stranger in society. The solitary individual is not threatened with the devaluation of his lived space and lived time. Lived space, in the experience of solitude, individuates without isolating. Time is not empty, as in loneliness, but filled with the memory of past fulfillments and with future anticipations which play a role in the creative thought and action of the present. The meanings extant in one's culture, both past and present, are appropriated without being uncritically accepted. They are weighed in the balance of contemplative consideration and taken over as the material for new creations. Through the use of my hands and through my critical reflection I can refashion the given and recreate the world. I can use tools in a way in which they have not yet been used, launch projects which have not yet been launched, think thoughts which have not yet been thought. Herein resides the creativity of solitude, a creativity which strives toward a unification and reshaping of experience. In solitude the self-mastery of consciousness is achieved. It is to this end that Nietzsche's Zarathustra summons his hearer: "Flee my friend into your solitude where the air is pure and strong." [9] The self-mastery of consciousness in the solitary mode of existence is achieved only through a hard struggle against the alienating threats of loneliness and conformism. Self-knowledge and self-affirmation are never presented as accomplished facts; they are won time and again in combat against the depersonalization of loneliness and the objectivizing influences of the other. Paul Tillich, in his phenomenological description of the "courage to be as oneself," has provided an illumination of what is at stake in this struggle for the self-mastery of consciousness. The solitary self is able to affirm the intentional structure of his personal existence against the objectivization and depersonalization of abstract thought, conforming tendencies, and idolatric technology. A creative mode of existence is maintained through the self-affirmation and originative thinking borne by the courage to be as oneself.[10]

As loneliness and solitude are, respectively, destructive and creative ways of being alone, so conformity and community are destructive and creative ways of being with others. In conformity and community there is an orientation toward the other, rather than toward oneself as in loneliness and solitude. This orientation toward the other can take one of two forms. It can take the form of a self-alienating submission to the look of the other, or it can posture a situation of creative participation. The former leads to conformity, which in the end threatens both the experience of self and the experience of other; the latter leads to community, in which the self and the other are mutually fulfilled. Conformity and community, as existential modifications of sociality, are configurations of experience which display dif-

9. *The Portable Nietzsche*, trans. and ed. Walter Kaufmann (New York: Viking Press, 1954), p. 166.

10. *The Courage to Be* (New Haven: Yale University Press, 1952), pp. 113–54.

ferent attitudes and different modes of inhabiting the horizon-forms of time and space. The conformist is unable to exert an existential claim on time and space as being uniquely his own. There is for him only the time and space of the generalized other —the *public*. Public space and public time inform his total behavior. His past merges with a mythical collective past in which his contributions are indistinguishable from the contributions of the group. His future becomes a generalized future which holds only possibilities for group actualization. Correspondingly, his space becomes public space. The self-identity borne by the individuating movements of the lived body is threatened, and space becomes a receptacle of bodies in general. Space becomes public property, owned by the public and inhabited by the public. No place remains where singular projects of thought and action might be actualized. The affirmative and unique self is displaced, and only the flattened space of the public remains. As time and space take on a public character so does the intentional structure of experience, for it is in the horizon-forms of time and space that intentionality is grounded. Sentience, volition, and thought no longer impute a personal experiencer. Feelings, volitions, and thought belong to everyone, and hence, to no one in particular. The conformist, as Kierkegaard had already so clearly seen, is an individual reduced to a mere numerical significance. He submits to the look of the other, thinks as others would have him think, and acts in accordance with the standardized norms of the group. Meaning itself becomes a public commodity and personal existence is placed under threat.

Community is the positive expression and existential fulfill-ment of the we-experience. The nihilistic threats of loneliness and conformity can be combated through the creativity of communal participation. Communal experience fills and expands time and space with shared memories and shared hopes. The other is neither expelled from my lived space nor permitted to absorb my lived space into his. His social space is acknowledged and respected, and my space is opened to him as the possible meeting place for a dialogic transaction. Communication requires the solicitation of contributions from the other through speech and action with the promise that these contributions in some manner will be reciprocated. The other is no longer viewed as a threat to my world-orientation but rather as an enrichment of it. Contrary to Sartre, the other ceases to be "the hidden death of my possibilities" [11] and becomes the midwife who aides in their birth. Within the perspective of community the other is seen to fulfill an ontological and not simply a psychological need, in that he contributes to the structure of meaning through which my projects are defined and my life is ordered; and in the developing reciprocity of dialogue he comes to an awareness that I fulfill an ontological need for him. By virtue of this reciprocity we are both enabled to participate in the wider cultural life of our society without loss of selfhood, either by loneliness or by conformity. Communal participation is a manner of *being-with* without the loss of existential individuality.

This participation requires both the exercise of a critical disposition and the transcending movement of love. The critical disposition provides a sheet anchor against fanaticism and dogmatism, and against the uncritical acceptance of institutionalized values and the use of power. Group hysteria is not communal participation. Genuine communication requires the distance of critical reflection, the ability to withstand absorption into any one ideology or any one social mode of existence. The transcendence of love constitutes another condition for the achievement of communication. Jaspers speaks to the point at issue when he says that love is "the source through which communication is illumined." [12] Communal participation requires the mutual acceptance of self and other. This acceptance makes possible the transcending of differences as to ideology and style of life. A genuine sense of community is achieved in spite of diverging ideologies and commitments. In the loving struggle of communication, the other, even though his life-style differs, is accepted as an associate in the search for communal meaning.

It is within this context of community that the constitution and emergence of personality occurs. In the final analysis, community and personality are coextensive. The self-integration of persons as persons occurs only in a community. In the communal context the other is addressed as a *person*. The presence of the other is illuminated in a new dimension. One can only

11. *Being and Nothingness,* trans. Hazel E. Barnes (New York: Philosophical Library, 1956), p. 264.

12. *Philosophie,* 2d ed. (Heidelberg: Springer, 1948), II, 356.

properly speak of a community of persons, and never of a community of things or even a community of selves. The elucidation of communal participation requires a shift from the language of self-other relation to the language of person-to-person encounter. The other as encountered in the drive for communication is neither an alienated other nor a neutral social presence. Community is sociality under the guise of creativity, and with this new mode of sociality a new perspective of the other is constituted. The existence of the other is viewed under a new determination or within a new existence modality. He is acknowledged as a person, as a unique and irreplaceable center of freedom. In the language of Martin Buber, the other is addressed as a "Thou," and in this dialectic of the "I-Thou" relation both I and Thou are constituted as persons. I cannot become a person myself without acknowledging the other as a person; and he achieves his status as a person through an acknowledgment of me as a person. Knowledge of oneself as a person is inseparable from the acknowledgment of the other as a person. Self-knowledge and acknowledgment of the person of the other are dialectical moments in the achievement of a sense of community. In this dialectic of mutual self-discovery the shift from the world of things to the world of persons becomes discernible and decisive.

[4] HISTORICAL EXISTENCE

OUR DISCUSSIONS OF HERMENEUTICAL THINKING and incarnated consciousness in previous chapters have already opened up the inquiry into the historical dimension of world-oriented existence. Hermeneutical thinking is attuned to historical contexts. Its centrifugal intentionality marks out nonobjectifiable life styles. Its centripetal intentionality implicates a contextualized historical experiencer. The historical was an issue in our discussion of incarnated consciousness, in which we were led to conclude that historicality is a phenomenal feature of consciousness itself. Incarnated in a world whose interstices of time and space are imbued with historical meaning, the contextualized experiencer apprehends himself as both a creature and a creator of history. The common memories and common aspirations which nurture the various forms of social interaction (family, civic organizations, professional and vocational groups, church, and state) coalesce in the structuring of *historical presence*. However, as we have seen, certain factors in our analysis of experience count against the postulation of a monadic subject securely positioned at a distance from the conflux of history. There can be no return to an insulated historical subject who might enjoy the transcendental privilege of surveying the historical from a standpoint of noninvolvement. The experiencer is already lodged in history and in some manner and degree constituted by it. He is never able to view history from above—only from within.

The task to be assumed now is that of further elucidating the dimension of the historical in light of our phenomenology of sociality. A broadening of the inquiry into social existence leads to the world-fact of historical existence. Sociality is not restricted to the dialogue of face-to-face encounter. There is a dialogue of wider range and reach. There is a region of social reality which extends beyond the intersection of lived time and lived space in my direct encounter with the other. In the background of this encounter there is a world of predecessors and a world of successors.[13] Although our predecessors are no longer encounterable in face-to-face situations and our successors are not yet encounterable, they impinge on our historical present in a decisive way. The dialectic that is operative in the face-to-face encounter of the we-experience is also operative in the experiencer's relation to the social world of yesterday and the world of tomorrow. Our predecessors have already charted formative influences that are at work in the present; thus the disclosure of the world of predecessors is not simply a matter of noting and recording the events of a dead past. The historical past lives on into the present. The historical past never appears as an isolated unit, as a collection of previous atomistic "nows" which are cut off from the present "now." Historical time shares in the ecstatic unity of

13. In his structural analysis and typification of the social world, Alfred Schütz has distinguished four interrelated regions: the world of close associates manifested in the face-to-face situation of the pure we-relation; the world of others who are contemporaries but more distantly and indefinitely known; the ancestral world of predecessors; and the world of tomorrow which includes all others who will succeed me. For a detailed discussion of this typification, see *The Phenomenology of the Social World*, trans. George Walsh and Frederick Lehnert (Evanston: Northwestern University Press, 1966), pp. 139–214.

the time of lived experience; indeed, it is a peculiar modification of it. The meanings which reside in our historical presence are conditioned by the worlds of our predecessors. And ultimately it is necessary to speak of "world" in the plural. The cultural worlds of the Egyptians, the Greeks, the Romans, and the Anglo-Saxons continue to contribute meaning to our experience of historical presence. Herein resides the existential basis for the science of history.

However, in becoming aware of the worlds of our predecessors it is necessary to recognize that the present also lives into and vitalizes the past. Originative thinking and decisive action in the present can reopen the past and reveal new perspectives. The meaning of the past—be it meaning associated with the family homestead or the storming of the Bastille—is never fixed and final. The emergence of new configurations of experience can reopen the past and expand its sense or significance. The historical experiencer is not mute in his confrontation with the world of yesterday. He addresses it, and is addressed by it, in a continuing project of interpretation. To interpret the past is to reopen and reenter it. The temporal span between present and past in historical time is not a vacuous or empty void which by necessity functions as a factor of negativity. To be removed from the past is not necessarily an unfortunate state of affairs for the interpreter. Admittedly, historical distance can conceal meanings, but it can also release a new understanding of what happened and give birth to new perspectives of meaning. This makes the interpretation of the meaning of the historical past a task to be perpetually achieved in the historical present.

The world of our successors enters our present concerns in a manner different from the impingement of the world of our predecessors, but also here the dialectic that structures the self-other encounter in the we-experience is operative. Through our thought and action we seek to shape in some manner the world of our successors. To experience historical presence is to act in such a manner that one plans for the world of tomorrow. We make wills, we legislate for soil conservation, we disseminate information on birth control, the total effects of which will not be experienced in our lifetime. The world yet to be fashioned exerts its own peculiar influence on us through the power of the possible. The anticipation of a future society already confers a meaning on our present existence. The anticipation of a certain social order (e.g., without class strife, without nuclear wars, with a minimum of poverty and disease, with a space-age consciousness) invests the present with particular configurations of purposive and goal-directed activity. The present influences the future and the future makes a difference for the present.

This dialectic of development, encompassing the worlds of contemporaries, predecessors, and successors, constitutes the sense of the historical. It enables one to speak of a "historical world" given equi-primordially with a "natural world." And these worlds of nature and history, although distinct, are not separable. The experiencer stands in history as he confronts nature, and nature is present in his historical existence. The time of man's evolutionary-biological development is illustrative of this interdependence of the historical and the natural. Evolutionary-biological time has both a historical and a natural dimension. The time of decision and historical action is interlaced with the datable sequences of the time of nature. The common distinction between historical time as irreversible and natural time as reversible, although valid as a kind of regulative abstraction, does not apply to evolutionary-biological time. Nor does it apply to the concretely experienced time of the life-world, for there is operative in the life-world a less abstract attitude toward nature as well as a less abstract attitude toward history. Concretely embodied consciousness has both historical and natural elements, and it is again in the phenomenon of the lived body that the interpenetration of history and nature is most clearly discernible. The dualism of history and nature is most decisively overcome through a dismantling of the mind-body dichotomy with a phenomenology of embodiment (see Chapter 4).

To grasp the full significance of the historical dimension of social existence a more precise explication of the meaning of "historical" is required. Although etymologically rooted in a common source, "historical" and "history" need to be technically distinguished. History is a story of past events. It is a selective account, either oral or written, of a succession of events in the development of a society. In providing such an account the historian makes use of a variety of materials (letters, documents, diaries, inscriptions, archeological discoveries) in an effort to reenter the past and understand a culture or period that once flourished. The historical indicates the events themselves, as they are lived through by the actors of history. There is a historical life-world which is always presupposed by the historian, and which is broader than his narration and interpretation of selected events. Clearly not all events find their way into the records of history. The historian must select and sift, generalize and classify, analyze and infer, in order to confirm or confute proposed hypotheses as to what actually occurred. It is through the inquiry into principles of selection, types of classification, and techniques of inference that the science of historiography is born. The issues of fact and interpretation, induction and inference, periodization, pre- and post-history, freedom and determinism, inevitably arise from such pursuits and lead to the discipline of the philosophy of history. A phenomenology of the historical is not as such a philosophy of history. It is an explication of the foundation for any philosophy of history, geared to an elucidation of that configuration of world-experience which first occasions a *sense* of history. It is this that we have in mind in speaking of "the historical." The historical is a frame of experience in which the horizon-forms of time and space and the intentional structure of world-orientation assume a certain texture and posture. Time and space are experienced as abodes of social meanings in which the already actualized possibilities in a world of predecessors and the not yet actualized possibilities in a world of successors can be taken over and anticipated in the here and now. Historical time is a qualification of lived time. It is time lived in awareness of the destiny of a social past which has already marked out interdependent, formative influences which conspire to produce historical trends. It is time lived in awareness of an open social future into which are projected goals and purposes yet to be actualized. It is time lived in awareness of an opportune present in which freedom comes to expression in decisive action. This is to say that historical time displays distinctive attitudes to the three modes of lived time. In historical time the past is something to be taken over through a running forward to the future as one grasps the opportunities for an actualization of presence. Historical space is a qualification of lived space. Lived space becomes a region of places where decisive historical action is to be carried out and common purposes achieved. The space of one's neighborhood, city, and nation are filled with historical memories (indicated by monuments, commemorative markers, battlegrounds) which are kept alive and with anticipations of the fulfillment of that which was begun by one's predecessors in a struggle to preserve their space. The actualization of a historical purpose requires a space where this purpose is to be brought to realization.

The intentional structure of world experience assumes a new texture within the historical perspective of lived time and space. The act of intentional consciousness becomes an *interpretive* act. Intending is already interpreting. Correspondingly, the figures as intended or as meant are understood as figures with a history. The background, in the figure-ground correlation that structures the intentional consciousness, also assumes a historical cast. In the background of every interpretive act of historical consciousness a community of interpreters is already at work, and this community provides its contribution toward the achievement and fulfillment of meaning. The contribution of the other is already inserted into every act of interpretation. Intentionality becomes embroidered with significations and values arising out of the historical facticity of being-with-others. It is at this point that the relevance and existential importance of studies in hermeneutics and the sociology of knowledge can be seen.

Time and space and the operating intentionality of world experience within the perspective of historical consciousness produce the *historical situation*. In this historical situation the experiencer is implicated in a special modality of his existence. He is implicated as historical actor or agent. The centripetal vectors of intentionality are thus again seen to be at work, intending a center of historical consciousness. This center is the experiencer as historically decisive actor. Phenomenology, in its return to the life-world, thus progresses to a *historically* contextualized experiencer. As already suggested, the experiencer as historical actor does not become phenomenologically transparent as the subject-pole of a subject-object relation. His self-awareness as historical actor is neither an interior movement within an encapsulated perduring substantial subject, nor does it issue from the basement of a transcendental subject. It arises out of the dialectic of the we-experience as this experience intends a world of contemporaries, predecessors, and successors. The difficulty in the application of the traditional category of substance to the historical actor resides in using a category of limited applicability to encompass the rich and varied modulations of world experience, reducing the concretely historical to an instance of finite substance in general. The difficulty in the postulation of a transcendental-historical subject, somehow positioned behind the concrete development of historical action, is that it places the historical actor at a distance from his action. Also, it ushers in a confusion of the nonobjectifying character of hermeneutical thinking with the objectifying movement of representational thinking, which first supplies the subject-object distinction. At this point hermeneutical phenomenology must simply abandon the quest for an undergirding metaphysical anchor (the soul-substance doctrine of traditional metaphysics) as well as a transcendental epistemological source (the ego of transcendental philosophy), and seek to elucidate the concrete movements of historical consciousness.

The experiencer in the mode of historical actor deploys such a breadth and variety of intentional behavior that any exhaustive description of this behavior remains problematic. In this dimension of existence, as in all others, the phenomenon is so proliferated with meaning structures that any schematic delineation of distinguishing features needs to remain open-ended. Nonetheless there are some such distinguishing features which characterize the experiencer as historical actor and require attention. The historical existence of the experiencer is textured by purposiveness, freedom, and uniqueness.

Purposiveness is a salient feature of historical consciousness. Historical action is action which intends a purpose. Even if this purpose does not enjoy actualization because of interruption or displacement, it enters into the constitution of the historical consciousness. Now the purposive character of the historical actor itself requires further elucidation. What precisely is purposive action? Here again one needs to be wary of the possible importation of nonhistorical modes of thought to explain the historical. Purposive action is action directed toward an end or goal through which some project of meaning is fulfilled. But this needs to be clarified independently of a metaphysics of cosmic teleology. The traditional doctrine of teleology, with its fixed ends and nature-bound course of development, sheds little illumination on the purposiveness displayed in a decisive historical action. The root difficulty in an application of the traditional teleological doctrine to historical reality is the same as that which disturbs the use of the category of substance. Designed as an explanatory principle of representational thought to account for the various types of objective movements and processes in nature, traditional teleology gets in the way of the phenomena when issues of the preobjective life-world are at stake. The experiencer as historical actor does not work with ends already given. The ends arise out of the rough and tumble of social experience. They are projected, modified, conserved, and displaced through the deliberation of dialogue and corporate action. Purpose is the child of human contrivance rather than the pseudohistorical expression of a cosmic teleology.

This leads to a second distinguishing feature of the historical actor—freedom. In the projection of purposive action freedom is already implied. Only because man is free can he propose and pursue value-bearing goals. Decisive historical action requires a liberation from the given. Although destined to be in some situation as long as he exists, the experiencer is not bound to any particular situation. He displays the power of self-transcendence by virtue of which he can reshape the given, vitalize a dead past, and project new goals for himself and his community. This power of self-transcendence is the primal ingredient of historical freedom. It provides the power to struggle against the dehumanization by technology, the threat of conformism, and the objectification of the past—all of which lead to a loss of historical identity. Historical consciousness is not an objectively given determinant. It is a task to be achieved time and again through self-transcending affirmation. The freedom displayed by the historical actor through this self-transcendence, however, is not absolute or infinite. We reject Sartre's claim, with which he himself does not remain consistent, that freedom is total and infinite.[14] Historical freedom appears only under the conditions of finitude. The finitude of lived time and lived space impose on freedom a limitation in which elements of facticity (an already actualized past, a biological and cultural environment, the existence of the other, transitoriness and death) are already in force. Historical freedom is *freedom-within-a-situation*, which makes possible variegated responses to given states of affairs, but which does not make possible the displacement of being situated in finite time and space. It is in historical freedom that the alliance of freedom and responsibility is most clearly illustrated. The historical actor is free to respond to prior action upon him and thus reshape the situation in which he finds himself. Re-

14. Sartre, *Being and Nothingness*, p. 531.

sponsible action is *responding to* a state of affairs by deliberating and deciding on alternatives. Freedom requires otherness in order to become real. Although the finitude determined by otherness excludes the freedom for creation *ex nihilo,* which could only belong to a non-finite being, it does not exclude the possibility of producing something qualitatively new through the projection and retrenchment of purposive goals. It is in this way that historical existence is able to enact the new and the untried.

The experiencer, implicated as historical actor, is unique and irreplaceable. He is not simply the embodiment of a transitory event within a generalizable scheme of becoming. He embodies significations and modes of action which "stand out" (*exist* in the root meaning of *"existere"*) from the universal process of successive change. The *significance* of the work of the historical actor resides in this power to stand out and display the unique. It is here where we see how the historical breaks out of the universality which characterizes the objectivity of nature. Admittedly this "break" is relative rather than absolute, for the historical continues to participate in the natural and the natural in the historical; nonetheless, the significance of the historical resides in its constitution of value-laden projects in a unique and incomparable manner. It was this which accounted for the bane of the historical in Aristotle's cosmologically oriented philosophy and led to his subordination of the historical to the poetical. Poetry, according to Aristotle, is still geared to the universal. We suggest that what is required is a different order of signification for grasping the meaning of a historical event and the role of the historical actor. In the methods of statistical analysis and hypothetical inference taken over by the natural sciences, anything which falls outside the range of generalizability and predictability has no significance. The scientific facts under scrutiny are replaceable and open to substitution; they do not stand out from the universal succession of occurrences. The historical actor and the fruits of his labors are not open to substitution in this manner. He structures human culture in a novel way by taking an inventory of his time and marshaling his unique potentialities in decisive action. He does this by grasping the unrepeatable moment as the opportune time for the actualization of a historical purpose. And it is in and through this deliberation and active participation that the self-consciousness of historical existence is achieved.

Purposiveness, freedom, and uniqueness, although they do not provide exhaustive characterizations of historical existence, indicate the posture that the experiencer as historical actor assumes. They supply additional determining features in the continuing elucidation of the contextualized experiencer. They are features of a particular mode of sociality. This sociality is inseparable from embodiment and speech, and the three together circumscribe open-ended contexts in which the experiencer achieves self-understanding.

PART III

*Metaphysics, Ontology,
and the Experienced World*

7 / Reflections on the History
of Metaphysics

My purpose is to persuade all those who think meta-
physics worth studying that it is absolutely necessary
to pause a moment and, regarding all that has been
done as though undone, to propose first the pre-
liminary question, "Whether such a thing as meta-
physics be even possible at all?"
—Immanuel Kant, *Prolegomena to Any*
Future Metaphysics

[1] THE STANDPOINT OF THE REFLECTOR

THE THIRD AND FINAL PART of our study has been
implied throughout the two preceding parts. The ontological
interest, which becomes thematically explicit here, was already
present in our explorations of the dynamics and structure of
experience and in our elucidation of the contextualized experiencer. Indeed, it could not be otherwise, for the general design of
the entire study is to propose an ontology of experience. Experience and being, in an ontological view of experience, are interwoven in such a manner that when either is at issue the other is
already implied. One does not arrive at being through inferences
from some kind of ontologically neutral experience. A sense of
being, however implicit, accompanies the upsurge of experience.
Being is neither the result of a deduction nor of an inference. It
is present in the first flush of world-awareness. Experience, in its
various modalities, is postured as a network of intentionalities

issuing from a contextualized experiencer whose presence is that of *being-in* and *being-at* the world.

The demand which now stands before us is that of explicating the peculiar connection between experience, being, and the phenomenal world. We have already developed in some detail a new approach to the dynamics and structure of experience in which the world *as experienced* provides the guiding theme. In working out this new approach to experience, in an atmosphere of critical contention with traditional versions, we found ourselves speaking of process and *Gestalt*, time and space, vitality and intentionality, the lived body and consciousness, nature and history. Quite clearly, in all this certain ontological features of experience are already marked out. But up to this point there has been no sustained reflection on the kind of question that is asked when one asks about being, nor has there been a clarification of the language of being. Further, the discipline traditionally entrusted with the responsibility of dealing with questions pertaining to the nature of that which is has not yet come under scrutiny. It is precisely these issues which will provide the focus of our attention and explorations in the concluding part of our study. Through these explorations we will hope to provide another stage of clarification as to the connection of experience and being, and sketch some prolegomena for a future ontology of experience.

Traditionally the so-called "problem of being" has fallen within the province of the discipline of metaphysics. Metaphysicians throughout history have assumed various inquiry-standpoints, proposed particular categories, and outlined certain conceptual schemes and models, all of which have played a decisive role in the manner in which the question about being has been asked. It is therefore unavoidable that our explication of the ontological character of experience should begin with reflections on the history of metaphysics. The purpose of these reflections, however, is not to enumerate the variety of metaphysical systems which have found their way into the history of philosophy, nor is it to provide an inventory of the main arguments that metaphysicians have devised. Such a task, motivated by the interests of historical research, possesses its intrinsic merit, but it involves a different endeavor than is at issue in our investigation. Our reflections will assume a somewhat more Kantian design, proceeding in such a manner that the question as to the *possibility* of metaphysics provides the direction. It will also be shown, however, that a questioning more radical than even that of Kant needs to be pursued. Kant accepts the inquiry-standpoint of traditional metaphysics more or less at face value, and within the context of its delivered categorial scheme he seeks to become clear about the possibilities and impossibilities of metaphysics as a special discipline. One might say that Kant accepts the traditional categorial scheme and restructures its applicability. What remains untried, or at best only suggested, in Kant, is the attempt to work one's way back through the traditional mode of inquiry and rostrum of categories to the ontologically imbued world experience which first occasioned the rise of metaphysics.

Before proceeding another step along the way, the project itself, namely that of reflecting on the history of metaphysics, needs to be made thematic. How does such an activity proceed? In what context and against what background does it take place? What occasions its requirement and what conditions determine its possibility? It would seem that the project, from the very beginning, presents one with difficulties of an unsurmountable kind. Is not the subject matter which has been staked out by traditional metaphysicians so variegated in scope and treatment that any assessment of the achievements and failures of the discipline remains an impossible task? Is the history of metaphysics already at an end, making it possible for the owl of Minerva to leave its perch and begin its flight of evaluation? Where does the reflecting thinker himself stand when he reflects on the history of metaphysics? Is not his thinking philosophical heir to the inquiry-standpoint and circumscribed problems delivered to him through the metaphysical tradition, and does this not color his interpretive stance even when he protests against metaphysics? Nietzsche read the history of metaphysics as an infectious growth of the "error of being," but his protest was itself shaped by that against which he protested. His transvaluation of value through an inversion of Plato provides a telling illustration of this. Marx sought to displace metaphysical thought to make room for a philosophy of action, but what emerged in the process was an inverted Hegelianism which resulted in a theoretical edifice of history that had its own peculiar metaphysical pillars. Logical positivism, with its celebrated verification-principle, sought to eliminate metaphysics once and for all, but in the process of elimination a *sub rosa* reductivist metaphysics made its appearance. The standpoints of Nietzsche, Marx, and the logical positivists—initially assumed as standpoints from which to attack metaphysics—were themselves conditioned by the historical destiny of metaphysical thinking that seems to infect all philosophical reflection. It is likely that it was some such state of affairs that Kant had in mind when he remarked that in matters metaphysical one has to do with "a *natural* and *inevitable* illusion," an illusion that is "inseparable from human reason."

The reflective thinker, as he reflects on the history of metaphysics, cannot escape his contextualism. This contextualism, as we saw in the preceding chapter, includes the solicitation of meanings and modes of inquiry by a world of predecessors. The reflective thinker is no more able to dissociate himself from his social past than he is able to dissociate himself from his personal past. The world of philosophical predecessors, with its metaphysical problems, arguments, categories, and systems, is already firmly entrenched when reflection begins. Happily or unfortunately, the discipline of metaphysics is already defined when the question about being is asked. The standpoint of the reflector is historically conditioned. The reflective thinker stands within the history of metaphysics when he begins to inquire about it. The thinker, contextualized as historical existence, is denied the unconditioned freedom to stand outside of the history of metaphysics as he makes judgments about it. However, it does not follow from this that no critical judgments of decisive import can be made. The historical situationality that infects the experienced world, insofar as it is structured by historical time and historical space, has a positive as well as a negative side. Clearly there is something that is negated by it. It negates the infinitude of presuppositionless thought. More concretely, it involves a rejection of the presumption that one can place oneself at the end of history and speak from the standpoint of a nonhistorical, disembodied logos. In reflecting on the history of metaphysics one is already immersed in it. But this inescapable historical situationality, which determines the finitude of the interpreter, has a positive as well as a negative expression. In his finitude the reflective thinker stands open to the discovery and creation of meaning. This is garnered through the recognition of the historical situation being at the same time a *hermeneutical* situation, a situation open to interpretation. In reflecting on the history of metaphysics we thus assume an *interpretive* stance. To interpret means to exercise critical judgment, to understand a text or a doctrine through the projection of untried perspectives of meaning. Not only does interpretation involve the clarification and making intelligible of particular points of metaphysical doctrine, it also involves—and this above all—a penetration to the kinds of questions that the metaphysican asked and the manner in which these questions were formulated. Not only do we need to learn to think Plato's thoughts after him, we need to become clear about the questions that Plato asked; and further we need to become clear about these questions through an imaginative projection of and comparison with alternative questions. Just as in perception one works with the perceived phenomena and develops knowledge of them through an imaginative variation of the constituting profiles, so in historical interpretation one works with the delivered modes of inquiry and varies the interpretive questions. Transcendence, as the power to think beyond any given question and delivered formulation, is at work in every project of interpretation. This transcendence defines the interpretive act as an act of freedom and an act of creativity.

It is thus that the reflective thinker as interpreter is able to loosen up the sedimentations of the tradition of metaphysics and reopen the question about being in such a manner that no particular question or mode of inquiry is accepted as ultimate and normative. Herein resides the critical function of historical interpretation, and it is by virtue of this that the interpreter can stand *in* the history of metaphysics without being *of* it. If indeed the subject-object dichotomy structures the inquiry-standpoint of traditional metaphysics, we can, as Jaspers maintains, think our way beyond the dichotomy while standing within it. We can work our way back to the experiential source from which the dichotomy springs through a patient examination of the conditions that underlie subjectivity and objectivity.

The standpoint of the reflector is thus characterized both by facticity and freedom. The reflection at issue involves interpretation, and interpretation carries with it a context of already delivered presuppositions and modes of inquiry. But the act of interpretation is not determined by these presuppositions and modes of inquiry. The hermeneutical situation is layered with possibility, transcendence, and freedom, which provide the conditions for criticism and imaginative insight. Through the exercise of this criticism and imaginative insight the destiny of metaphysics can be transfigured, its external development as a discipline or an area of knowledge can be critically questioned, and the primordial experience of being which occasioned its rise can be uncovered and brought to light.

[2] METAPHYSICS AND COSMOLOGY

WHAT ARE THE FEATURES of that metaphysics in the history of which the reflective thinker stands as he reflects upon it? It would appear that to embark on an answer to this question would already thrust one between the Scylla of banal generalization on the one hand, and the Charybdis of partiality through omission on the other. Metaphysicians have been known to quarrel with one another, and what emerges in the history of metaphysics is by no means a continuous and undisturbed unfolding of common insights and formulations. Yet the above-mentioned perils might, to a great measure, be avoided if one stays on the path of searching for distinctive and basic inquiry-standpoints and presuppositions, rather than striving for an enumeration of doctrinal details. It is towards a reflection on the inquiry-standpoint of traditional metaphysics that our analysis is geared. And reflections on matters such as these can at best offer tentative suggestions for further and continuing understanding and critical insight.

Our first suggestion is that the project of metaphysics, from Aristotle to Russell, proceeds within a cosmological frame of orientation. Admittedly Aristotle and Russell address themselves to quite different specific problems and emerge with quite different answers to these problems, but in the thought of both there is the effort to give an account of what there is in the universe and what it is like. To do metaphysics, whatever else is included, is to render such an account. Clearly there is a spectrum of boldness and scope in rendering such an account, but the metaphysical program seems to be motivated largely in the interests of providing answers to cosmological inquiries. In the bolder expressions of these interests efforts have been made to use reason so as to deduce or infer the origin of things in the universe and the structure that such a universe must have. The metaphysicians whose claims are less bold tend to settle for regulative principles. But in either case the metaphysical lenses are adjusted so as to yield a view of the universe, either telescopically, to open up a vision of the whole, or microscopically, to lay bare the constitutive elements.

Proceeding from such an inquiry-standpoint and projected program, it is hardly surprising that the history of metaphysics became intertwined with the history of science, and was destined at times to take on the form of a superscience. Metaphysics has often quite freely borrowed methodological procedures and epistemic principles from the special sciences, and there are recurring efforts in the development of the discipline to provide, on the one hand, a synthetic conceptual frame which would unify the sciences, and, on the other hand, a conceptual analysis of their foundations. It is particularly in the development of metaphysics in the modern period that this alliance of metaphysics and science has recurred. But already in classical metaphysics the question about cosmology was intertwined with the question about science, and in answering it a sedimentation of perspectives on being, meaning, and the world developed.

Aristotle had proposed an understanding of being as the most universal of all concepts, subsuming all things in the world as instances of it. Quite literally everything, real or imaginary, actual or merely conceptual, was given some status in being. Being, according to Aristotle, is all-inclusive in scope, transcending even the status of a genus, which is restricted by its exclusion of differences. Being is marked off only by nonbeing, and even nonbeing in the speculations of some metaphysicians (notably Plato) is seen as maintaining some relation with being. Meaning, in the development of metaphysics, came to be allied with the significations of representational thinking and was defined as a property of propositions within a subject-predicate scheme of analysis. The world was understood as the universe of material and formal objects of nature, and this gave rise to the distinction between the material existence of something and the nature or essence which defines it. The attempt to account for the presence of mental activity or mind in such a universe led to the introduction of the subject-object dichotomy as primary and normative.

These approaches to being, meaning, and the world have recurringly accompanied projects aimed at the formulation of a kind of superscience, particularly in modern philosophy.

Descartes, enthralled with the beauty and certainty of mathematics, was astonished that up to his time no firmer metaphysical edifice had been built with the use of the method of mathematics as the touchstone. Our astonishment is of a somewhat different sort than that of Descartes. We are astonished about his uncritical acceptance of the traditional cosmologically oriented approaches to being, meaning, and the world, and about his serene and untroubled faith in the demonstrative unification of the sciences. It is this that we understand as the first feature of traditional metaphysics. Traditional metaphysics in asking the question "What is the universe like?" has assumed a specific standpoint on the issues of being, meaning, and world; it has tended to look to mathematics and the special sciences for help in formulating its methodological principles; and it has moved in the direction of a superscience.

Closely allied with this question and range of interests has been the drive to formulate a system. Metaphysics has been pretty much synonymous with system-building, and has thus exhibited claims for comprehensiveness, completeness, and certainty. Admittedly, there are weaker and bolder applications of the systematic principle, but it would be difficult to identify an approach as metaphysical if no drive to proceed beyond the limitations of point-of-view philosophizing were discernible. Traditional metaphysics displays an inner drive to move beyond the limitations of finite experience and to find a standpoint beyond perspectival knowledge so as to be able to survey the totality of that which is. The history of metaphysics has offered us systems of idealism and realism, supranaturalism and naturalism, mentalism and materialism, and numerous versions of these types. But in all of these types and versions of types the will to formulate a system is present. The proposed goal is to lay bare the structures of being and view them in their totality. Traditional metaphysics, as Kant so clearly saw, displays a yearning to unify all the conditions of experience and thought within an architectonic of cosmological, psychological, and theological ideas. It may well be that the later philosophy of Hegel provides us with the most illustrious instance of this drive toward total unification and completeness. The fundamental project in Hegel's absolute idealism (which may, admittedly, constitute only one strand in Hegel's thought), is that of comprehending or grasping (*begreifen*) the totality of life within a unity of concepts (*Be-*

griffe). In such a project whatever stands outside of this unity of concepts stands outside of reality itself. The rational becomes the real and the real becomes the rational. It was by virtue of such an understanding and use of reason that Hegel was able to formulate a metaphysical system which is undoubtedly one of the more awesome feats of metaphysical speculation in history. As is well-known, it was through an impassioned attack on Hegel's system of idealism that existentialism as a protest movement emerged. Kierkegaard led the attacking forces, and the situation of the nineteenth century produced a distinguished array of field marshals in the persons of Feuerbach, Stirner, the early Marx, and Nietzsche. The story of this anti-Hegelian protest cannot be rehearsed here.[1] Mention of it, however, does provide an occasion for distinguishing systematic analysis from metaphysical system-building. Kierkegaard never tired of harpooning the Hegelian system, and Nietzsche spoke of the "will-to-system" as a disease, but their rejection of Hegel's project did not entail a rejection of systematic analysis. Indeed, at bottom, their elucidations are informed by a rather rigorous systematic analysis of the problem of existence. Their writings, far from being a series of disconnected and sporadic utterances, display an underlying thematic consistency. A philosopher can be systematic in his analysis and elucidation without aspiring to construct a metaphysical system.

A third characteristic feature of the cosmological orientation of traditional metaphysics is the use of argumentation. Metaphysicians have attempted to support their claims about the origin and structure of the universe through some manner of argument. They have not remained content with a recording of insights and an enumeration of isolated claims. Both in metaphysics and in certain varieties of mysticism, comprehensive views of man, the world, and God have been presented; but whereas the mystic, satisfied that the ultimately real is ineffable, takes the path of intuitive insight and evocative description, often making use of poetic imagery, the metaphysician takes the path of argumentation. Admittedly mysticism and metaphysics have at times been synthesized (as in the emanationist sys-

1. For an illuminating discussion of the versions of anti-Hegelianism and their historical roots the reader is referred to Karl Löwith, *Von Hegel zu Nietzsche*, 3rd ed. (Stuttgart: Kohlhammer, 1953).

228 / METAPHYSICS, ONTOLOGY, & WORLD

tem of Plotinus), but an essential distinction between the two would seem to turn on the use or rejection of argumentation. That metaphysicians make use of arguments is readily apparent through even a cursory glance at the history of metaphysics, and may be regarded as nothing more than a truism. Yet the truism becomes philosophically interesting when one asks "What constitutes a metaphysical argument?" It would appear that there is no one thing that answers to this question.

Although every noteworthy metaphysics displays movements from premises to conclusions, gathering argumentative force, there is a wide variance with respect to precision and rigor in these movements. In the metaphysics of Spinoza the arguments are formalized, compact, and conclusive; in the metaphysics of Plato they are less formal and more a matter of suggestion and adumbration. Also there is a variance with respect to the use of inductive and deductive procedures. Although it would appear that traditional metaphysical arguments are neither of an unalloyed inductive nor pure deductive variety, they do tend to assume the form of one or the other. Some metaphysical arguments strongly resemble the inductive form. Aristotle's argument for the existence of the Prime Mover as the ultimate explanation for the fact of motion would appear to be of an inductive type. It must be remembered, however, that for Aristotle induction as a rational inference culminated in the intuition of a necessary and real causal bond, which provided a certainty that would not be acknowledged in contemporary theories of inductive probability. So if induction is understood as providing only a calculus of probability, it could hardly be said that Aristotle's argument, and others like it, are of a pure inductive kind. The force of metaphysical arguments does not rest on considerations of probability and a collection of generalizable facts. The metaphysician is interested in something more necessary and more universal. Yet certain metaphysicians, possibly because of the lure of a possible superscience, have been tempted to employ arguments that are remarkably similar in form to the straightforward inductive inferences found in the special sciences.

But if the metaphysician, as we have suggested, is looking for something more necessary and more universal than can be garnered through the use of inductive inference, then why does he not look to the deductive form of argumentation? It is precisely there, we suggest, that metaphysicians have for the most part looked. More often than not, metaphysics has been a kind of deductive enterprise, working from an axiomatic base. Deductive metaphysics is very much like, but again not the same as, a formal logical system. In a formal logical system one proceeds from a set of axioms which are accepted as being true, at least with respect to their applicability to the particular system at issue. From his axioms, the logician, if he is careful, is able to move to conclusions which *must* be the case and which are *always* the case as long as the axioms are accepted. It is this talk of necessity and universality that is appealing to the deductive metaphysician, and there are systems of deductive metaphysics which have been patterned quite consciously after an axiomatic model. The system of Spinoza is possibly the best example. Yet deductive metaphysics is not the same as a formal logical system. The metaphysician is concerned about the necessity and universality of his axioms as well as his conclusions. But such support for one's axioms cannot be provided by the logical system itself. Hence the metaphysician must seek such support outside the procedures of deductive inferences as such and garner the necessary truth of his axioms in some other way. Descartes, as is well known, appealed to the intuitive self-evidence of the "I think," which according to him was delivered by the pure light of reason alone. Spinoza establishes his axioms by fixing what he considered to be the proper definitions of substance, attribute, and mode. Leibniz lays the foundations with an analysis of unity and diversity. Although each of the deductive metaphysicians may establish his axioms in a different way, they are all striving for a content in their axioms which is necessarily true. The deductive metaphysician is interested not only in the necessity and universality of forms of reasoning, he wishes to have this necessity and universality fit the content. He wants to say something about the world that is necessarily true.

There is yet another type of metaphysics, less deductive by nature, in which argumentation proceeds somewhat differently. One might speak of this type as empiricist metaphysics. Now in speaking of this type, the suggestion might be conveyed that the mode of argumentation is of an empirical kind and hence strictly inductive. But this would be misleading. In the use of the empiricist's argument from perceptual illusion, to make use of a particular example, the basis of the argument is provided through an inspection of visual experience, but the force of the argument does not rest simply with a generalization from collected visual facts. It involves a rather intricate analysis of concepts such as "perception," "illusion," "recognition," and "experience" itself. Yet the argument is not simply of a deductive variety. The conclusion—namely, that sense-data are the ultimates of that which exists—does not follow from the conceptual analysis in the way that conclusions follow from the axioms in a formal system. The conclusions seem to be justified in another manner. All along the empiricist is working with the facts of visual experience, and the concepts which he uses and analyzes and the conclusions drawn from such a use of concepts are validated to the extent that they do not distort the facts of our ordinary visual experience. And insofar as the question of what constitutes ordinary visual experience and the more basic question of what features of experience should be selected as the point of departure appear to remain open-ended, then the claims of an empiricist metaphysics would be significantly more tentative than those offered in a system of deductive metaphysics.

A fourth feature of metaphysics as a cosmological program has to do with the derivation and use of a categorial scheme. Metaphysicians, throughout the colorful history of their discipline, have been intent on setting forth certain very general concepts which have become known as "categories." The number of categories never became definitely fixed because of disagreements among metaphysicians themselves as to precisely how long the list was to be. Aristotle delineated ten such basic concepts as fundamental types of classification, which he believed provided a complete inventory of the definable aspects of any given subject. Kant, working out from an ingenious table of judgments, deduced twelve categories. Hegel, of course, had many, many more. What is of central importance, however, is not the number of categories that any particular philosopher derived or deduced, but the function that these key concepts performed in their philosophical formulations. The two categories that have played more than an innocent role in the history of metaphysics are the categories of *substance* and *causality*. There is indeed a sense in which the history of metaphysics from Aristotle to the present day could be understood as the history of the categories of substance and causality. The substance-attribute distinction became fixed early in the history of metaphysics. Although the varied meanings of "substance" in the philosophy of Aristotle still remains something for textual scholars to puzzle over, it is evident that substance, as the king of the categories, plays a dominant role in Aristotle's definition of first philosophy. Substance provides the classification whereby one identifies the thing in question as the subject of discourse. First we identify any given thing with respect to its substance, in both the primary and secondary sense, and then we can proceed to characterize it in terms of the nine other categories, appropriately called attributes. Of these attributes, that of relation—specifically causal relation—is of singular importance for Aristotle. Through the use of this category we can render intelligible the causal connections between various substances and account for the very existence of finite substances through a causal inference to an Unmoved Mover. It is thus that substance and causality, in a very basic way, become the key general concepts for providing a picture of the universe. The universe is pictured as a composite of finite and eternal substances which are related through causal bonds.

Differences in the tradition as to the understanding and use of substance and causality—e.g., Spinoza *vs.* Aristotle and Leibniz *vs.* Descartes—were differences within the framework of presuppositions that determined traditional metaphysics. Substance and causality, and the categorial scheme more generally, continued to be employed in the service of a preconceived notion of the world as a totality of entities. The main presupposition that remained in force and unquestioned, at least up to the time of Kant, was that not only is metaphysics possible but substance and causality provide the key categories for answering the question "What is there in the universe and how is the universe structured?"

There was no sustained critical inquiry into the possibility of metaphysics and the applicability of its traditional categorial scheme until the time of Kant. So it is with Kant that we come to a decisive stage in our project of reflection on the history of metaphysics. The effects of Kant's "Copernican revolution" continue to register in the philosophical world. These effects are discernible not only in the continuing tradition of transcendental philosophy but also within traditions that have been markedly non-Kantian and non-transcendental in orientation.[2] A legion of post-Kantian attacks on metaphysics have emerged in the nineteenth and twentieth centuries, making various uses of Kant's texts and insights. Of these one of the more vigorous efforts is that of Heidegger, who has proposed (although not carried through) a "destruction" of the history of metaphysics through a new interpretation of Kant. His book *Kant and the Problem of Metaphysics* provides the central themes which were to govern this project of destroying metaphysics. It need, however, be kept in mind that by "destruction" Heidegger does not mean annihilation. It is not that metaphysics, according to Heidegger, is to be annihilated or displaced. Rather the project of destruction involves a process of shaking loose certain sedimented standpoints and categorial schemes that have accrued in the history of metaphysics, in order to disclose a more primordial questioning about being. Now whether Heidegger's interpretation of what Kant *intended* to say but "recoiled" from saying does or does not do violence to the texts of Kant is an issue over which some controversy has already taken place.[3] The third section of Heidegger's book on Kant, in which Kant's recoil is discussed, is clearly the most problematic in Heidegger's interpretation. It was this section which elicited from Ernst Cassirer the rejoinder that here Heidegger no longer speaks as a commentator but rather as a usurper. The pursuit of the complex of issues involved in this debate remains incidental to our present concerns.[4] What is of interest at this juncture is Heidegger's recognition of the need for rethinking and reevaluating the project of metaphysics in light of Kant's critical philosophy so as to reopen the question about being from a new perspective.

2. This is particularly the case with P. F. Strawson's book, *Individuals: An Essay in Descriptive Metaphysics* (London: Methuen, 1959), and it is evident also in many of the essays contributed by leading British philosophers and compiled in D. F. Pears, *The Nature of Metaphysics* (London: Macmillan, 1960). In the latter, see particularly the essays by S. N. Hampshire, "Metaphysical Systems," and G. J. Warnock, "Criticisms of Metaphysics."

3. See particularly Ernst Cassirer's critical review of *Kant und das Problem der Metaphysik* in *Kant-Studien*, vol. XXXVI, nos. 1, 2, (1931).

4. Some of these issues have been explored in an article by the author. See Calvin O. Schrag, "Heidegger and Cassirer on Kant," *Kant-Studien*, LVIII, no. 1 (1967), 87–100.

Before pursuing further the internal critique of metaphysics launched by Kant, and the external critiques that emerged in various post-Kantian developments in scientific and religious thought, another characterizing feature of the nature of metaphysics needs to be considered. This has to do with the traditional link of metaphysics to theology.

[3] METAPHYSICS AND THEOLOGY

CLOSELY ALLIED with the cosmological orientation of traditional metaphysics is what one might call its theological thrust. We will need to discuss whether the connection between metaphysics and theology is an intrinsic or an extrinsic one. There are alleged non-theological varieties of metaphysics and alleged non-metaphysical varieties of theology. The disclaimers of each with respect to the influence of the other will need to be examined. But before this task is undertaken, an attempt at a clarification of the traditional link between theology and metaphysics needs to be made. From the very beginning of metaphysical thinking, as we characterized it in the preceding section, it has at least been expected of metaphysicians to address themselves to the question of the existence and nature of God. The link between theology and metaphysics was already articulated in the philosophy of Plato when he interrogated the relation of his ultimate metaphysical principles—the Good, the Forms, the Psyche, the Receptacle, and God. In book 10 of the dialogue, *The Laws*, Plato adumbrates what has become known as the cosmological argument for the existence of God. But it was primarily Aristotle's *Metaphysics* that solidified metaphysical inquiry with theology. The title of this work was initially a descriptive designation simply characterizing it as the work which followed the *Physics*, but it soon became a designation of the content of "first philosophy" discussed therein. This content consisted of two distinguishable aspects. On the one hand first philosophy was defined as an inquiry into "being qua being" (IV. 1. 1003a. 20); on the other hand it was defined as knowledge of the "most divine being" (XII. 9. 1074b. 16, 27). Metaphysics as a distinct philosophical discipline was given birth and cradled in the ambiguity of this two-fold definition of its central task. In post-Aristotelian developments these two definitions of metaphysics become institutionalized, and in the confrontation of metaphysics with Christian modes of thought in the patristic and medieval periods, Aristotle's second definition of first philosophy moved into the forefront. Metaphysical knowledge found its supreme exemplification in knowledge about God. Metaphysics and theology were synthesized, and the history of metaphysics suffered the destiny of becoming a theo-metaphysics. The pinnacle of metaphysical knowledge was to be found in speculative theology. Admittedly Aristotle's first definition of metaphysics was not displaced, but rather integrated with his second definition and the emerging theological interests (mainly of a Christian variety) into an architectonic of speculative theology, speculative cosmology, and speculative psychology. Within this architectonic the distinction between the terrestrial-human and the celestial-divine, already present in the philosophies of Plato and Aristotle, came to be understood as a distinction between created and uncreated being. This established itself as the fundamental distinction of the philosophy of being, and further solidified the inquiry-standpoint of speculative metaphysics. This conceptual scheme continued to determine the development of metaphysics through the modern and into the contemporary period. The philosophies of Descartes, Spinoza, Leibniz, Hegel, Fichte, Bradley, and Whitehead—to mention only a few who have achieved metaphysical renown—are virtually unintelligible with respect to their comprehensive projects without attention to the distinction between finite-created being and infinite-uncreated being. Clearly, not the same significance is attached to this distinction by each of these metaphysical stalwarts—one needs only compare Spinoza's intrinsic Infinite Substance with Descartes' extrinsic Divine Cause to discern a wide range of modulation in the orchestration of the distinction. Yet, the distinction continues to define for these and other metaphysicians the basic conceptual scheme in the context of which the basic problems of metaphysics are to be pursued. Metaphysics thus continues to proceed from an inquiry-standpoint in which the distinction between created being and uncreated being is in force. The requirement then becomes that of mustering support, through some form of argument, for the existence of uncreated being, as well as that of discovering the conceptual structures of both realms and establishing the peculiar nature of the connection between them. It is thus that the cosmological orientation of metaphysics, with its ideal of a superscience, its drive toward a system, its peculiar use of argumentation, and its employment of a categorial scheme, becomes integrated with a more or less explicit theological design.

That traditional metaphysics in its alignment with speculative theology should undertake the difficult project of supplying arguments for the existence of God would appear to be inevitable. Given the presupposition of a subject-object structure of thought and a view of the universe as a totality of entities, the stage is already set for an attempted demonstration of the existence of God as a supranatural being. The questions as to whether such an enterprise can indeed succeed, what form of logic is employed in the demonstration, or whether such an effort from the "religious standpoint" is irrelevant or indeed blasphemous, are not at issue here. That judgments pertinent to the above issues can, or even should, be made is in no way contested. Rather our interest is in probing the conditions which occasioned the search for demonstrations of the existence of God and investigating within a broader context the inquiry-standpoint and complex of presuppositions that underlie a metaphysics of theism.

The history of metaphysics of theism has offered curiously diversified portraits of God and a variety of ways which lead to knowledge of his existence. Already in the patristic and in the medieval periods two general tendencies had become fixed. On the one hand there was the "ontological approach," developed mainly within the Augustinian-Anselmic tradition; on the other hand there was the "cosmological approach," stemming mainly from the Aristotelian-Thomistic tradition. The peculiar use of terminology in distinguishing these two traditions may confuse as much as clarify; for, according to our interpretation of traditional metaphysics, cosmological and ontological considerations remained interfused. Yet a distinction as to orientation with respect to the two types is discernible. Representatives of the so-called ontological approach—particularly Augustine—were considerably more cautious with respect to their use of metaphysical principles of explanation. Augustine made use of metaphysics in a rather oblique manner. Metaphysics did not provide him with rational demonstrations of the existence of God, but provided, rather, an apologetic context for illuminating and supporting that which was apprehended in the act of religious faith.

Anselm, who continued the Augustinian tradition, in formulating his ontological "proof" for the existence of God made it quite clear the proof is a stage in the process of "faith seeking understanding." In this tradition faith retains its primacy over philosophical reason. The cosmological approach, on the other hand, was from the very beginning much bolder in its use of philosophical reason and metaphysical principles. Representatives of this approach used metaphysics not only as the proper context for the asking and pursuit of theological problems, but as providing the means for the resolution of these problems, involving principally the problem of the existence of God and the problem of the immortality of the soul.[5]

In the development of the metaphysics of theism in modern and contemporary philosophy, the picture became even more diversified. The teleological argument for the existence of God, which in the medieval period tended to be subsumed under the cosmological argument, began to develop as an independent argument and gathered up about it a more or less distinctive theistic approach. Paley and Butler, in the eighteenth century, provided formative influences for this development. But the most articulate spokesman for the teleological approach as a distinct variety of theism was the contemporary British philosophical theologian F. R. Tennant. He sought to provide theism with an explicit empirical basis. The empiricistic theist, according to Tennant, is cognizant of the developments in modern and contemporary science (particularly biology) and makes use of its discoveries. He is urged to remain in dialogue with the special sciences, yet he must not confuse the fundamental projects of science and philosophy. According to Tennant what philosophy needs to account for, in its dialogue with science, is the fact that our world is a *uni*-verse rather than a fortuitous concourse of accidental variations and randomness. He argued that the postulation of a supreme Cosmic Intelligence would explain this general feature of the world, its harmonious interrelations and adaptations, more reasonably and more persuasively than would an appeal to reductive materialism. This was the intent of his

5. For a more detailed discussion of the distinction between the cosmological and ontological approach in the history of the metaphysics of theism the reader is referred to Paul Tillich, "Two Types of Philosophy of Religion," in *Theology of Culture*, ed. Robert C. Kimball (New York: Oxford University Press, 1959), pp. 10–29.

"wider teleological argument," which was wider by virtue of its attempt to account for the general order of nature rather than the particular cases of adaptedness, which he conceded could be explained well enough by the proximate causes supplied by the special sciences. This focus on the general order of nature, rather than on particular instances within it, served to differentiate Tennant's teleological argument from the "narrow" varieties of classical thought.[6]

Another distinctive approach to the existence of God emerged in the developments of modern and contemporary philosophical theology. This approach might be termed the axiological approach, for it revolves around considerations of value. Its unique feature has to do with the effort to construct a moral argument for the existence of God. Admittedly, this approach is not a clear example of theistic metaphysics. It proceeds more specifically out of the context of moral considerations than metaphysical ones. Yet that which emerges is a species of a metaphysics of morals in which a benevolent Deity provides the basis for value experience. The inspiration and underpinnings of this approach were supplied by Kant in his *Critique of Practical Reason.* Specific versions of the argument were later worked out by a variety of nineteenth- and twentieth-century thinkers.[7] In all of these versions the argument proceeds not from the cosmic facts of adaptedness and design, as does the teleological argument, but rather from the facts of moral consciousness and judgments about these facts. The thrust of the argument is to demonstrate the existence of a benevolent Deity, who functions as the ultimate source of the "ought" and as the ground for the objective validity of moral judgments.

The above briefly delineated approaches—ontological, cosmological, teleological, and axiological—comprise the dominant expressions of the metaphysics of theism, from the classical period up to the present. Sundry versions and reformulations of these approaches have appeared in the contemporary literature

6. See particularly his book, *Philosophical Theology,* Vol. II (London: Cambridge University Press, 1930).

7. Two of the more interesting of such versions are those formulated by H. Rashdall and A. E. Taylor. For the relevant discussions of this issue the reader is referred to H. Rashdall, *Philosophy and Religion* (London: Gerald Duckworth, 1909) and A. E. Taylor, *The Faith of a Moralist* (London: Macmillan, 1951).

on philosophy of religion.[8] What interests us in these various approaches is not the question as to the validity or nonvalidity of the different arguments which have been proposed—a question more germane to the special discipline of philosophy of religion —but rather the question concerning the linkage of traditional metaphysics to the theistic program. We have already suggested how the traditional cosmological orientation, with its more or less distinct understanding of the world as a totality of entities, its drive toward the completeness of a system, and its implementation of a categorial scheme, is put into play in the project of theism, defining it as a metaphysics of theism. In particular, the category of "existence," one of the more troublesome categories in the history of metaphysics, figures rather decisively. Clarity as to what it means to say that God exists is not always forthcoming in the formulations of the traditional approaches. The use of the categories of possibility and necessity is very much in evidence in the ontological proof, particularly in its more formalized aspect; and without the category of causality the cosmological argument remains unintelligible. But it would seem that of even greater significance for the metaphysics of theism than the implementation of a certain categorial scheme is the stance that it assumes with respect to the meaning of world. Kant did well to probe the issue concerning the meaning and use of the category of existence in the metaphysician's theological designs (or the theologian's metaphysical designs), but surprisingly he left the issue of the meaning of world undisturbed. He was content to show that the use of the idea of God to complete the unification of the objective and subjective conditions of experience could lead only to regulative principles and never to constitutive knowledge. But Kant's interpretation and criticism of this use of the idea of God was still conditioned by a cosmological inquiry-standpoint, as is evidenced by the questions which underlie the

8. To mention only a few, Charles Hartshorne has reformulated the ontological proof within the context of his pantheism (*Vision of God* [New York: Harper, 1941]); Jacques Maritain (*Degrees of Knowledge,* trans. G. B. Phelon [New York: Scribner's, 1959]) and Fernand van Steenberghen (*Ontologie,* [Louvain: Nauwelaerts, 1946]) have reformulated the classical cosmological argument in light of modern and contemporary criticisms of it; and P. Bertocci has reconstructed the wider teleological argument and integrated it with the moral argument (*Introduction to the Philosophy of Religion* [New York: Prentice-Hall, 1951]).

fourth antinomy. The meaning of "world" in the God-world distinction of the metaphysics of theism is determined by the view of the world as a totality of entities within an extensive continuum. Not only does speculative theology inherit a table of institutionalized metaphysical categories, it also takes over a derived and abstracted view of the world. Assuredly there are suggestions in Kant's philosophy, particularly as one moves to his second *Critique*, that other versions of the world are possible, but it would seem that the meaning of world in the designs of theistic metaphysics is never focused on by Kant as an explicit theme.

We would now suggest that this same inquiry-standpoint which lies behind the program of theistic metaphysics, in its manifold expression, has informed some of the more illustrious nontheistic varieties of metaphysics. Metaphysical naturalism and metaphysical materialism, as spokesmen for the autonomy and self-sufficiency of the finite realms of being, have repeatedly raised their defiant heads in the development of Western philosophy. Yet these metaphysical programs appear to share the same concept of world and categorial scheme as that implemented by theistic metaphysics. The naturalist and the materialist simply propose a different use and application of the categories and carry through a program of reductionism by virtue of which entities in the world (and the world continues to be viewed as a totality of entities) are pruned of their supranatural reference and signification. But in carrying out these programs of reductionism, naturalism and materialism define themselves largely through a protest against theistic metaphysics. Nontheistic metaphysics thus achieves the determination of its nature by making use of that against which it protests. This is most decisively illustrated in the program of Marxian materialism, which took over many of the governing insights and categories of Hegel's theo-metaphysics in protesting against it. Thus although it could not be said that theology is an essential feature of metaphysics, it would seem that both the theistic and nontheistic varieties of metaphysics are shaped through a dialectical interplay within a common framework of presuppositions and a common inquiry-standpoint.

It would thus appear that metaphysicians have not only been expected to ask theological questions, but in many cases they have defined their basic conceptual frames of reference in terms of theological distinctions and notions. And even in the protest of metaphysicians against such distinctions and notions, the result seems to be a program which is itself shaped by them, leading to a kind of secularized theo-metaphysics. Correspondingly, it has been expected of theologians to ask metaphysical questions, and often theologians have invested a great deal of capital in the metaphysical enterprise. For the most part, traditional theology has been willing to assume the risks of this investment and has moved rather boldly in the direction of a metaphysics of theism. Yet it is evident that theology has not always been willing to align itself so comfortably with metaphysics, and, as we shall see in the following section, some rather far-reaching suspicions as to the handmaiden services of metaphysics have arisen in modern and contemporary developments of theological and religious thought.

[4] SKEPTICISM AND CRITICISM

IT IS PERHAPS INEVITABLE that every bold application of a conceptual scheme and every emphatic affirmation of some belief or mode of life should be followed by a reaction of skepticism. This would appear to be the case both in man's cultural and in his personal history. It happened during the period of the widespread political and cultural change that determined the transition from Hellenic to Hellenistic civilization. With the rise of universal empires the Greek city-states lost their autonomy. Greek cultural life expanded and reached out to those who were not of Greek origin, bringing into question the traditional importance of the distinction between Greek and barbarian. Religious cults from Egypt and Asia Minor were introduced into the Greek-speaking world; barbarian scholars made their presence felt; questions about the validity of the conceptual schemes of Plato and Aristotle were asked. All this conspired to produce what Gilbert Murray has so aptly characterized as a widespread "failure of nerve." [9] Doubt erupted and what had heretofore been considered as stable political theories, secure religious beliefs, and trustworthy conceptual schemes, were confronted with a

9. *Five Stages of Greek Religion* (New York: Doubleday Anchor, 1951).

skeptical reaction. A similar pattern of development seems to be evident in the history of personal consciousness. An emphatic affirmation of some ideational content or moral imperative succumbs to the threat of doubt. The intellectual development of Augustine affords a marvelous illustration of the emergence of skepticism in the wake of uncontested certitude. Admittedly this doubt may remain latent, to which the prevalence of dogmatism and fanaticism testify, but at any moment in the life of one's culture and in one's personal history it can become manifest. Indeed, it would seem that doubt is an essential condition for wonder and reflection, and hence for the spirit of philosophical inquiry itself. This doubt can become the basis for the establishment of a distinct school of thought, as occurred in ancient Greece at the hands of Pyrrho of Elis; or it can receive expression as an attitude or a stance operative within a variety of philosophical positions. In both cases something about the human condition and something about the nature of philosophy itself is revealed. The emergence of doubt points to the finitude that pervades human experience and suggests that philosophy cannot surmount its open-ended and perspectival character. The interrelated finitude of human existence and perspectivity of philosophy resist the coming to rest of any conceptual project in final and fixed formulations.

The phenomenon of doubt, which underlies both skepticism as a philosophical program and an attitude, itself needs to be made the topic of philosophical investigation. Reflection on doubt as the chief ingredient of skepticism is required. Two distinct, although not unrelated, expressions of doubt are discernible. First to be distinguished is what one might call methodological doubt. Methodological doubt is a movement within theoretical consciousness and representational thought. Presupposing the subject-object dichotomy, it places into question both the sense and reference of any object of consciousness. The sense of an idea, the validity of a theoretical judgment, or the referent of a sensory perception can be questioned in the movement of methodological doubt and a search for verification undertaken. Descartes and Hume, in differing degrees of intensity, have provided us with illustrations of methodological doubt. Descartes, in the implementation of his procedure of systematic doubt, attempted to suspend the whole ideational structure of preceding philosophy so as to arrive at a foundation from which one might build anew. A rather sizeable amount of this idea-tional structure, however, was reintroduced as Descartes' sys-tem-building proceeded. Hume's methodological axe, on the other hand, had a sharper edge, cut deeper, and left considerably less for philosophers to reflect about. But in both cases the species of doubt exercised was similar. Doubt, for both philoso-phers, was a movement within representational thinking, determined by the subject-object dichotomy, geared to the establishment of apodicticity in the interests of founding an adequate theory of knowledge.

Existential doubt is the second type of doubt to be distin-guished. It is broader in its scope and located more primordially within the structure of experience. Historically, existential doubt is illustrated by Pascal rather than by Descartes. Existential doubt infects not only the movement of representational thought, calling into question the noetic meanings therein in-tended. It pervades the whole structure and dynamics of experi-ence and threatens the intentional structure of felt and willed meanings as well as noetic meanings. Existential doubt reaches into every region of world-experience and radically questions the meaning of life itself. The question in existential doubt is not what type or criterion of meaning is adequate for a specific form of theoretical knowing, but rather whether one's being-in-the-world can share in any meaning whatsoever. Not only one's theoretical projects, but one's practical life and one's total exist-ence is rendered problematic. The extreme expression of this existential doubt occurs in the experience of despair and the world view which accompanies it is that of nihilism.[10]

Criticism, although related to skepticism and dependent upon it for the conceptual dismantling and existential disquietude occasioned by doubt, nonetheless moves beyond it. Criticism is the effort to explore new conceptual territory and experi-ment with different styles of life in light of the disturbances of doubt. Critical philosophy, as Kant had already made explicit, is that philosophy which moves beyond skepticism while stopping

10. Albert Camus has provided a striking elucidation of the phenomenon of despair as it relates to the question of nihilism in *The Myth of Sisyphus* (London: Hamish Hamilton, 1955). Camus places nihilism into the center of philosophical concern and proposes that "there is but one truly serious philosophical problem and this is suicide" (p. 11).

short of dogmatism. Criticism strives for elucidation and meaning, seeking not so much to displace skepticism as to appropriate it in a positive way. The method of systematic doubt needs to be performed time and again, and all theoretical judgments need to be made to testify at its bar. Correspondingly, the ineradicable reality of existential doubt needs to be acknowledged, its pervasive character courageously faced, and a style of life assumed in which it is taken over in projects of decisive self- and world-affirmation. The critical stance thus becomes a precondition both for the truths of representational thought and for that mode of existence through which the threat of nihilism is overcome.

It is this critical stance which we assume in our reflection on and assessment of the history of metaphysics. Kant and Nietzsche are of particular importance for our project for in different and yet correlative ways they attack metaphysics from within and provide *internal* critiques of it. Kant's critical considerations move out from an examination of pure reason as the pinnacle of representational or objective thought. Nietzsche's critique of metaphysics is nourished by a passion to combat the threat of nihilism to which traditional metaphysics itself had contributed.

Kant's internal critique of metaphysics takes the form of a demonstration of how the very project of metaphysics leads to presumptive claims which cannot be justified by a finite knower. Human reason, he argues, is so enmeshed in its own finitude that any attempt to unify the totality of experience through the formulation of a superscience simply breaks down. Kant's attack at the same time calls into question the main features of traditional metaphysics, its superscientific character, claim for a system of all-inclusive knowledge, mode of argumentation, use of the categorial scheme, and liaison with theology. More specifically, Kant undertakes in his first *Critique* to show that pure reason—in its effort to found constitutive principles of speculative psychology, speculative cosmology, and speculative theology —loses its way in a maze of paralogisms, antinomies, and transcendental illusions. The root difficulty, according to Kant, lies in the misapplication of the categorial scheme. In traditional metaphysics a greater burden was placed on the categories than they could manageably carry. As long as the finite knower is content to apply the categories to the world of phenomena he is able to achieve knowledge, but when the categories are applied to a world beyond the phenomena then concepts become empty and argumentation becomes specious. Reason in the service of metaphysics is thus rendered problematic and its aspirations are condemned to difficulties which remain unsurmountable. Determined by its ineradicable finitude, reason is unable to supply constitutive and rationally compelling knowledge of a substantial and immortal soul, a unified cosmos, or a transcendent God. It is thus that both aspects of traditional metaphysics—knowledge of being qua being and knowledge of the most divine being—are undermined by Kant's critical reflections.

Nietzsche wages his attack on metaphysics from another front. The "error of being" resides not so much in an illegitimate use of a categorial scheme as it does in the stultification and devitalization of human existence through the imposition of a metaphysics of virtue and vice. Through this imposition man's vitality is cut off and his drive toward creativity thwarted. Nietzsche's interests, from the start, are ethical in character, and it is from this standpoint that his critique of metaphysics is undertaken. He is led by virtue of his ethical interests to define the fundamental problem of philosophy as that of nihilism, and he undertakes the task of indicting metaphysics not so much for failing to solve the problem but for veritably contributing to its rise. The problem of nihilism arises, according to Nietzsche, principally through an institutionalization of a supersensible realm which is then set over against the sensible. Whereas the project of Kant was to show that our finite knowledge is not adequate for an apprehension of the supersensible, Nietzsche was concerned to show that the very notion of a supersensible realm, expressed in the form of a Christianized Platonic metaphysics, has its origins in the distorted projections of a bad conscience. It is well known that out of this violent attack by Nietzsche on traditional theo-metaphysics there arose a species of inverted voluntaristic metaphysics, which indicates that Nietzsche's critique still moved partly within the presuppositional scheme of metaphysics itself. In the last analysis Nietzsche still fights metaphysics with metaphysics. Although he stands at the end of traditional theo-metaphysics, he was unable to overcome its determining inquiry-standpoint.

The internal critiques of metaphysics, illustrated in the philosophies of Kant and Nietzsche, helped spark the external critiques of metaphysics by science and religion. Science, in its self-conscious coming of age, took over theories of explanation that once bore the copyright marks of metaphysics. Metaphysical causality was transposed into the language of the special sciences and operationally defined. Scientific explanation took over, reformulated the canons of induction and inference, and settled for knowledge about useful probabilities while remaining silent about issues of ultimate explanations. This development in the investigations of the methodology of the special sciences, far from being viewed as an "encroachment," needs rather to be understood in light of its purifying function. It has pruned away certain empty metaphysical categories and vacuous theories of explanation which explained the facts badly, or as was more often the case, explained nothing at all. In defining its own domain and clarifying its methodology science was able to mark out its distinction from philosophy, strive for autonomy, and thus undermine the attempt on the part of traditional metaphysics to erect a superscience with quasi-scientific methods and principles. Admittedly, sporadic efforts to found a new "scientific philosophy," occasioned by the liberation of science from metaphysics, were carried through. This was the case in the early stages of the development of logical positivism. But the result of this particular effort was the inauguration of a program of *scientism* which simply took over a new set of metaphysical commitments, proffered an exhaustive classification of types of meaningful discourse, projected a unification of all the sciences, and made dogmatic knowledge-claims not unlike those expressed within traditional metaphysics. In seeking to eliminate traditional metaphysics by casting it out of the door, a *sub rosa* metaphysics in the form of scientism reentered by way of the window. Scientism, however, is not a necessary implication of the drive toward autonomy on the part of the special sciences. Awareness of methodological presuppositions and clarity as to methodological procedures in any particular science can be won without commitment to problematic conceptual schemes which purport to unify the sciences as an exhaustive body of absolute knowledge.

The external critique of metaphysics stemming from developments in modern science was paralleled by a corresponding critique voiced within religion. Particularly in the history of Protestant theology from Adolf von Harnack to Karl Barth, a disenchantment with the theo-metaphysical structure of pre-

Kantian thought is discernible. Clearly the program of liberal theology which Harnack inaugurated, culminating in an attack on the appropriation of Greek metaphysics to substantiate theological claims, is of a quite different cloth than the Biblically oriented neo-Reformation theology of Barth. Harnack was led to a virtual displacement of theology by ethics; Barth returns to the theology of the "Word of God" and the Christological accent that undergirded the theological interpretations by Luther and Calvin. However, a break with the traditional metaphysics of theism is readily discernible in both of these theological expressions and may even be said to constitute a distinctive feature of Protestant theology itself. So within religion itself a protest against the liaison of theology with metaphysics, if not against metaphysics itself, has been registered. Religion, becoming more and more suspect of its self-styled helper and more skeptical about the status of theology as the "queen of the sciences," began to look for its justification either in ethical commitments or self-authenticating revelation. Religion, like science, began its fight for independence from traditional metaphysics, and with this revolt a particular feature of traditional metaphysical thought was rendered problematic.

Our reflections on the ventures of some of the metaphysician's most ardent critics force us to ask again the question of the possible ground of metaphysics. Not only does the history of metaphysics need to be interpreted and assessed time and again, but the question about being, which purportedly occasioned the rise of metaphysics, needs to be reopened so that one can become clear as to the kind of question it is. The arguments of the critics need also to be brought under scrutiny and the alternatives which they propose examined. However penetrating and incisive Kant's attack on traditional metaphysics might have been, it will hardly do to simply accept his conclusions as definitive and final and consider the question about the possibility of metaphysics irrevocably closed. This would yield little more than a reactive absolutism which would no longer be cognizant of the fractures and frailties of human reason to which Kant himself so forcefully called our attention. But of even greater interest and relevance to our concluding task is the alternative to metaphysical speculation which Kant sketched. Kant's critique, as we have already suggested, moved within the inquiry-standpoint of traditional metaphysics. There is a sense in which Kant attacked metaphysics with metaphysics, as Feuerbach attacked theology with theology. Feuerbach attacked the supranaturalism of theism in the name of "atheistic theology"; Kant's critique of traditional deductive and dogmatic metaphysics, in the final analysis, was predicated on a "metaphysics of experience," in which the proper uses and limits of reason, which traditional metaphysics failed to acknowledge, were to be defined.

The positive fruits of Kant's critical labors cluster around the suggestion that metaphysics is possible only as a metaphysics of experience. It is precisely at this point that both the greatness and weakness of Kant's program is discernible. The summons which his program issues to return to experience and the warning about possible pitfalls that await us when we try to step outside of this experience, are to be heeded. Any "future" metaphysics proceeds at its peril if Kant's critical questions are suppressed. Clearly this does not mean that the doctrinal details of his *Critique of Pure Reason* must be accepted as incorrigible, but in assessing any particular metaphysical endeavor, the critical question as to the possibility of metaphysics needs to be re-asked and followed through in depth. This means that Kant's suggestion of an alternative and minimal kind of metaphysics itself needs to be assessed and reinvestigated from bottom up. Kant's metaphysics of experience would seem to have its own peculiar defects, having to do principally with the fact that it is still a "metaphysics," founded on a still too restricted and narrow view of "experience." It is still a metaphysics because it projects as possible a complete and final characterization of the absolutely fundamental features of any possible human experience. Kant's metaphysics of experience still employs a traditional categorial scheme, which is proposed as being exhaustive and necessary for an understanding of any and every given portion of experience. Admittedly, there is for Kant no such necessary and universal knowledge of the thing-in-itself, but there is such knowledge of the phenomenal or experienced world. It is, however, problematic as to whether the table of judgments from which he derives his categorial scheme is as general and complete as he assumed. Clearly there are forms of ordinary speech, which articulate manifold meanings within everyday experience that do not fall under the neat classification that Kant supplied. Kant, like metaphysicians of old, was still deceived by the beauty of formalization, particularly that bent on providing a delineation of the conditions for objective knowledge of nature. The disposition toward the inclusiveness of a system (although admittedly of an immanental sort) and the use of definitive categories, characteristic of traditional metaphysics, still remain much in evidence in Kant's metaphysics of experience. Kant, in the end, provides only a narrowing of the range of metaphysical thinking and an attenuation of its traditional presumptive claims rather than a fundamental reassessment of its inquiry-standpoint relative to possible new approaches to being, meaning, and world.[11]

The theory of experience which accompanies Kant's minimal metaphysics, we have already suggested, is saddled with certain confining determinations. There is first of all the restriction imposed on experience by virtue of its subordination to an epistemological role. Kant elaborates his view of experience, particularly with regard to its perceptual mode, in the interests of locating a secure foundation for a theory of objective knowledge of nature. Used for purposes such as these, it was unavoidable that Kant should give primacy to the subject-object structure of experience. That such a structure of experience, at least on one level of analysis, is unavoidable remains uncontested. But we have shown in our explorations in Part I that one can rechart the map of experience in such a manner that the subject-object structure is seen as secondary and derivative. Also to be questioned is Kant's understanding of perceptual experience as the reception of inert and nontendential sensory qualities. Kant never arrives at an intentional view of consciousness. On this point his indebtedness to the tradition of British empiricism is clearly visible. He more or less takes over the empiricist's granular theory of perceptual experience as a serial succession of sensations. Given such a view on sensation and perception, it is not surprising that Kant is led to define his categories as transcendental concepts which provide perceptual experience with conceptual understanding. What is not recognized by Kant is that, all along, experience—by virtue of its sentient, volitional, and noetic intentionality and its gestaltist structure—is able to see, feel, will, and comprehend the world.

11. Even if Heidegger's interpretation of Kant, with its claim that Kant was struggling to work his way through metaphysics to a fundamental ontology, is accepted, the fact remains that Kant nowhere develops or even sketches the main features of such an ontology.

The remaining task which lies before us is that of reassessing the positive and constructive results that follow from a critique of traditional metaphysics. This will lead us to a sketch of a possible ontology of experience, proceeding from our previous analysis of the dynamics and structure of experience in such a manner that new perspectives on being, existence, and world will be suggested.

8 / Toward an Ontology of Experience

> *Insofar as a thinker sets out to experience the ground of metaphysics, insofar as his thinking attempts to recall the truth of Being instead of merely representing beings as beings, his thinking has in a peculiar sense already left metaphysics.*
> —Martin Heidegger, *The Way Back into the Ground of Metaphysics*

[1] MOVING BEYOND METAPHYSICS

THE DESIGN OF THIS CONCLUDING CHAPTER is to sketch the characterizing features of a possible ontology of experience. This chapter, and indeed the whole of Part III, should properly be understood as a proposal of prolegomena for a future ontology. It is both a project of prefatory elucidations and an invitation to further investigation of the ontological features of experience. These prolegomena, unlike those of Kant, are geared not towards a future metaphysics, in which the traditional cosmological categories remain in force with limited applicability; rather, they are geared towards a future ontology in which organizing notions of lived-through world experience take precedence over traditional cosmological categories. This will entail not so much an elimination of traditional metaphysical questions and categories as a relocation of them within a broader philosophy of experience.

[250]

Our prolegomenon initiates a movement toward an ontology of experience. This movement *toward* ontology is at the same time a movement *beyond* metaphysics. The underlying and governing distinction in such a program is that between ontology and metaphysics, and the first requirement is to achieve clarification as to what it is that is being distinguished. To a very great extent the crux of the distinction turns on what we have spoken of as the cosmological orientation of traditional metaphysics, which carries with it a particular viewpoint regarding the world as a totality of entities neatly parceled into material and mental kinds. Metaphysics thus becomes, as Heidegger has correctly seen, an inquiry into beings as beings, with an eye to discerning their peculiar natures and relationships. Metaphysics, properly speaking, is an inquiry which "comes after" the inquiry into *physis* or nature and provides a capstone for it. Metaphysics investigates the same realm of beings as does a philosophy of nature, but it approaches this realm in the interests of delineating the more general features, universal structures, and causal connections pertinent to the beings at issue. It should be made clear, however, that *physis* as understood by Aristotle, was not restricted to "physical nature" in the modern understanding of it. *Physis* as the "self-emerging of what is" included mental as well as physical phenomena. At this juncture the Cartesian dichotomy of *res cogitans* and *res extensa* had not yet become institutionalized; but already among the ancients the philosophical focus of attention was on beings as components of a totality, and an effort was made to derive the abstractable determinations of these beings and locate their range and connections. It was thus that being was understood as the most abstract and most universal of all concepts, overriding all differentiations. The meaning and use of ontology which we propose undergoes a shift of focus of attention from the abstractable qualities and structures of beings, viewed in their totality, to a concrete experience of being-in-the-world which antedates any speculation about the natures and relations of objectifiable entities. Ontology comes *before* rather than *after* the investigation of the realm of *physis*. As we propose its use in an ontology of experience, ontology is *ta pro ta physica* rather than *ta meta ta physica*.

This shift from abstractable qualities and relations to concrete experience is accompanied by a new approach to the meaning of world, and it is this approach which provides the distinctive inquiry-standpoint for our ontology of experience. World is no longer conceived as a universe of entities, a totality of physical and mental beings with their generic and transcendentalist traits. By world we mean a contextual posturing of experience vitalized with concern, illustrated, for example, in the speech of everyday life when one speaks of the "business world," the "political world," and the "academic world." World is where man's concerns are. These concerns achieve multiple expressions and vary with human existence itself. That which is indicated by the notion of world never comes to rest as a definable object or totality of objects. It is always on the way insofar as the human concerns and involvements which vitalize it and determine it as a *life-world* are always on the way. The variegated expressions of these concerns prohibits the use of the expression *"the* world" to refer to a substantive reality. Our account of world is an account of worlds in the plural. There are many regions of concern, and each particular region is bounded by the actuality and possibility of other regions. Each region is thus surrounded by an indeterminate horizon that encompasses other possible configurations of world-engagement. The locution, *"the* world," may be suitable as an indicator of this awareness of a surrounding, indeterminate horizon. But it must be kept in mind that "the world" has no substantive reference, nor is it simply an abstraction from the phenomena of worlds in the plural. It indicates a texture of experience in which the intentionality within any particular region of concern points beyond the constitutive elements of the region to a horizon of indeterminate and possible perspectives.

A phenomenological elucidation of the sense of world at issue here was already carried through in Chapter 1. Our present task is that of explicating its ontological relevance and distinguishing it from the metaphysical sense of world as a totality of beings. It is through the use of the above-delineated sense of world, as a region of human concern, that we are able to locate the distinctive inquiry-standpoint on which an ontology of experience stands. This inquiry-standpoint is able to disclose the correlation of being and world. The experience of being is coeval with the experience of world. That which comes to presence in the first flush of experience is the phenomenal complex of being-in-the-world. The peculiar task of ontological analysis is that of explicating this phenomenal complex. Thus ontology, of the type that we are suggesting, marks itself off from traditional metaphysics not only by relocating the inquiry-standpoint so that the experience of world as a region of concern is given primacy but also by abandoning the quest for a supranatural world behind the natural world. The abandonment of supranaturalism, however, does not result in a commitment to the equally dubious program of naturalism. An ontology of experience is indeed an ontology of immanence, but not an immanence of a metaphysical-reductionist variety. It is an ontology of immanence in that it proceeds within the structures of finitude that determine the human grasp of reality. The traditional metaphysical distinction between immanence and transcendence—involving a separation into realms, each with its peculiar entities—is suspended. Neither "this world" nor a possible "other world" is conceptualized as a totality and ordination of entities.

Our ontology of experience, however, differs not only from traditional metaphysics but from a post-Kantian "metaphysics of experience" as well. To make this differentiation clear, further considerations need to be put into play. A crucial consideration at this point has to do with the historical character of world experience. We have already given attention to historical understanding in our discussion of the intentionality of hermeneutical thinking and to the phenomenon of historical existence in our discussion of the contextualized experiencer. Hence, the problematic of the historical has already been brought to light, but its direct relevance to our present task of sketching prolegomena for a future ontology of experience still needs to be explicated.

Since the time of Hegel it has become fashionable to contrast "metaphysical approaches" with "historical approaches." The emergence of this contrast and the accompanying dichotomy of nature and history may well have been inevitable, given the inquiry-standpoint of traditional metaphysics. Given a cosmological frame of reference as somehow normative, it is exceedingly difficult to take historical consciousness and the meaning structures of the wider socio-historical world seriously without reducing them to expressions of a cosmic scheme of things. It was because of this inability of metaphysics to deal with the meanings in man's historical existence that historicism emerged as a protest movement. The proponents of historicism sought to interpret both history and nature in terms of historical rather than cosmological concepts. But historicism in its return to man as the *subject* of history still remained within the subject-object framework of thought, and it introduced a relativism and a subjectivism which was more the result of its protestations than of a careful and patient examination of historical phenomena.

An ontology of experience, in its return to the concrete life-world, seeks to provide an account of the historical meanings in world-experience. Both traditional metaphysics and Kant's metaphysics of experience were impoverished to do so. This was due mainly to the fixity and closed character of their categorial schemes, which in both cases were formulated from the standpoint of considerations that took their rise from a philosophy of nature. In traditional metaphysics such a scheme was formulated in the interests of establishing a superscience that would yield knowledge of both finite and nonfinite substance; in Kant's metaphysics of experience the scheme was employed so as to provide a grounding of the necessary conditions for finite knowledge. Admittedly, the possibility of such a Kantian metaphysics of experience is here acknowledged, if not in the form that Kant's categories prescribe, possibly in some other form. It is not at all our task to deny such a minimal metaphysics, aware of the factors of finitude and the limited applicability of the categorial scheme. We are suggesting, however, that such a project would remain subordinate to an ontology of experience which would first be able to account for the primordial experience of being-in-the-world in such a manner that man's involvement with nature and history are seen as nonreducible perspectives. Such an ontology requires the reformulation of categorial functions so as to make room for organizing notions which are more consonant with the originary experience of both nature and history.

Our difficulty with Kant's philosophy has to do not with his attack on deductive metaphysics and its effort to deduce by pure reason principles which would explain the origin of entities and the structure of the universe. His arguments against such a program would seem to be well founded. Clearly, as Kant pointed out, there is a limit to the applicability of cosmological categories, and traditional metaphysics, it would seem, was prone to overstep this limit. But there is also a limitation in Kant's listing and use of categories. They seem not to be found operative within the actual context of human life and historical world-experience. They seem to be useful only for an investigation of the indispensable conditions for objective knowledge of nature; and even here Kant may still have been too obsessed with the ideal of completeness. Admittedly certain key concepts are required for an understanding of the natural world, but why only twelve? And why the particular twelve that Kant deduced? [1]

The fundamental limitation of Kant's metaphysics of experience, however, resides within the very nature of his project. His project remains a project of metaphysics, a project which follows "the physics" and assumes an inquiry-standpoint commensurate with the designs of representational thinking and objectifiable knowledge. An ontology of experience relocates the inquiry-standpoint within the life-world and searches for organizing notions which are operative in the contextuality of human experience. Heidegger has made an effort to delineate such notions in his doctrine of "existentials," which he differentiates sharply from "categories." [2] This distinction may have been drawn too sharply, inviting a bifurcation of human existence and objective nature on another level. But an effort such as Heidegger's possesses its intrinsic merit and points the way to a new and fresh approach to the elucidation of experience through "pre-objective" notions. It provides an invitation to think beyond the stock categories of both traditional metaphysics and traditional psychology.

These organizing notions cannot be specified in advance. They emerge in the actualization of concrete experience and are

1. The difficulty in Kant's doctrine of the categories would seem to be twofold. The claim for completeness in his logical table of judgments, which directs the delineation of his *a priori* concepts or categories, remains problematic. To justify his categorial scheme, Kant must first represent the varied operations of judging in general and the corresponding varied functions of the understanding which accompany judgment. He attempts this in his logical table of judgments which is proffered as a *complete* table. But he fails to provide justification as to why the table of judgments is to be ordered in the way that it is or even why twelve, and only twelve, types of judgment are permissible. Even more problematic is the underlying assumption in Kant's doctrine of the categories that meaning (and categories for Kant are the source of meaning) is derived only through judgmental operation. Meaning is already operative in the ordinary usage of commands, interrogations, and exclamations which fall outside of a table of judgments strictly defined. The basis for conceptualization would thus seem to be broader than Kant's table of judgments would allow. Had Kant recognized this he would have been able to allow for a more open-textured employment of his categorial scheme.

2. *Sein und Zeit* (Tübingen: Max Niemeyer, 1953), p. 44.

disclosed as structures of this actualization. As such they are capable of elucidating the concrete history of human experience in a way in which the traditional metaphysical categories failed to do. There is no exhaustive list of such organizing notions, nor are there *a priori* rules for their application. Their application and meaning varies with the configurations of world experience. The meaning of freedom is different for the understanding of a political revolt than it is for an understanding of a liberation from compulsive neurosis. Alienation, creativity, anxiety, guilt, hope, and resolve—to mention only some of the governing notions in an ontology of experience—are subject to a variation of intentional meaning as experience moves from one configuration to another. Whereas the categories of traditional metaphysics are fixed and complete, the organizing notions of an ontology of experience are fluid and open-ended.

A peculiar characteristic of these organizing notions is that they stand on the hither side of the distinction between concepts and percepts, intellection and sensation, at least as these distinctions are commonly employed. Organizing notions are not subsumptive concepts nor are they categories or transcendental concepts which are, *a priori*, resident within the mind. They evolve with the dynamic development of world experience and are constituted through the interplay of the various presentative acts as these acts respond to the solicitations of figure and background. In the interplay of these presentative acts perception, imagination, memory, volition, desire, and conception are already at work, but not in such a manner that they appear as isolated movements of the mind. Perceptions are infected with volitions; imagination is at work in remembering, and it directs the formation of concepts; and concepts remain vacuous if separated from the structure of perception. The organizing notions at issue arise only within this intercalating movement of the various presentative acts that determine the experience of having a world, and it is to this experience that these notions need to return time and again for their validation. The justification of an organizing notion resides in its success in elucidating the actual context of human life.

These notions are neither objectifying nor subjectifying. They perform their job independently of any separation of experience into objective and subjective poles. Admittedly such a polarity is illustrated in the development of experience, but it remains a distinction within experience. What is denied is the metaphysical status which commonly attaches to this distinction, whereby reality is sectioned into an interior or subjective sphere on the one hand, and an exterior or objective sphere on the other. That which is intended by anxiety, for example, is not an object; nor is anxiety an encapsulated mood within a sphere of interiority. Anxiety is the experience of *being-in* a condition or state of affairs in which presentative acts and solicitations are consummately reciprocal. Anxiety as an organizing notion elucidates this consummate reciprocity in the configurative development of world experience.

Yet, despite their fluid and open-ended character, the organizing notions of experience are not arbitrary or free floating. They are rooted in a common center. This common center is not the transcendental ego of the philosophy of Kant, which synthesizes the operations of perception, imagination, and conception; nor is it the transcendental ego of the philosophy of Husserl, which functions as the ultimate source of intentional consciousness. Indeed, it is no transcendental ego at all, the use of which we have already at numerous times found to be acutely limited. The common center, as we have seen in Part II, is the experiencer contextualized by virtue of his embodiment, speech, and sociality. And although the issue of the unification of these contexts has been implied in the preceding discussions, it has not been explicitly focused. These contexts, we suggest, are unified in "existence," and it is this which functions as the source of the interpretive notions which organize experience. It is at this juncture that existentialism—understood as a philosophy of *Existenz*—and our philosophy of experience merge. In order to distinguish our use of "existence" from its use as a traditional metaphysical category, we will employ the already familiar terminology of *Existenz*. The meaning and ontological weight of *Existenz*, as the common center in which organizing notions are rooted, will hence need to be discussed next.

[2] SUBSTANCE, SUBJECT, AND EXISTENZ

THE TASK WHICH WE HAVE INHERITED from our discussion in the preceding section is that of carrying through an elucidation of the use and meaning of *Existenz*. *Existenz*, we propose, provides the unification of the embodiment, speech, and sociality of the contextualized experiencer. In our ontology of experience this *Existenz* functions as the source or ground of those organizing and interpretive notions which we recommend as being more originative than the traditional metaphysical categories. Our elucidation will begin with an examination of substance and subject as possible candidates for such a role, suggesting in the end that they will need to be disqualified. *Existenz,* we will then argue, is better able to fulfill the role.

The difficulties in the use of the concept of substance as a cosmological category are notorious. As is well known, there are numerous senses of substance in Aristotle's *Metaphysics.* Sometimes substance is understood as a principle of individuality. At other times it is a designation of actuality as distinct from potentiality. Then again it is a principle of unity, or a principle of intelligibility, or "source of being" in the sense of cause. Substance would seem to mean all of these things for Aristotle —and possibly more. Any interpretation and evaluation of these senses in the use of substance by Aristotle, as well as by other classical metaphysicians, requires careful attention to the kinds of questions that were posed by these metaphysicians as they addressed the world as a cosmos or totality of beings. And at this juncture it strikes us as patently premature to claim, as does Whitehead, that Aristotle's doctrine of substance is a complete mistake. That the category might be useful for an organization of one's theoretical knowledge of nature, as Kant for example maintained, is not as such contested here. The merits and demerits in the use of the category of substance need to be discussed within the context of questions which occasioned its rise. But in moving from metaphysics to ontology of experience we are moving to another context of questions and another inquiry-standpoint for addressing the world. The chief difficulty in the category of substance emerges precisely at this juncture. It does not appear to be applicable within the project of organizing lived experience without introducing certain alien features.

We begin with a question about the question as to substance. What inquiry-standpoint is presupposed when one asks about substance? What form does the questioning take and what is it that is addressed in the questioning? The question as to substance, on its most elemental level, is a *"what"* question; and that which is addressed is the cosmos, understood as a totality of entities. At the source of Aristotle's philosophy of substance we thus find a peculiar question coupled with a peculiar world-picture. The question "What is the nature of that which is?" is asked within the context of an understanding of the world as a totality of that which is. The various entities of this totality are singularly addressed so as to give up their peculiar *natures*. We perceive an entity as a particular *this*, and then proceed to say *what* it is. We thus characterize it as a particular "this-what," and in doing so we characterize it with respect to the category of substance. Now the procedure of explicating "what is" involves the assignment of different kinds of predicates to the thing in question, specifically essential predicates, propria, and accidental predicates. It is in this way that a doctrine of essence is given birth in Aristotle's philosophy of substance. Becoming clear about what something is involves, to a great measure, becoming clear about the essential nature of that thing. A kind of essentialism thus accompanies Aristotle's doctrine of substance.

Now that which at the same time interests and puzzles us about Aristotle's philosophy of substance is its use in the formulation of a theory of experience, and more specifically a theory of human existence. Leaving for the moment the applicability of substance to nonhuman reality uncontested, it does seem that something dissonant occurs when the category is applied in the interests of establishing a theory of human nature. It is precisely at this point that certain difficulties in the use of the category of substance emerge. In applying the category of substance in the service of a theory of human existence, man becomes an instance of finite substance in general. Admittedly such a determination of man might well yield information about the general features of man as a biopsychological entity within objective nature, but little is learned about that which contributes the distinctively human—the uniqueness and personal idiosyncrasy of man as historical consciousness. It would thus seem that in the application of the category of substance to man some rather decisive features of what it means to be human are concealed.

Now to point out certain shortcomings in the application of the traditional category of substance in the interests of securing a theory of man, and more broadly an ontological foundation of world-experience, is but a feeble beginning in achieving comprehension of the problem at issue. After all, it is quite common today to snipe away at the doctrine of substance and find it wanting for many different reasons. And in doing this the snipers are often oblivious to the many-faced character of their target. Substance means different things for different philosophers. An attack, for example, on the Cartesian doctrine of substance would not necessarily constitute an attack on the Aristotelian doctrine. The static "standing-in-itself" and self-containedness of the Cartesian concept of substance would appear to be even more alien to the concrete historical deployment of human life than the more dynamic *ousia* of Aristotle. Yet there is an inquiry-standpoint, a way of asking the question about man, assumed both by Aristotle and Descartes which seems to impose certain restrictions on the showing of the phenomenon itself. This inquiry-standpoint legislates in advance a world-picture whereby man is viewed as some type of entity located in the midst of a totality of entities. One then addresses this entity with the objectifying question "What is it?" So Aristotle's dynamism would still seem to characterize only the dynamism of entities at large. Dynamism itself remains a cosmological concept. As a substance man is an entity among other entities, differentiated from them principally through the assignment of essential predicates. It is thus that a doctrine of essence straightway accompanies the doctrine of substance. There are some well known difficulties connected with such a resultant essentialist view of man. There is first the difficulty of justifying the claim that there indeed is an "essence of man" or a "human nature." Searching for such an essence seems to end up as a project not dissimilar from that of peeling away the layers of an onion; no real core is discovered. But even granting for the moment that such an essence could be localized as a kind of formal and bare common denominator—such as rational animality—another difficulty would make its appearance. How would one derive or in some way establish exhaustive or even adequate *propria* which would provide one with the distinctive properties of rationality? What does it mean to be rational? Does not the meaning of rational behavior vary with human existence itself? How much of the irrational can be taken up into the concept of rationality before it becomes vacuous as an essential determinant?

It would seem that what is required to overcome the difficulties is not further investigation into possible property candidates so as to give the essence some content, but rather a reassessment of the inquiry-standpoint which lies behind the whole project. Can the question "What is the nature of man as an entity amidst other entities?"—asked within the perspective of a world-picture in which the world is represented as a totality of entities—even so much as put us on the path toward an understanding of man and the unifying source of experience? Admitting that the category of substance and the language of essential and property predication may have some applicability to the realm of objectifiable nature (and even this would need to be explored in depth), man in his concrete, lived experience does not appear or come to presence as such an objectifiable nature. The substantializing and essentializing of man thus seems to involve a mistaken use of concepts generated by a fixation and absolutization of a particular inquiry-standpoint. In the final analysis such substantializing and essentializing leads to a concealment rather than disclosure of that which is distinctively human. It would thus seem that the unity of the contextualized experiencer and the source of our organizing notions cannot be secured with a doctrine of substance.

The "turn to the subject," which may well characterize the distinctive thrust of modern philosophy, would seem at first glance to offer an attitude and program for surmounting the difficulties inherent in the classical philosophy of substance as it attempts to deal with the source of human experience and its organizing notions. A closer view, however, reveals that many of the traditional difficulties are simply reformulated in a new guise. Admittedly, with the turn to the subject the inquiry-standpoint shifts from the standpoint of objectivity to the standpoint of subjectivity, but this shift still occurs within a framework of presuppositions in which the world is addressed as a totality of entities. The primal question, asked from the standpoint of subjectivity, is more determined by epistemological concerns than was the case in the classical philosophies of substance. Now one asks "What can man know?" rather than "What is man's nature?" The subject comes into its own principally as epistemological subject—the subject as knower seeking some kind of commerce with the object as known. Yet the picture of the world as a totality of entities remains in force. In the philosophy of Descartes this world-picture is little more than a refurbished traditional metaphysical picture of the world, neatly divided into thinking and extended substances. Descartes still sought to secure his knowing subject with the supports of a traditional doctrine of substance. In British empiricism, particularly in its culmination in the philosophy of Hume, these supports are swept away and the subject is understood as a bundle of sense-perceptions. But in pruning away the traditional metaphysics of substance, British empiricism, even in its post-Humean developments, continued to move about within the framework of cosmological designs in which the traditional approach to the meaning of world remained normative. For example, when Russell asks "What is there in the world and what is it like?" he is asking an admittedly metaphysical question, a question that presupposes that the world is a totality of entities. Clearly these entities are not substances, according to Russell, as they were for Aristotle; they are ultimate "facts" reducible to properties and relations. The reductive analysis of Russell (and the early Wittgenstein) yields a world pictured as a "totality of facts." But such an inquiry-standpoint introduces the dilemma of locating the epistemological subject. Does the subject remain within the world as part of the fabric of facts? Then it would appear that the subject is in some way an instance of facts in general, and one is saddled with the old problem of differentiating the peculiar fact-character of the subject so as to arrive at that which is peculiarly human in the act of knowledge. Or does the subject remain outside the world of facts as a condition for facts being known? It would seem that the latter is the path most often pursued by epistemologically oriented philosophies of subjectivity, but in pursuing this path a whole host of familiar problems is brought to the fore. By formulating the problem in terms of a breach between the knowing subject and the world as known objects, an account of the commerce between subject and object still remains to be given. Is the subject indeed capable of bursting its cocoon of private sense-data and proceeding to a world of objective facts? What can be said about the character of the subject *as knower*? What is mind? What is consciousness? What is the nature of mental activity? Assuredly various answers to these questions can be given, and indeed have been given, in the course of the development of subject-oriented philosophies. Our task, however, is not that of pursuing and evaluating specific answers to these questions, but rather that of interrogating the inquiry-standpoint which first gives rise to the questions. It is not yet clear that these questions, emerging from a subject-object framework, are the basic questions, or indeed the proper questions for achieving clarification and insight into the ontological foundation of experience.

The return to the epistemological subject thus moves within a particular inquiry-standpoint. The problem of knowledge is defined in such a manner that the subject-object dichotomy is installed as the basis of experience, and a metaphysical commitment to the world as a totality of entities or reductive facts becomes evident. Some of the notorious difficulties connected with locating and defining the epistemological subject seem to follow from an uncritical acceptance of such a view of the world. We will suggest here (and develop later) that this view of the world is only one of the possible ways of organizing one's experience of the world, and may not at all be as primary and foundational as has sometimes been claimed. The world can also be viewed as an evolvement of events, as a series of situations, as a region of concerns. And it would seem that in the ordinary language of everyday experience the world is mostly spoken of in terms of events, situations, and concerns. So one might do well to consult the meanings in this ordinary usage in the effort to become clear about the meaning of world in its initial presentation.

The return to the subject, inaugurated by modern philosophy, was given an ethical as well as an epistemological expression. Ethics, as an increasingly specialized discipline, began to narrow its focus on the moral *subject* or the moral *self*. Some of the peculiar and defining properties which were proposed for an understanding of the moral subject were agency, the power of deliberation, and free will. But the search for a moral subject seems to be afflicted with the same problems as is the search for an epistemological subject. Where and how within the subject-object scheme of things is such a subject to be located? Attendant with the difficulty of locating the moral subject is that of delineating the defining properties of the subject and specifying the peculiar objects of the subject. The very use of subject-language is unintelligible without corresponding objects from which subjects are distinguished. But what are the objects that stand over against the moral subject? One might be tempted to say that they are duties, obligations, and commitments; but such as these do not appear to be objects in either an ordinary or technical sense. They seem rather to be forms of behavior or styles of life. Further, it has been claimed by the advocates of the moral subject theory that, in the exercise of duties and the fulfillment of obligations and commitments, free will is in some sense operative. But the theory seems to be peculiarly impoverished in providing an account of this free will. The main difficulty, again, is that freedom is considered to be a property which attaches to an entity. But if indeed the moral subject is an entity, either of a metaphysical or logical variety, it partakes of the abstract fixity of a substance or a logical concept and remains determined by its own constitution. In the last analysis the moral subject becomes a thing or a concept, a species of objectified reality, and to speak of the freedom of a thing or a concept involves a curious and meaningless combination of words. Freedom, as it is experienced in the actual context of human life, remains unaccounted for in a theory of man as moral subject.[3]

We have examined substance and subject as possible candidates for the source or common center from which organizing notions of experience issue, and have found that neither is qualified. We are now in position to suggest a third alternative which seems to hold some promise for a more proximate approach to that which is in question. This is the alternative which moves out from an investigation and elucidation of *Existenz* as the primal source or origin of world experience and its organizing notions. To speak of *Existenz* immediately indicates indebtedness to certain contemporary continental philosophers, notably Jaspers and Heidegger. Yet, the similarity of terminology can be deceptive. The *Existenz*-philosophies of Jaspers and Heidegger, which themselves differ significantly in detail, carry with them particular doctrinal contents to which our philosophy of experience remains uncommitted. In the case of Jaspers this doctrinal content is bound up with his appropriation of certain

3. Admittedly there is no one single usage of subject-language that has dominated modern and contemporary philosophy. Of particular relevance for the present context is Kierkegaard's use of the vocabulary of subject and subjectivity. Kierkegaard's use of "ethical subject" and "concretely existing subject" is recurrent, but it needs to be understood within the context of Kierkegaard's use of irony in lampooning the Hegelian dialectical terminology of subjective and objective spirit and the metaphysics of absolute idealism which accompanied it. Kierkegaard counters Hegel's essential dialectic with an existential dialectic and he does this by using Hegel's terminology against him.

features of German Idealism. In the case of Heidegger, particularly the Heidegger of the later writings, there is an appeal to a kind of *Seinsmystik* reminiscent of the traditions of Boehme and Eckhart. Without however as such minimizing the contributions of Jaspers and Heidegger to the development of a philosophy of *Existenz* (and there is a sense in which they, along with Kierkegaard and Nietzsche, first asked the question about *Existenz* in a decisive manner) we wish to suggest a clarification of *Existenz* which remains in closer touch with the dynamics and structure of experience.[4] Much less is our project to be considered consonant with that of Sartre. Sartre's dualism of *en-soi* and *pour-soi*, which in the final analysis seems to be but a refurbished Cartesianism, is difficult to install within the intentional flow of experience. His existentialist protest never fully succeeds in unmasking the root difficulties of essentialism and his program continues to be defined in terms of the classical metaphysical distinction between essence and existence. Consequently his alleged phenomenological ontology remains a tortuous exercise in metaphysics.

In seeking to clarify our use and meaning of *Existenz* we need first to distinguish it from the traditional metaphysical category of *existentia*. Existence as *existentia,* in the Scholastic usage which tended to become normative for the developing metaphysical tradition, is a designation of *thatness* (*quid est*), by virtue of which something is marked off from nothing. *Essentia,* as its conceptual partner, is a designation of *whatness* (*quod*

4. Heidegger never succeeds in formulating a consistent position on the role of experience in his *Existenz-ontologie*. For the most part, particularly in his earlier writings, he is discernibly critical of any "philosophy of experience." In *Being and Time,* he relegates—probably without due consideration—all philosophies of experience to the limbo of subjectivism. In his book on Kant he takes pains to distinguish the design of the *Critique of Pure Reason* from the program of a possible philosophy of experience. Admittedly, in his later work, *Unterwegs zur Sprache,* he speaks more approvingly of experience, and suggests a close connection between experience and language. But the fact remains that the question about the structure and dynamics of experience is never squarely faced by Heidegger. This is partly the result of the fact that his philosophical project (particularly in *Being and Time*) still moves within the confines of transcendental philosophy, and partly due to his identification of philosophy of experience with the traditional epistemologically oriented version of it.

est), by virtue of which existing things are marked off from each other. *Existentia* as a designation of brute thatness applies without exception (although not necessarily univocally) to all entities marked off from non-being, and provides the basal assertion about things in the world. First one asserts existence, then one defines what exists by locating its essence, and then one derives the determining properties. Again what is at issue in our thesis is not a rejection of the possible use of this metaphysical distinction in becoming clear about what there is in the objective world of nature and what it is like. We wish to suggest, however, that *Existenz* is not a category in the traditional sense. It is not an element of a world-picture in which the world is divided into existential and essential entities. *Existenz* is a mode of comportment, indicative of a *how* rather than a brute cosmological fact, and is applicable uniquely to the manner in which the contextualized experiencer is postured in his lived-through experience. *Existenz* indicates the projective character of the experiencer as he uncovers the world not as a totality of entities but as a plurality of regions of concerns, as an interpenetrating complex of places and times for tasks to be assumed. As contrasted with substance, *Existenz* is not an entity which stands-within-itself. Nor is it a hermetically sealed epistemological subject. *Existenz* is the center of concerns projected against a background of natural and historical meanings.

It may be of some help in elucidating the intended sense of *Existenz* as the projective character of the contextualized experiencer and the source of his organizing notions by following through certain etymological leads suggested by the Latin root *existere*, which means "to emerge" or "to stand out." Hence, to speak of *Existenz* as the central determination of the experiencer suggests the emerging, developing, and projective character of life which lies behind every concrete experiential act, whatever the contents of this experience might be. A lived-through experience—whether of a sentient, volitional, or noetic variety (or, more aptly, an interlacing of all three)—is an emerging process, a happening or an event lodged in a world which is pregnant with meaning and structured by intentionality. It is *Existenz*, understood in this sense, which provides a philosophy of experience with an ontological grounding for its organizing notions.

As the ontological source of world experience, *Existenz* provides the unifying center for the horizon-forms of lived time and lived space. Lived time and space, as we have seen in an earlier chapter, are forms in which experience emerges and, also, horizons into which experience is projected. They are textures of experience itself rather than dead frames of reference somehow given prior to experience. The emergence of experience is at once temporalized and spatialized. Not only, however, are the horizon-forms of time and space ontologically grounded in the emergence of experience; the vectors of intentionality, as bearers of meaning, also issue from *Existenz* as an emerging and projective event. The intentionality of experience, in its varied deployment, has its source in *Existenz*. It is at this juncture that one of the chief merits for the selection of *Existenz* over *subject* as the ontological ground comes to the fore. Whereas the language of subjectivity, particularly in the dress of a transcendental ego, is able to account only for a selected configuration of experience—the noetic-noematic structure of representational thought—*Existenz* provides the unifying source for pretheoretical intentionality as well. The epistemological subject, as a condition for representational thought, is a late arrival and "exists" only *in abstracto*. *Existenz* recaptures the primordial unity in which sentience, volition, and thought are interpenetrating and reciprocal movements.

The shift from philosophies of substance and subjectivity to a phenomenology of experience which takes its point of departure from an analytic of *Existenz* introduces a new approach to the meaning of world. When one asks about the world one is no longer asking about a totality of entities, each sharing in some kind of common nature. Nor is one asking how the world as external object can be known by a subject. The world in its primitive presentation to *Existenz* is neither pictured as a totality of entities (things or facts) nor is it postulated as the *terminus ad quem* of a cognitive act. The world in its primordiality is neither pictured nor postulated. It is an experienced life-world. This is world in the sense of regions of concern, appropriate places for the execution of tasks, direction of interest, occasions for involvement, and accessibility to utensils and tools for the actualization of projects. World, understood in this manner, already enters into the constitution of *Existenz* and is inseparable from it. *Existenz* and world are correlative. Experience as the articulation of *Existenz* is world-oriented. The experiencer is never mute in the presence of world. He always already addresses the world through intentional and meaning-laden concerns. In such an inquiry-standpoint the bogus dichotomy of knowing subject and world as object is undercut, and world is permitted to show itself in a more primordial sense, a sense given expression by ordinary language when one speaks of the "business world," the "political world," the "world of sports," the "academic world," and the like. The world as a region of concerns and situations of involvement takes priority over the world pictured as a totality of abstractive entities. The return to *Existenz* is thus also a return to a more primordial sense of world.

We have sought to clarify our use and meaning of *Existenz* and have spoken of it as the ontological ground for a philosophy of experience. It is in *Existenz* that the organizing notions of an ontology of experience find their common seat or center. But is not *Existenz* simply one organizing notion among others? In what sense is it the basis or ground of these notions? The formulation of an analogy with the traditional metaphysical category of existence may serve to clarify the issues at hand. In the metaphysical tradition, existence is basic in the sense that the defining of essences and the assigning of properties requires a prior stipulation that something exists. One asserts existence, determines the essence of that which exists, and makes an inventory of its properties. In our ontology of experience, *Existenz* is basic in an analogous manner. It is necessary, however, to underscore the analogical character of the relation; for *Existenz*, unlike the traditional category of existence, is neither a simple designation of a *quid est* nor a designation of finite existents in general. It has to do with the emerging of experience in the contextualism of its embodiment, speech, and sociality, whence organizing and interpretive notions arise and whither they return for their justification.

Thus far we have spoken of the task of ontology as principally that of searching for organizing notions applicable in the actual context of human life. The question which may well be unavoidable at this juncture is: Why speak of ontology at all? Is not what we have been proposing simply a disguised form of "conceptual" analysis in which organizing notions are substituted for categories? Where does discourse about being enter the project? And if it does not enter, then one had better dispense with talk about ontology, for whatever else ontology may be, it is assuredly the *logos* (discourse) of *onta* (being). It is to this issue that our attention will now turn.

[3] THE QUESTION ABOUT THE QUESTION OF BEING

OUR ADUMBRATION OF A POSSIBLE ONTOLOGY of experience has thus far yielded two results. There is first the requirement to search for organizing notions through which experience achieves a partial unification. It is important to underscore that this attempted unification remains partial and incomplete, due to the finitude of the experiencer. This finitude precludes any definitive and complete delineation of organizing notions. But ontology is more than an analysis of organizing notions. It involves some kind of commitment to that which the organizing notions elucidate, to the world-fact of the emerging of experience in its varied intentionalities. As an appropriate indicator of this emerging of experience we have suggested the use of the term *Existenz*. It is in *Existenz* that an ontology of experience has its source or foundation. But in all this the crucial import of the use of the term "ontology," designating a discourse about being, remains as yet only implicit and unexplored. So it is now to a radical questioning of the use of the language of being that our attention turns. Why speak of an ontology at all, and not simply about a phenomenology of experience proceeding from an analytic of *Existenz*?

When one asks about being, what kind of question is it that one asks? The question of being has not only been posed in the history of philosophy, very often it has been posed as *the* question of philosophy. The question has been reiterated time and again, sometimes with an air of religious fervor, other times with evident disdain. But in this reiteration of the question, either approvingly or disparagingly, for the most part little awareness has been displayed as to the kind of question that is at issue, as to what is addressed and how it is addressed. We have already provided a characterization of the general features of traditional metaphysics, in which the question of being is very much at the center of things. What remains to be carried through in this section is an interrogation of the question itself as it has been asked and re-asked from the inquiry-standpoint of traditional metaphysics. Through this interrogation we hope to bring into relief another interpretive meaning of the question, specifically as it pertains to an ontology of experience.

It is evident that the question of being, as asked by a metaphysician, is not an ordinary kind of question, and what is called for by the question appears not to be an ordinary kind of answer. When one asks "How does the crystalline structure of copper differ from that of zinc?" or "What processes of photosynthesis occur in the growth of an oak tree?" or "What are the genetic factors in the evolutionary development of the sea lion?" one is asking questions whose sense can be readily understood, for the path to be followed in achieving an answer is clearly marked out. These questions are rather straightforward scientific questions about the nature of particular entities in the realm of objectifiable fact. They are questions about this and that. Yet it might seem as though something very basic remains unexplored in our interminable inquiries about this and that. The very presence of "thises" and "thats" which can be inquired about may elicit astonishment. Copper and zinc, oak trees, and sea lions are present as investigable particulars by virtue of sharing a common status which marks them off from nothing, a status which permeates their differentiating characteristics. The presence of investigable entities is itself an occasion for wonder. Copper and zinc, oak trees, and sea lions can be picked out from a manifold of entities and can be investigated not only in the interests of scientific explanation but also in the interests of discovering their more general features. It is through this type of questioning that such metaphysical distinctions as particular and universal, existence and essence, actual and potential are given birth; and the world of objectively investigable entities is addressed in the language and viewed in the perspective of these distinctions. To ask a metaphysical question is thus to ask about entities or beings which populate the world in such a manner that something can be learned about what they are like with respect to their general structure and features. Metaphysical inquiry is geared to knowledge about beings. But metaphysicians have also been prone to use "being" as a singular noun-term or grammatical substantive. Used in this manner, being suffers the fate of becoming an extraordinarily general designation, including within its scope all individual entities, structures, relations, and properties, real and merely imaginary. The conceptual distance between such an extraordinarily broad designation and a vacuous concept is very short, as Nietzsche had already recognized. As long as one talks about particular beings, their structures, relations, and properties, then meaningful contents can be specified, but when one begins to talk about "being in general" meaningful contents seem to evaporate.

The problem areas occasioned by the traditional use of the term "being" would seem to arise primarily through the employment of the distinction between beings and being and the effort to move from beings to being through abstraction and inference, either of a deductive or inductive variety. More specifically, the beings from which a general concept of being is to be abstracted or inferred are drawn from the realm of external objects and things. The categories which are derived from an inspection of such beings are cosmological in character, geared toward a unification of these beings in their totality. The inquiry-standpoint and the various presuppositions about world and meaning which inform such a philosophy of being have already been discussed in Chapter 7. Our present task is that of suggesting another approach to being as this approach is implicated in a philosophy of experience which, as we have already seen, assumes a different inquiry-standpoint. Proceeding from the inquiry-standpoint of our philosophy of experience the world is addressed not as a totality of beings but rather as a manifold of regions of concern; open-ended organizing notions replace fixed categorial determinations; and the phenomenon of human reality or *Existenz*, rather than nonhuman external objects and things, provides the point of departure for the search of the meaning of being. An ontology of experience proceeds from an elucidation of the being which we ourselves are.

Ordinary usage testifies of a singularly wide range of senses which attach to various grammatical forms of "being." The verb form is used in multiple ways. It is used as a copula in statements about objects and things, as when one says "There is an oak tree in my backyard" or "There are sea lions off the coast of Alaska." It is used with reference to facts as is the case when one says "Sugar is soluble" or "Arsenic is poisonous." It is used to designate historical events, as when one says "There is a revolution in China" or "Nationalism is increasing in France." And it is used to express involvement in situations, as illustrated in the locutions "He is in the army," "She is in love," and "He is in dire need of help." Correspondingly, the infinitive and the substantive (which in English is participial) display a variety of senses, in one case having to do with things, in another case with facts, and in yet another with historical events, and still in another with situational involvement. Coupled with this variety of grammatical verb forms are varieties of tense, number, and person. Yet the logic of grammar is such that substantives are derived from the verb form which is itself a definite form of the indefinite infinitive (*modus infinitivus*). The infinitive "to be," itself indefinite, is rendered definite through a determination of verbal forms, such as "I am," "you are," "he is," and the various tenses, numbers, and persons which accompany these forms. It would thus follow that the infinitive of the word being (to be) is a *grammatically preliminary* form. The various verb forms and the substantive are derived from the infinitive.

As such, however, the grammatical analysis of the word "being" yields little of philosophical importance. The philosophically significant question is first raised when one inquires into the connection of grammar with the experiential act of speaking in which meanings through various usages are put into play. The concrete usage of terms in the actual context of speech introduces considerations that go beyond the formalization of a logic of grammar. A logic of grammar is constructed through a process of abstraction from the concrete act of speaking. The form of a *modus infinitivus* and the resultant substantivizing are abstractive and late arrivals. They are abstractions from ordinary usage, in which the verb form in its various tenses is primitive. One speaks of that which is, that which was, and that which will or might be; and the topic of discourse centers either on objects, facts, events, or situations.

In clarifying the language of being in our ontology of experience, it is imperative that the focus of attention be directed to the use in its tensed, verbal form. This is the use put into play by the contextualized speaking experiencer in his daily expression and communication. Speaking about objects, facts, events, and situations, he announces and discloses their *presence*. It is this announcement and disclosure of presence that is at issue in the verb form of being, and it is at this juncture that the question about being becomes philosophically interesting. To say that there is an object or an event is to say that such an object or event is present, and to say that something is present implies at least two things—that it is *presented* to an experiencer and that it is located and occurs in a spatio-temporal horizon. Being as presence is thus inseparable from an experiencer and from spatio-temporal determinations. To say that something *is* is to specify it in the context of its mode of presentation and apprehend it against a temporal and spatial horizon.

But as we have seen, that which is can be divided up in various ways. One speaks of objects, facts, events, and situations. Yet one must proceed with caution in making use of the metaphor of division with respect to the components of experience. These divisions are never as neat and clear-cut as may at first appear to be the case. Situations involve objects, and objects are always situated, both with respect to their background and their relation to an experiencer. Objects and situations can both be apprehended as events, and facts can be asserted about them. Objects, situations, events, and facts thus seem to intermingle in a curiously mosaic manner, and in speaking about them a kind of diversity in unity seems to emerge. In following through the philosophical significance of this we are led to a kind of regulative principle, a principle which prohibits both the normativizing of any one of the sectors of that which is and the taking as definitive and exhaustive the key categories or organizing notions which are appropriate to it. This seems to be precisely the root difficulty in traditional metaphysics in its easy linkage of being with entities which are present as instances of an objectifiable scheme. The world as experienced is never simply a totality of objects nor a totality of facts. It is also, and in certain respects first and foremost, a world of events and a world of situations. These are different versions of the world and constitute equally appropriate and equally valid ways of talking about that which is present.

An ontology of experience which takes as its point of departure an elucidation of experience will thus establish a close connection between being and world. Indeed the sense of that which is present already presupposes world. Objects, facts, events, and situations, and their corresponding meaning structures, come to pass and pass away in a wider frame or field of concern which we call the world. Hence, John Wild's argument, against Heidegger's claim that being remains the primary topic in philosophical thinking, would seem to have some justification. Wild's central thesis is that the "world-horizon" is a more ultimate factor, broader in its range and prior to both being and meaning.[5] Yet this thesis requires further qualification and possibly a restatement. Admittedly the world already conditions the various senses of that which is present and provides for their ultimate background. Yet without the variety of that which is present, articulated in the manifold ways of speaking about it, the notion of world would remain vacuous. Without objects, facts, events, and situations, there would be no meaning to world, just as without world there would be no way of ascribing meaning to objects, facts, events, and situations, or even to judgments about them. The connection between being—understood as the coming to presence of that which is—and world is not found through an interrogation that presupposes that one must be primal. The connection is a dialectical one, and it is to the project of speech that one must turn to discern this connection. In speaking about that which is present we implicate a world, and in speaking about world our discourse inevitably turns on some region of that which is present. Herein resides the significance of the already well-known hyphenated expression "being-in-the-world" which we can now understand more explicitly as the presence-of-that-which-is-in-the-world. The sense of being resides in the coming to presence of that which is, and this coming to presence requires a world.

A connection of an equally vital and dialectical sort obtains between *Existenz* and being, and correspondingly between *Existenz* and world. We have already clarified our use of *Existenz* and have indicated how it functions as the grounding for the organizing notions within experience. The task that remains is that of explicating the interdependent relatedness of *Existenz*, being, and world. Stated somewhat formally, *Existenz* is the configurative location in which being and world appear. The world comes to presence, is rendered manifest and meaningful through the open and projective presence of *Existenz*. The coming to presence of that which appears against the background of world is located in *Existenz* in a privileged way, for it is the elucidation of the *presence of Existenz* that provides the point of departure. It is by virtue of the emerging, open, and projective character of *Existenz* that one is first enabled to speak of the presence of objects, facts, events, and situations. But is not

5. See John Wild, "Being, Meaning and the World," *Review of Metaphysics,* XVIII, no. 3 (1965), pp. 411–29.

Existenz then simply another instance of that which is present, and possibly reducible to an object or a fact? If *Existenz* is not an instance of that which is, it would seem difficult to avoid the rather odd conclusion that *Existenz* is in some sense separable from being. This problem, however, arises only when one takes as normative the traditional view of being as a universal, or at least a very general, concept under which the various entities can be subsumed as instances or examples. So long as the traditional metaphysical distinction between universal and particular continues to be invoked in establishing the connection between *Existenz* and being, the crux of the issue will remain concealed. In an ontology of experience, that which is at issue in the meaning of being as presence, relative to the regions of object and fact, is the role that *Existenz* plays in the determination of presence. It is not that *Existenz* is an object or fact alongside other objects or facts. *Existenz* marks out the horizon of world in such a manner that objects and facts can appear or become manifest. Objectification itself is made possible through the projective character of *Existenz*. Incarnate consciousness spatializes and temporalizes its environment in such a manner that objects are made to appear, occasioning the operation of a theoretical intentionality whereby objects can be identified, defined, and reduced to facts. So *Existenz* is not simply an instance of objectivized being; rather it is a condition for it. Nor is *Existenz* an instance of events in general. It is through *Existenz* that events and situations are rendered present. That which is comes to presence against the background of world by virtue of *Existenz*.

As *Existenz* and being remain dialectically related, so do *Existenz* and world. Only by grasping the dialectical interplay between *Existenz* and world does one avoid the splitting-off of the self from the world which has plagued traditional metaphysics. Already in classical metaphysics we are able to discern the separation of the psyche from the world as its proper object. The world, as a totality of entities, is external to the mind and is that which is known by the mind. In the fateful turn of modern metaphysics, this separation becomes a veritable dichotomy. The *res cogitans* of Descartes is sharply marked off from the world as a continuum of extended substance. Even in the transcendental philosophy of Kant the ego is securely situated "behind" the world as an *a priori* condition for knowledge. Our elucidation of

Existenz, as we have distinguished it from substance and subject in the previous section, reformulates the inquiry-standpoint so as to make possible the reinsertion of *Existenz* into the world as the center of concernful thought and action. *Existenz* emerges in the world and pursues its projects in the world. *Existenz,* being, and world are thus dialectically interpenetrating ontological features which are at work in every lived-through experience, and the intelligibility of any one of these ontological features is dependent upon the intelligibility of the other.

[4] ONTOLOGY AND PERSPECTIVITY

AN ONTOLOGY OF EXPERIENCE, as we have sketched it, must at some time or other come to terms with the issue of perspectivism. Is it possible for a philosophy of experience, even if the ontological features of this experience are acknowledged, to proceed beyond the perspectivism of point-of-view philosophizing? We will argue in this concluding section that, although the perspectivity of experience cannot be surmounted, the recognition of this need not entail the subjectivism and relativism that is commonly associated with perspectivism. Much of the force of the argument will depend upon a careful analysis of the meaning of perspectivity as it relates to a philosophy of experience.

In becoming clear about the meaning of perspectivity, a rather firmly entrenched prejudice needs to be suspended. One might call this the intellectualist prejudice of using as one's paradigm the perspectives of conceptual thought. The intellectualist hurriedly, and without due consideration, grants a priority to the mind and the workings of abstract representational thought. Hence, the perspectives that are at issue for him are unavoidably abstract and, in the last analysis, definable as conceptual constructs. On this abstract level of conceptual construction, the primary focus of attention readily falls on the patterns and possibilities of the *conceptual act.* The stage is thus set for an understanding of perspectives as the product of a conceptual engineering. Making use of the subject-object dichotomy— which the intellectualist does not for a moment question—the attention is directed to the role of the subject and the act of conceptual patterning. The inquiry-standpoint assumed by intellectualism thus directs the inquiry rather decisively in the direction of an idealistic, if not subjectivistic, definition of a perspective.

What is required, we suggest, is the pursuit of the meaning of perspectivity within a more primordial context of considerations than that of conceptual perspectives. This more primordial context is that of the contextualized experiencer and his lived-through experience. In the genealogy of meaning in lived-through experience, perceptual and praxis-oriented perspectives take priority over conceptual ones, and it is in the life of perception and practical concerns that the *structure* of a perspective is more clearly discernible. There is a facticity and concreteness in a perceptual perspective from which conceptual perspectives inevitably prescind. The structure of a perceptual perspective is concretized within the *configurative* development of world experience. A perceptual perspective is always a perspective *of* or *on* a figure surrounded both by an inner and outer horizon. Perceiving the house from the front is a determinate perspective within the actual context of perceiving. But the sense of this perspective, as a perspective of the house from the front, is already conditioned by the possibilities of other perspectives within the inner horizon, such as perspectives of the house from the side, the back, and the top. Then there is the outer horizon that surrounds the figure. The house is within a woods, on a hill, by a brook, in the city, or in the country—all of which provides the figure with a background that enters into the constitution of any profile within the inner horizon. What becomes apparent in the exploration of this structure of perceptual perspectives is that perspectives are always in some manner solicited by the figure and background, and never simply engineered by the perceiver. In perceiving the house from the front it is not in my power to perceive the house from the back while perceiving it from the front. The interlacing of figure and background conspire to solicit the sense of any particular perspective. Admittedly the perspective is always a perspective *from* a perceiver, but the perceiver is himself a part of a wider context of solicitations in which figure and background interplay. Perspectives are *from* a perceiver and *of* a figure-with-background. Neither idealism, with its regression to a transcendental subject as the source of perspectives, nor realism, with its postulation of an objective realm of essences, is able to account for the bipolar structure of perspectives as this structure emerges in the genealogy of perception. Perceptual perspectives are neither subjectivistic nor objectivistic. They are neither mere constructs within an enclosed sphere of subjectivity nor do they have a structural status within the object which can be handily "read off" through pure description. Subjectivism and objectivism are already intellectualistic prejudices which prohibit the seeing of the phenomena as they presents themselves. If indeed one makes use of subject-object language on this level at all, it will need to be said that perspectives are both subjective and objective. But to speak of the subjective and the objective as polarities which interplay in the genealogy of a perspective is not yet to speak of subjectivism and objectivism as metaphysical alternatives. Perceptual perspectives are borne by the conspiring of presentative acts with the solicitations from a presented figure and background.

We have used as our illustration of the structure of a perspective the phenomenon of perception, and we have done this because perceptual perspectives adhere more closely to the actual context of lived-through experience than do conceptual perspectives. And conceptual perspectives, if they are to withstand the danger of becoming vacuous and contentless, need to be related time and again to their experiential source. We concur with Kant's celebrated insight that concepts without percepts are empty, but we believe that our view of world-experience as an intentional structure provides a broader and more adequate perceptual base.

Our illustration of the structure of a perspective by placing it within the context of perception, however, should not be misconstrued to mean that we are advocating a doctrine of the primacy of perception. Admittedly, in relation to conceptual perspectives, a kind of primacy of perception is suggested, but even here it would seem to us that it is more a matter of dialectical interplay between percepts and concepts than a matter of granting primacy to the one over the other. But the central point at issue is that caution must be exercised in articulating the genealogy of the structure of experience through consultation of one's perceptual life alone. Lived-through experience is also praxis-oriented, imbued with a sentient and a volitional intentionality which respond to solicitations from figures and backgrounds of wider reach and range than mere perception. What is required, as we have suggested in an earlier chapter, is a reinsertion of perception and conception into the broader context of intentional experience. This leads to a primacy of experience with the contextualized experiencer at its center. And it is in this primordial experience that the peculiar structure of a perspective as an interplay of presentative acts and solicitations finds its genealogy.

A plurality of perspectives is displayed in world experience, and within this plurality there is a great deal of diversity. A recognition of this plurality and diversity should legislate in advance an attitude of caution with respect to the possible unification of perspectives. It would seem at this juncture that a unification of the manifold perspectives within world experience remains at best an ideal to be approximated. Any scaffolding or ordination of these perspectives remains a tentative project. Not only are there perceptual perspectives and praxis-oriented perspectives, there are scientific perspectives, ethical perspectives, esthetical perspectives, religious perspectives, perspectives on man's socio-historical life, and undoubtedly other possible configurations. Each of these perspectives can become a special topic of inquiry and investigation. The task of an ontology of experience is to pursue questions with respect to the structure and meaning of perspectives in each of these areas of inquiry in such a manner that their relevance to lived-through experience can be discerned. We have suggested that the structure and meaning of a perspective can be more readily seen in an examination of the phenomenon of perception and man's praxis-oriented life. Whether the structure of a perspective that shows itself on these levels can be rediscovered on every other level, and in what manner it can be discovered, can be decided only after careful analysis and description of the other levels has been carried through. Yet such an analysis and description of some other possible level will need to be cognizant of the discoveries on the perceptual and praxis-oriented level if it is to avoid severance from a region which circumscribes much of man's lived-through experience.

It would seem that whatever we perceive, think, and do, we perceive, think, and do within the context of certain perspectives. Man may indeed be condemned to freedom, as Sartre maintains, and condemned to meaning, as Merleau-Ponty maintains, but there is a sense in which man is first and foremost condemned to perspectives. The actualization of personal freedom and the apprehension of meaning occurs only within a perspective. To be sure, one is able to shift perspectives, move from one to another, which is itself an indication of the measure of man as open to transcendence, but this openness to transcendence does not result in a nonperspectival standpoint. This would suggest that an ontology of experience will need to remain a philosophy of human finitude, not because a nonperspectival standpoint is necessarily unthinkable, but because it does not appear to be realizable within the actual context of lived-through experience. The attempt at a God-like survey is thus abandoned for the less presumptuous and more mundane description and interpretation of the human hold on reality. The world is approached always from the side of finite experience, and never as a reality or totality of entities open to the vision of a disembodied, nonhistorical, and nonfinite mind. Meanings are achieved and fulfilled only within the manifold and operating intentionality of experience as this experience is determined by finite structures. The most decisive testimony of this finitude which is illustrated by the perspectivity of one's being-in-the-world is supplied by the finite horizon-forms of time and space, which are present in any given portion of experience.[6]

This apparently ineradicable finitude and unavoidable perspectivity furnishes our projected ontology of experience with a kind of regulative principle. It regulates our search for a unification of the various perspectives in such a manner that no particular version of world experience becomes absolutized. It provides, if you will, a safeguard against metaphysical idolatry. It cautions against the reduction of the various perspectives to a single perspective, much less to a feature within a single perspective. The metaphysical reductionism of the ethical to the esthetical, the religious to the ethical, or the religious to the scientific—to provide but a few illustrations—involves a presumptive transgression of the limits of experience. It involves an absolutization of a particular standpoint and a particular version of the world, which belies an unspoken claim for absolute knowledge. A philosophy of experience which seeks to remain in touch with that which shows itself in the manifold of lived-through experience must remain uneasy about such absolute claims. Franchises must be granted to the multiple ways of speaking about the world and to the varied styles of existing in the world.

6. *Supra,* chap. 2, §4.

What is required is elucidation of these multiple ways and varied styles and a justification of their meaning before the tribunal of lived-through experience.

The operation of this regulative principle in our ontology of experience can be illustrated through an investigation of some different possible perspectives on the socio-historical dimension of man's being-in-the-world. In dealing with the various patterns of the wider cultural life of man the perspectivity of the life-world is illustrated with a peculiar poignancy. Here one is dealing with more general perspectives, each of which displays an interlacing and determinate configuration of the more specific perspectives within perception, conception, and valuation. With our regulative principle we will be able to safeguard the prolific character of these wider perspectival patterns without proffering the claim that one is more objectively true than the other. There appears to be no one meaning that can be attached to the cultural and historical life of man. The historical life-world comports a plurality of meanings, each of which emerges from an attentive explication of the phenomena as they show themselves.

The myopic character of deterministic interpretations of history (be they psychoanalytical, economic, or theological) resides precisely in the solidification and absolutization of a particular perspective and the consequent screening-off of all other possible perspectives. In such a program any imaginative variation of historical profiles is excluded. Admittedly, every cultural and historical phenomenon has some economic significance, and it will not do to say that the historical life of man can be understood independently of conspiring economic forces. But to recognize that history can never fully transcend economics is by no means tantamount to a reductionist claim that history is simply determined by the interplay of economic forces of production and exchange. It is the latter claim that leads to the presumption of the Marxist interpretation of history. As economics enters into every structural configuration of historical development, so does sexuality. Sexuality is a mode of bodily comportment, and history is an expression of embodied consciousness. However, to say that history is conditioned by the varied expressions of sexuality is not yet to legislate a pan-sexualism whereby the socio-historical life of man is restricted to the perspective of libidinal forces. The latter constitutes the basis and error of the classical Freudian interpretation of history. The religious perspective has unquestionably played a role in the assessment of the meaning of history. The historical life-world offers intentional contents which are open to religious interpretations. But to picture history as the necessitation of Divine volition pure and simple involves an idolatry of a perspective which does not do justice to the structural interdependence of conditioning factors in world experience. This idolatry of the religious perspective constitutes the undemonstrated and problematic claim of theological determinism. Every cultural and historical event involves a network of meanings supplied by economic, sexual, and religious perspectives (among others) which are mutually implicatory within the unity of the event.

An ontology of experience which thus remains sensitive to the breadth and variegated character of experience will abstain from any reductionism of human relationships and historical life to any one set of formative factors, be they economic, sexual, or religious in character. It may of course well be that in any given sector of society and in any given period of history, one of any number of perspectives would be dominant, but dominance does not as such entail the exclusion of other perspectives. What lurks in the background of a deterministic view of history with its easy reductionism is a metaphysical urge to explain the phenomena from a God-like vantage point, making use of the category of causality in a somewhat cavalier fashion so as to establish an objectivistic view of what the historical world is like and why it develops as it does. An ontology of experience, when it deals with the question of historical patterns and life styles, resists this metaphysical urge. It proceeds from an inventory of the times, searches for elucidating descriptions rather than architectonic explanatory theories, settles for the human grasp of reality, and sees the realms of objectivity and subjectivity as derivative rather than primary. Ontology, understood in this manner, takes its rise from the proliferating breadth of lived-through experience, and returns to this experience for the justification of its organizing notions through a continuing project of elucidation.

Index

Absolute Spirit, 75, 148, 199
Action: and decision, 101–8; historical, 209, 212
Adventures of Ideas, 86n, 91
Aisthesis, 19–20, 22
Alienation, 94–95, 98, 143–49, 189, 198–200, 256
Aloneness, 200
Ambiguity, 3–4
Analogy, 195–96
Anselm, 236
Anti-Hegelianism, 143–44, 197–98, 227
Anxiety, 76–78, 92, 94, 256, 257; and fear, 93–95; and finitude, 11, 76; and intentionality, 92–99; and space, 98; and time, 96–97
Apodicticity, 242
A priori, 50, 96, 125, 171, 256, 275
Aquinas, 139
Aristotle, 26, 27, 66–69, 78, 79, 88, 91, 139, 224, 225, 228, 230, 231, 233–34, 240, 251, 258–60, 262
Aristotelian-Thomistic tradition, 235
Auden, W. H., 201
Augenblick, 79
Augustine, 68, 139, 235, 241
Augustinian-Anselmic tradition, 235

Barth, K., 245, 246
Behaviorism, 121, 127, 195

Being: "error of," 221, 244; and *Existenz*, 274–75; grammar of, 270–72; and meaning, 225–26; as presence, 269–76; question about, 246, 269–76; as traditional problem, 220, 225, 269–76; and world, 273–74
Being-in-the-world, 136, 220, 252, 254, 274, 280, 281
Being and Nothingness, 146
Being and Time, 9, 29, 43, 71n, 91, 97, 153, 265n
Bergson, 26, 27, 68–69, 71n
Berkeley, xii, 8
Binswanger, 65
Boehme, 265
Bodily comprehension, 133–41
Body: as lived, 71–73, 130, 131, 134, 135–37, 142, 145, 151, 166, 167, 170, 175, 192, 220; as myself, 151–57; as object, 130; phenomenological investigation of, 132, 133
Boredom, 76–78
Bradley, 234
British empiricism, xii, 7–9, 21, 22, 118, 126, 127, 248
Buber, 206
Butler, 236

Calvin, 246
Camus, 79, 201, 242n